INTERNATIONAL AGRICULTURAL TRADE AND DEVELOPMENT

INTERNATIONAL AGRICULTURAL TRADE AND DEVELOPMENT

DRAGAN MILJKOVIC
EDITOR

Nova Science Publishers, Inc.
New York

For permission to use material from this book please contact us:
Telephone 631-231-7269; Fax 631-231-8175
Web Site: http://www.novapublishers.com

LIBRARY OF CONGRESS CATALOGING-IN-PUBLICATION DATA

International agricultural trade and development / Dragan Miljkovic, editor.
p. cm.
Includes index.
ISBN-13: 978-1-60021-965-8 (hardcover)
ISBN-10: 1-60021-965-9 (hardcover)
1. Produce trade. 2. International trade. I. Miljkovic, Dragan.
HD9000.6.I525 2008
382.41--dc22 2007033445

Published by Nova Science Publishers, Inc. ✦ New York

CONTENTS

In: International Agricultural Trade and Development
Editor: Dragan Miljkovic, p. 1-2 ISBN 978-1-60021-965-8

Chapter 1

INTRODUCTION: MODELING GLOBAL FOOD AND AGRICULTURAL MARKETS

David Abler[*]

This edition of the *Journal of International Agricultural Trade and Development* contains papers and selected discussant comments from the Theme Day of the annual meeting of the International Agricultural Trade Research Consortium (IATRC), held in December 2005 in San Diego. Most IATRC members are developers or users of models of food and agricultural markets, and yet it has been twenty years since IATRC last devoted a Theme Day to modeling at its annual meeting. The modeling of food and agricultural markets has changed dramatically in the intervening years as new theories and modeling techniques have been developed, and as new policy issues have arisen. The 2005 Theme Day focused on new dimensions and emerging issues in modeling global food and agricultural markets.

Two papers in this issue revisit standard theories of international trade in the presence of product differentiation and economies of scale, one by Ian Sheldon and the other by Rakhal Sarker and Yves Surry. Sheldon's paper lays out how theories of trade under product differentiation and scale economies can be and have been empirically tested, with a focus on food and agriculture. Sheldon devotes significant attention to how different formulations of the gravity equation can be used to test among alternative theories of trade. Sarker and Surry's paper surveys the literature on product differentiation models applied to food and agricultural trade, including the Armington model and models of horizontal and vertical product differentiation. Discussant comments on the two papers are provided by Philip Abbott and Julian Alston.

The paper by Pat Westhoff, Scott Brown, and Chad Hart addresses stochastic modeling of agricultural and trade policy. They establish that point estimates often paint an incomplete or even misleading picture of policy impacts, and that estimating a distribution of outcomes is important in many cases, particularly when policies have asymmetric effects or when there is interest in the tails of distributions. Using a stochastic version of the FAPRI model, they find

[*] Professor of Agricultural, Environmental and Regional Economics and Demography, Penn State University

that both of these factors are important in evaluating WTO commitments on internal support measures.

The paper by Jesús Antón focuses on modeling partially decoupled farm payments, or "more decoupled" payments as he refers to them. Even though they may be largely decoupled from production, Antón concludes that there are a variety of mechanisms through which these payments can affect farmers' decision making. Antón reviews how "more decoupled" payments are represented in several simulation models of global agricultural markets. He notes that the magnitude of the production impacts of decoupled payments is an empirical question that deserves significantly more econometric research than has been done to date.

The paper by Scott Bradford analyzes non-tariff barriers (NTBs) for food and agricultural products. Bradford presents a new method for estimating tariff equivalents of NTBs for final food goods in OECD countries that exploits detailed and comprehensive price comparisons between countries. He then uses an applied general equilibrium model to assess the impact of these NTBs. His results imply that NTBs significantly restrict trade in OECD countries and that removing them would bring large gains to them and to developing countries. Linda Young provides discussant comments on Bradford's paper.

In: International Agricultural Trade and Development
Editor: Dragan Miljkovic, p. 3-32

ISBN 978-1-60021-965-8

Chapter 2

MONOPOLISTIC COMPETITION AND TRADE: DOES THE THEORY CARRY ANY EMPIRICAL 'WEIGHT'?

Ian Sheldon

ABSTRACT

This paper revisits the theory of trade in the presence of product differentiation and economies of scale, and lays out how such a theory can and has been tested for empirically using the gravity equation. Initially, the empirical phenomenon of intra-industry trade is discussed, followed by an outline of the standard monopolistic explanation for intra-industry trade, along with a discussion of how this is embedded in a general equilibrium trade model. Then, the theoretical foundations for the gravity equation are developed, and the empirical strategy for testing the increasing returns/product differentiation story is outlined, indicating that it could be applied to processed food and agricultural trade.

Keywords: Monopolistic competition, gravity model, trade

In a recent paper, Cho, Sheldon and McCorriston (2002), using a panel of bilateral trade flows across ten developed countries between 1974 and 1995 explored the effects of exchange rate uncertainty on the growth of food and agricultural trade as compared to other sectors such as manufacturing, machinery, and chemicals. Based on the use of a standard gravity model controlling for other factors likely to determine bilateral trade, the results of their analysis showed that real exchange rate uncertainty had a significant negative effect on food and agricultural trade over this period. In terms of the standard gravity model, a puzzling result of this research though is that when all countries were included in the analysis, the impact of country-pair incomes on bilateral trade was significant for all sectors except food and agriculture. In contrast, when the panel was split into separate samples of members of the European Monetary System (EMS), and all other non-EMS countries including the United

States, the income variable was found to be statistically significant for the food and agriculture sector in the EMS sample, but not in the non-EMS sample.

One possible reason for this result is that the underlying model of trade may differ depending on the sector and sample of countries involved, and hence the expected size of the income variable. A recent study by Feenstra, Markusen and Rose (2001) used the gravity equation to focus on this issue. They found that there is a 'home-market' effect whereby an exporting country's income has more of an effect on its net exports of differentiated products than the importing country's income. In contrast, this effect is reversed for the case of homogeneous goods, whereby there is a reverse 'home-market' effect, although the average effects of both countries' incomes are higher for differentiated than homogeneous products. In the context of Feenstra *et al.*'s (2001) categorization of trade into homogeneous and differentiated goods, it should be noted that countries in the EMS have generally exported processed food and agricultural goods while the United States and Canada, major non-EMS countries, have exported bulk agricultural commodities (McCorriston and Sheldon, 1991), which may explain the differences in the income parameter between these two samples in the Cho *et al.* study.

In addition, McCorriston and Sheldon, Hirschberg, Sheldon and Dayton (1994), and Hirschberg and Dayton (1996) have all noted high levels of intra-industry trade for processed food and agricultural products, particularly involving European Union (EU) countries, intra-industry trade being defined as the simultaneous import and export of products that are very close substitutes in terms of factor inputs and consumption (Tharakan, 1985). The existence of intra-industry trade is typically associated with increasing returns to scale, product differentiation and monopolistic competition (Helpman and Krugman, 1985), and the volume of such trade is expected to be higher the greater the equality of trading partners' GDP per capita (Helpman, 1987). Helpman (1987) has also argued that the volume of trade among a group of countries as a percentage of their aggregate income, should be larger the more similar the countries' income levels. Using a gravity-type equation, Helpman (1987) found support for this hypothesis using data for a sample of OECD countries, noting that such a result is consistent with a model where specialization is a function of the connection between economies of scale and brand proliferation (Helpman, 1999). Hummels and Levinsohn (1995), however, in repeating Helpman's (1987) analysis for a sample of non-OECD countries, found that the gravity model still worked well for a group of countries whose bilateral trade was more likely characterized by homogeneous goods.

In analyzing bilateral trade data, there appears to be a model identification problem: the gravity equation works well empirically for both differentiated and homogeneous goods. Evenett and Keller (2002) have argued that the gravity model can nest both the increasing returns/product differentiation story as well as a more conventional homogeneous goods/relative factor abundance story. With appropriate theoretical restrictions on the income parameter, it is possible to use the gravity model of bilateral trade to discriminate between different theories of international trade. In addition, following Feenstra *et al.* (2001), one can place further restrictions on the home and foreign income parameters in order to assess the 'home-market' effect and also allowing identification of the correct trade model.

In this context, the overall objective of this paper is to revisit the basic theory of trade in the presence of product differentiation and economies of scale, and to lay out how such a theory can and has been tested for empirically. The paper proceeds as follows: first, the empirical phenomenon of intra-industry trade is discussed; second, the standard monopolistic explanation for intra-industry trade is briefly laid out, along with a discussion of how this is embedded in a general equilibrium trade model; third, the apparent contradiction between the findings of Helpman (1987), and Hummels and Levinsohn is resolved through a discussion of the theoretical foundations for the gravity equation; and finally, the empirical strategy for testing the increasing returns/product differentiation story is outlined, indicating ways in which it could be applied to processed food and agricultural trade.

THE EMPIRICAL PHENOMENON OF INTRA-INDUSTRY TRADE

Measurement

Neo-classical trade theory predicts that trade between two countries will take place on the basis of comparative advantage generated by differences in some primitive such as technology and/or relative factor endowments. As a result, it is expected that the pattern of trade will be of an inter-industry nature. However, empirical work on the evolution of the European Economic Community by Verdoorn (1960), Drèze (1960, 1961) and Balassa (1965), and later work by Grubel and Lloyd (1975), indicates that a considerable part of the growth in world trade in the post-war period, particularly between developed countries, has been of an intra-industry nature, i.e., the simultaneous export and import of products which are very close substitutes for each other in terms of factor inputs and consumption (Tharakan, 1985).[1]

The early work on intra-industry trade essentially focused on its measurement. As the various indices of intra-industry trade have been carefully reviewed in Tharakan (1983) and Greenaway and Milner (1986), only the main indices are outlined here. Following Kol and Mennes (1986), measures of intra-industry trade can be grouped under two main headings; the first and most common type of index includes both imports and exports for a given country at an industry/sector/country level, hence the concept being assessed is overlap in trade flows. The second type of index compares patterns of imports and exports separately, focusing on a single country relative to a group of countries for an industry/sector/country.[2] This type of measure can also be used to assess the degree of intra-industry specialization, i.e., the extent to which factors of production are being used to produce specific products within an industry at the expense of other products.

The focus here is on the most-commonly used measure of overlap in trade flows, the Grubel and Lloyd (*GL*) index, which can be written as:

---

[1] Helpman (1999) reports that trade overlap within industries has remained high, e.g., the share of intra-industry trade in the UK was 53 percent in 1970, increasing to 85 percent in 1980, and for Germany the equivalent shares were 56 percent and 72 percent respectively.

[2] The most common index of this type is that suggested by Glejser, Goosens and Vanden Eede (1982). Their index is one of either export or import specialization, based on measuring changes in an individual country's trade relative to changes in total trade of a group of countries. For example, if a country's exports increase at a rate equal to or less than that for the group, this represents intra-industry specialization in supply. However, if exports change at a faster rate than that for the group, this is inter-industry specialization. This index has been applied to food and agricultural trade by McCorriston and Sheldon.

(1) $$GL^j = \frac{(X^j + M^j) - |X^j - M^j|}{(X^j + M^j)},$$

and re-arranging:

(2) $$GL^j = 1 - \frac{|X^j - M^j|}{(X^j + M^j)}, \qquad 0 \le GL^j \le 1$$

X^j and M^j being a country's exports and imports respectively, j is a given level of aggregation, and GL^j takes a value of unity for pure intra-industry trade.[3] In aggregating across goods/industries/sectors, it is important to note the weighting characteristics of the index, particularly if it is used as a summary measure of intra-industry trade at a country-level. Suppose j is an aggregate across two industries $i = 1$ and 2, (2) can be re-written as:

(3) $$GL^j = 1 - \left[\frac{|X_1 + X_2 - M_1 - M_2|}{(X_1 + X_2 + M_1 + M_2)}\right].$$

If each industry i has the same sign on its trade balance, then GL^j is a weighted average of the two industries. If, however, the two industries have opposite signs on their trade balances, this weighting effect is lost. In order to guarantee the weighting property, GL^j should be adjusted to:

(4) $$GL^{j'} = 1 - \frac{\sum_{i=1}^{n} |X_i^j - M_i^j|}{(X_i^j + M_i^j)}.$$

Given this index, it is important to recognize three technical problems that arise in the measurement of intra-industry trade. The first concerns the adjustment for aggregate trade imbalance. Given that products/industries/sectors can be chosen at a particular level of aggregation, it may be the case that there is no overall trade balance such that, $\sum_{i=1}^{n} X_i^j \neq \sum_{i=1}^{n} M_i^j$, which implies that, $\sum_{i=1}^{n} |X_i^j - M_i^j| > 0$. Looking at $GL^{j'}$, it means that it must take a value less than one.

This characteristic of the index has raised the question as to whether it is a fundamentally biased measure of intra-industry trade. Both Grubel and Lloyd and Aquino (1978) argue that there is a bias and have suggested adjustments. Focusing on Grubel and Lloyd, they argue that intra-industry trade should be derived as a proportion of total trade imbalance:

---

[3] Prior to Grubel and Lloyd, Balassa (1966) derived a similar index, $B^j = |X^j - M^j|/(X^j + M^j), 0 \le B^j \le 1$, which is simply the analogue of GL^j, where B^j is equal to zero for pure intra-industry trade.

(5) $$GL^{j''} = \frac{(X^j + M^j) - \sum_{i=1}^{n} \left| X_i^j - M_k^j \right|}{(X^j + M^j) - \left| \sum_{i=1}^{n} X_i^j - \sum_{i=1}^{n} M_i^j \right|},$$

which can be re-written as, $GL^{j''} = GL^{j'}/(1-\omega)$, $0 \leq GL^{j''} \leq 1$, where: $\omega = \left| \sum_{i=1}^{n} X_i^j + \sum_{i=1}^{n} M_i^j \right| / (X^j + M^j)$. Hence the value of the adjusted $GL^{j''}$ index increases as ω increases and it indicates what would have been the level of intra-industry trade in the absence of a trade imbalance. Greenaway and Milner (1981, 1986) have questioned whether such an adjustment is actually necessary. In particular, the adjustment presumes *a priori* that the observed trade imbalance reflects trade disequilibrium. However, for a particular group of industries, trade imbalance is not necessarily inconsistent with macro-equilibrium. Therefore, some care should be taken when making the above type of adjustment.

The second technical problem that arises is known as categorical aggregation.[4] This occurs when products are aggregated together in inappropriate trade groups and is essentially the same problem that occurs in applied industrial organization, i.e., what is the correct way of defining an industry? Given that intra-industry trade is defined as trade in similar but differentiated products, the researcher needs to be sure that is what is being measured, as opposed to industry misspecification.

Essentially two procedures have been adopted to deal with the problem. First, researchers have re-grouped trade data into their own concepts of an industry. For example Balassa (1966) grouped third and fourth-digit SITC data into 91 industries. Clearly such a method is open to subjective bias. Second, researchers have selected a particular level of statistical aggregation in the published data that best conforms to their concept of an industry. In principle, such a technique should make use of external evidence on factor inputs and elasticities of substitution. Greenaway and Milner (1983, 1985) note that there appears to be a fair degree of consensus over which level of SITC category to use, most researchers adopting the 3-digit classification. Although consensus does not imply correctness, casual tests indicate that the choice of the 3-digit level is not unreasonable. For example, Greenaway and Milner (1983) regrouped 3, 4 and 5-digit SITC data into SIC Minimum List Headings for the UK and found, for the Grubel and Lloyd index, a high degree of correlation between the two classifications. They also indicate that in moving from the 3 to the 4-digit level of the SITC, while there is a decline in the recorded values of intra-industry trade, it is not a substantial decrease. The general conclusion drawn by Davis (1995) is that, "...While all observers acknowledge that actual industrial classification does not mesh neatly with the theoretical demarcations of industries, most would argue that this does not eliminate the puzzle since intra-industry trade is important down to quite fine levels of disaggregation..." (p. 205)

The third problem relates to the fact that the *GL* index is essentially a static measure based on trade data for one year only (Brülhart, 2000). Hamilton and Kneist (1991) have argued that

---

[4] For example, Finger (1975) argues that goods of heterogeneous factor proportions are placed in a single industry. Davis and Weinstein (2001a) recently concluded that, "...Much of what we call intra-industry trade is simply a data problem that reflects the failure of our industrial classification system to capture the fact that very different goods are being lumped together..." (p. 12)

even if the *GL* index increases between periods, it may actually hide an uneven change in trade flows which is characterized more by inter-industry than intra-industry adjustment. Brülhart (1994) has suggested the following adjustment to the *GL* index designed to capture the concept of marginal intra-industry trade:

$$A_I = 1 - \left[\frac{|\Delta_I X_t - \Delta_I M_t|}{(\Delta_I X_t + \Delta_I M_t)} \right], \qquad 0 \le A_I \le 1 \tag{6}$$

where for a given industry, Δ denotes changes in *X* and *M* in constant prices, *t* is the base year, and *I* denotes the time period between the base and end years. A_I varies between zero for marginal trade that is exclusively inter-industry and one for marginal trade that is exclusively intra-industry. Importantly, Brülhart(2000) has shown that A_I is not correlated with levels and first-differences in the *GL* index, so that the distinction between marginal intra-industry trade and intra-industry trade is empirically meaningful.

This adjustment of the *GL* index has some bearing on evaluation of the so-called 'smooth adjustment hypothesis', whereby it is claimed that if industries are characterized by intra-industry trade, then adjustment to competitive forces will be easier than if it were inter-industry in nature (Greenaway and Milner, 1986). Specifically, if industries are characterized by product differentiation, then it is easier to adjust product lines than it is to undertake the restructuring implied by inter-industry trade. In addition, the labor economics literature indicates that the cost of adjustment is substantially higher under inter-industry adjustment, due to the fact that accumulated human capital is portable between firms in a sector but not across sectors (Lovely and Nelson, 2000). Brülhart(2000) has tested the 'smooth adjustment hypothesis' using a panel data set for 64 Irish industries over the period 1977 to 1990, finding that, intra-industry job turnover, a proxy for labor market adjustment, was positively and significantly related to A_I, but was unrelated to the *GL* index.

Evidence of Intra-Industry Trade in Food and Agriculture

Most empirical work on intra-industry trade has focused almost entirely on manufactured goods. For example, Balassa and Bauwens (1987) explicitly excluded food products from their sample. However, empirical work by McCorriston and Sheldon, Christodolou (1992), Hart and McDonald (1992), and Hirschberg *et al.* has shown that intra-industry trade does exist in this sector, and that the level has been growing over time. While Carter and Yilmaz (1998) do a nice job of summarizing these studies, it is worth noting the key findings reported in McCorriston and Sheldon, and Hirschberg *et al.*

In the latter study, an unadjusted version of the *GL* index was used to generate sectoral values of intra-industry trade for a sample 30 countries over the period 1964-85 based on 4-digit SIC data.[5] Over the sample period, average values of the index for bilateral trade with all partners varied from 0.19 for the UK to 0.03 for Taiwan, the countries exhibiting higher levels intra-industry trade being developed. In the former study, the authors used an adjusted version of the *GL* index to analyze trade patterns in a sample of processed food products for the US and

[5] The sectoral values of the *GL* index were derived following a method suggested by Bergstrand (1990).

nine members of the European Community (EC). Using 3-digit SITC data for 1986, the average value of the index across the sample of processed food products was 0.42 for the US compared to 0.87 in the EC9, although a good deal of the EC's trade was accounted for by trade among the EC member countries. Importantly though, where the results indicate intra-industry trade, they are of a similar order of magnitude to other industrial goods and higher than values recorded for agricultural products. This emphasizes the importance of choosing suitably disaggregated data when measuring intra-industry trade, since aggregated product groups such as 'food and live animals' may hide the existence of intra-industry trade at a more disaggregated product definition.

MONOPOLISTIC COMPETITION AND TRADE

Leamer (1992) has argued that other than the Leontief (1953) paradox, Grubel and Lloyd's work is the only empirical finding presenting an important and substantive challenge to the neoclassical orthodoxy, and in his view has been, "...at least partially responsible for the large theoretical literature on models with increasing returns to scale and product differentiation..." (pp. 5-6)[6] Essentially, the traditional model of comparative advantage, based on the assumptions of homogeneous goods, constant returns to scale and perfect competition, was not thought capable of rationalizing intra-industry trade, whereas scale economies provides a motivation for specialization and hence, two-way trade in differentiated goods, where the market structure is one of monopolistic competition.

Two types of monopolistic competition model have evolved. Krugman (1979, 1980, 1981), following Dixit and Stiglitz (1977), assumes individuals derive utility from variety *per se* and therefore consume all differentiated goods being offered in a particular group. Consequently, product differentiation takes the form of producing a variety not yet in supply, although scale economies at the firm level, constrains the number of goods that can be produced in equilibrium. In contrast, Lancaster (1980) and Helpman (1981) assume that individuals demand goods that embody bundles of characteristics and they are assumed to have an ideal bundle. Consequently, only one type of differentiated good is purchased by consumers, but given diversity of tastes, there is an aggregate demand for variety. Therefore, product differentiation in this case takes the form of a firm offering a variety of good with a different bundle of characteristics to those already on offer. Again, scale economies limit the number of products in equilibrium. Importantly, both types of model generate intra-industry trade.

Basic Monopolistic Competition Model

Following Krugman (1980), the initial focus is on the autarky equilibrium. An economy consists of one industry which produces a variety of goods from a continuum of potential goods.

---

[6] The monopolistic competition model has been widely used in computable general equilibrium (CGE) trade modeling, e.g., Francois, van Meijl, and van Tongeren (2005), and has been used in a variety of other settings, including, amongst others, innovation and endogenous growth models, e.g,, Grossman and Helpman (1992), and spatial models, e.g., Fujita, Krugman and Venables (1999).

On the demand side, the goods produced enter each consumer's utility function symmetrically and all consumers have the same homothetic utility function of the form:

$$U = \sum c_i^{\theta}, \qquad 0 < \theta < 1 \qquad i = 1, \ldots, n \tag{7}$$

where c_i is the consumption of the ith good, the elasticity of substitution between any two goods being equal to a constant $\sigma = 1/(1-\theta)$. If w is income, consumers maximize utility subject to a budget constraint, $w = \sum_{i=1}^{n} p_i x_i$, the first-order condition being:

$$\theta c_i^{\theta-1} = \lambda p_i, \qquad i = 1, \ldots, n \tag{8}$$

where λ is the shadow price on the budget constraint.

Labor is the only factor, all goods being produced with the same cost function:

$$l_i = \alpha + \beta x_i, \qquad \alpha, \beta > 0 \qquad i = 1, \ldots, n \tag{9}$$

where l_i is labor used in production of the ith good and x_i is output of the ith good. This function implies a fixed cost element α, constant marginal costs β and hence decreasing average costs.

The output of any good x_i must equal consumption in equilibrium, so assuming consumers are also workers, output of any good is simply the consumption of one individual multiplied by the labor force L:

$$x_i = Lc_i, \qquad i = 1, \ldots, n \tag{10}$$

and assuming full employment:

$$L = \sum (\alpha + \beta x_i), \qquad i = 1, \ldots, n \tag{11}$$

Under autarky, equilibrium in the economy is derived by assuming monopolistic competition where no two firms produce the same good and free entry drives profits to zero. In addition, assume equilibrium is symmetric with prices and quantities being identical across goods. Dropping subscripts and using (8) and (10), the inverse demand curve facing any firm is:

$$p = \theta \lambda^{-1} (x/L)^{\theta-1}. \tag{12}$$

Given a sufficiently large number of goods are produced in equilibrium, the pricing decision of one firm has no impact on the marginal utility of income λ, consequently the elasticity of demand is $\varepsilon = 1/(1-\theta) = \sigma$. Profit-maximization implies:

$$mc = mr = p(1 - 1/\varepsilon), \tag{13}$$

so that the profit maximizing price for any firm will be:

(14) $$p = \theta^{-1}\beta w,$$

firms' profits being:

(15) $$\pi = px - (\alpha + \beta x)w,$$

Using (14), (15) can be solved out for x:

(16) $$x = \alpha/(p/w - \beta) = \alpha\theta/\beta(1-\theta).$$

From the full employment condition (11) and (16), the equilibrium number of goods is:

(17) $$n = L/(\alpha + \beta x) = L(1-\theta)/\alpha,$$

i.e., the number of goods is a function of the size of the labor force L, the level of fixed costs α and the value of θ from the utility function.

Suppose there is another economy identical to the one just described such that there is no reason for conventional trade to occur. From (17), it can be seen that the number of goods produced in equilibrium will be $2n$ because effectively the labor force L has doubled. Trade occurs because of the production technology, i.e., each good will only be produced by one firm in one country but is sold in both countries, generating pure intra-industry trade. Consequently, the gains from trade are greater diversity for consumers as they spread their incomes over twice as many goods, which, given the symmetry in the model, implies that in equilibrium each firm's output is the same as under autarky, i.e., (16) holds before and after trade.[7] Also, in the trading equilibrium, the prices of any good in either country are the same, and real wages are the same, i.e., there is factor-price equalization. The volume of trade in the model is determinate in that each country exports half of the output of its products, however the direction of trade is not determinate, i.e., it is arbitrary which country produces which goods.

General Equilibrium and Monopolistic Competition

With these micro foundations in place, it is possible to lay out a general equilibrium trade model due to Helpman and Krugman (1985). Assume two countries, j and k; two factors, capital K and labor L; two industries, one perfectly competitive producing a homogeneous

[7] In Krugman (1979), a different specification of the utility function is used, and the elasticity of demand facing each firm is assumed to vary negatively with consumption. Consequently, with trade, consumers spread their expenditure over a wider range of goods, which in turn lowers the elasticity of demand for any specific good, reducing equilibrium prices, and raising real wages. In addition, while the total number of goods increases with trade, each country produces fewer than under autarky, implying that each firm's output increases and greater scale economies are realized.

good Z under constant returns to scale, the other monopolistically competitive producing a range of differentiated goods X, nx under increasing returns.

First define the set of world resource allocations that generate a trade outcome similar to an integrated equilibrium, i.e., the outcome that would arise if all factors were perfectly mobile.8 Following a figure popularized by Dixit and Norman (1980), the dimensions of figure 1 show the combined factor endowments of the two countries. With full employment, this endowment $\bar{V}$ will be fully utilized in the two industries: OQ will be the vector of resources used in the differentiated goods sector, assumed to be capital-intensive in production, and OQ* will be the vector of resources used in the homogeneous good sector, which is labor-intensive in production. In addition, the vector OO* represents aggregate employment, and with appropriate units of measurement, it can be interpreted as world gross domestic product (GDP), denoted as Yw.

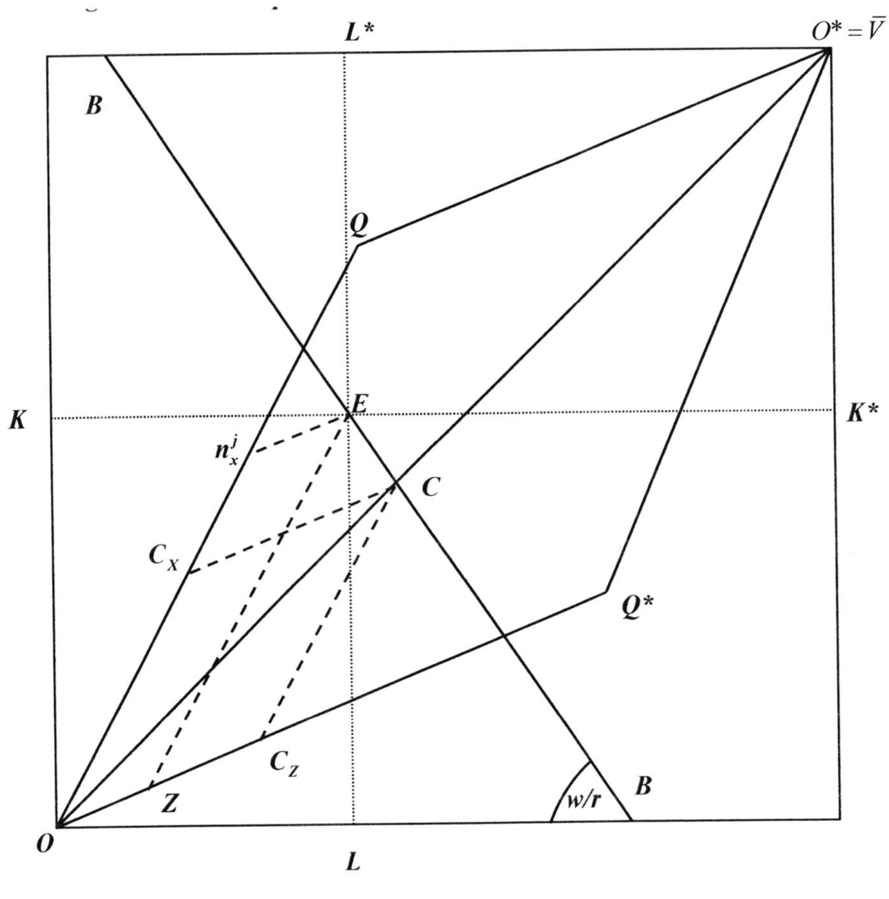

Figure 1. Trade Equilibrium.

Assuming common knowledge of technologies and identical, homothetic preferences, trade can generate the full employment, integrated equilibrium. Suppose that country j is evaluated from the origin O and country k from the origin O*, and define the area OQO*Q*

[8] See Krugman (1995) for a good discussion of the integrated equilibrium and its relation to Samuelson's so-called 'angel'.

as the factor price equalization set. If the allocation of factors is given by the endowment point E, country j will devote On_x^j resources to the production of n varieties of the differentiated good and OZ to the production of the homogeneous good. This solution is derived by constructing a parallelogram between O and E, where a line parallel to OQ* is drawn through E and a line parallel to OQ is also drawn through E. A similar process is followed to derive country k's production levels.

In order to describe the pattern of trade, a negatively sloped function BB is drawn through point E, the slope of which is relative factor prices, w/r. This line passes through the diagonal OO*, giving the home and foreign countries' income levels of Yj=OC and Yk =CO* respectively; all income being paid to the factors of production and all income being spent. Constructing a parallelogram between O and C, the consumption level of country j can be derived, with country j consuming OCX of the differentiated goods and OCZ of the homogeneous good. By a similar process, the consumption levels of country k can also be shown. In this particular equilibrium there is simultaneous inter-industry trade and intra-industry trade. Country j imports the homogeneous good, and is a net exporter $(n_x^j - C_X)$ of differentiated goods, while country k is an exporter of the homogeneous good and a net importer of differentiated goods. The concept of net trade flows in the differentiated goods sector follows from the fact that country j produces and exports n_x^j varieties, and imports n_x^k varieties from the foreign country, where $n_x^j > n_x^k$.

The trading equilibrium described in figure 1 is of course just a re-statement of the Heckscher-Ohlin (H-O) theorem, i.e., the capital-abundant country j is a net exporter of the capital-intensive good X, while the labor-abundant country k exports the labor-intensive good Z. This can also be re-interpreted in terms of the net factor content of trade. With identical homothetic preferences, the composition of the factor content of consumption is the same for both countries, and is identical to the world endowment $\overline{V}$. Consequently, vector OC is country j's factor content of consumption, while the vector *EC*, the difference between the endowment *E* and the consumption of factor services, is the factor content of net trade flows, i.e., country *j* is a net exporter of capital services and an importer of labor services, while country *k* is an exporter of labor services and a net importer of capital services.[9]

Empirical Analysis

A key empirical prediction of the Helpman and Krugman (1985) model is that the share of intra-industry trade is expected to be larger between countries that are similar in terms of their factor endowments and also their relative size. Helpman (1987) evaluated the empirical validity of these predictions using 4-digit SITC data for a cross-section of 14 OECD countries over the period 1970 to 1981, estimating a regression of the form for each year:

[9] An interesting empirical literature has evolved testing for the factor-content of trade theorem, important contributions being by Trefler (1995), Davis and Weinstein (2001b), and Debaere (2003).

$$(18) \qquad GL^{jk} = \alpha + \beta_1 \log\left[\frac{Y^j}{N^j}\right] - \left[\frac{Y^k}{N^k}\right] + \beta_2 \min(\log Y^j, \log Y^k)$$
$$+\beta_3 \max(\log Y^j, \log Y^k) + \mu^{jk},$$

where GL^{jk} is the Grubel and Lloyd index for each country pair j and k, Y^j and Y^k are their respective GDPs, and N^j and N^k are their respective populations. The results provide support for the predictions that that $\beta_1 < 0, \beta_2 > 0$, and $\beta_3 < 0$, although the negative correlation between intra-industry trade and dissimilarity of GDP per capita weakens over time.

Hummels and Levinsohn note two key problems with Helpman's (1987) empirical analysis: first, there are potential problems with using GDP per capita as a proxy for relative factor endowments, and second, the empirical methodology ignores the panel characteristics of the data. In terms of the former, GDP per capita is only a reasonable proxy if, the number of factors is limited to two[10]; and, second, there is a possibility that GDP per capita captures differences in demand structure rather than relative factor endowments. To address these concerns, Hummels and Levinsohn initially ran (18) for the same sample of OECD countries for each year in the period 1962-1983, replacing GDP per capita with GDP per worker. Their results replicate those of Helpman (1987), the negative correlation between intra-industry trade and dissimilarity of GDP per worker weakens over the sample period, and the parameters on the minimum GDP and maximum GDP variables are consistent with the theory. They then re-ran (18) with actual factor data, replacing GDP per worker with capital per worker and land per worker. The results indicate land per worker is negative and significant throughout the period, while capital per worker is initially negative and significant, but then turns positive and significant. Hummels and Levinsohn suggest that the sign on land per worker is picking up the possibility that there is little intra-industry trade in agricultural products, i.e., countries that are relatively well-endowed with land trade agricultural products for manufactured goods.

Hummels and Levinsohn also estimated (18) by pooling all 22 years of their sample, using either GDP per worker or capital per worker, and also country-pair fixed effects to pick up idiosyncratic differences across country-pairs such as geography and language that do not change much over time. Their results suggest that Helpman's (1987) earlier findings may not be robust. In particular, use of country fixed effects reverses the negative sign on both GDP per capita and capital per worker and the explanatory power of the regressions increases substantially, i.e., country fixed effects produce results exactly opposite to what theory predicts.[11] Hummels and Levinsohn are led to conclude, "…If much intra-industry trade is specific to country-pairs, we can only be skeptical about the prospects for developing any general theory to explain it…" (p. 828)

Interestingly, Hummels and Levinsohn did try to decompose the country-pair effects into land and distance effects, finding that a distance effect is quite important in understanding intra-industry trade. In this context, Hirschberg et al. in their study of intra-industry trade in the food processing sector for a sample of countries over the period 1964-1985, conducted a test of the Helpman and Krugman (1985) model using several other variables, including

[10] Helpman and Krugman (1985) show for any country j that, $Y^j = \pi(p, L^j, K^j)$, where π, p, L^j, and K^j are profits, prices, labor and capital respectively. Re-arranging gives, $Y^j / L^j = \pi(p, K^j / L^j)$.

distance, exchange rate uncertainty, and dummies for country-pairs having common membership of a customs union/free trade area, and a common border. In addition, country-pair fixed effects were used to capture any remaining unobserved factors, as well as time fixed effects. Based on a weighted tobit model estimation, the results indicated that although the relative size of trading partners' GDP was statistically insignificant12, dissimilarity in their GDP per capita has a negative impact on intra-industry trade in the food processing sector13, while exchange rate uncertainty, distance, membership of a customs union/free trade area, and a common border all have significant and correctly signed effects on the level of intra-industry trade. These findings provide some support for Helpman's (1999) contention in commenting on the Hummels and Levinsohn results that there is, "...an obvious need to broaden the theory to arrive at a better empirical specification..." (p. 136) 14

Competing Explanations for Intra-Industry Trade

While the focus of this paper is on the monopolistic competition explanation for intra-industry trade, it is worth briefly mentioning some competing theories. Perhaps the most convincing alternative to the monopolistic competition model is that of Davis, who introduces elements of Ricardian theory into a Heckscher-Ohlin setting. In this model, preferences are assumed identical and homothetic across countries; there are two factors of production, capital and labor; and there are three goods, X1, X2, and Z, where goods X1 and X2 have identical factor intensities, but are more capital-intensive in production than good Z.15 Importantly, there are technological differences across countries such that for country j, the production function for good X1 is $X_1^j = Af(K_{X1}, L_{X1})$, and for country k it is $X_1^k = f(K_{X1}, L_{X1})$, where A>1 represents a Hicks-neutral shift in the production isoquants of country j. In equilibrium, country j produces the entire supply of good X1 in which it is has an absolute advantage, and the structure of trade then depends on the location of relative endowments in the factor price equalization set, with four possibilities: (i) pure inter-industry

[11] Hummels and Levisohn get similar results using a random effects model.

[12] Following Noland (1989), Hirschberg *et al.* measure relative size of countries *j* and *k* by the variable $GDPSIZE^{jk} = \left(\frac{GDC^k - GDC^j}{GDC^k + GDC^j}\right) \cdot \left(\frac{GDP^j}{GDP^k}\right)$, where *GDC* is GDP per capita. If $GDC^j > GDC^k$, then the ratio $GDPSIZE^{jk} < 0$, and the larger the difference in size between *j* and *k*, the smaller the level of intra-industry trade.

[13] Following Balassa and Bauwens (1987), Hirschberg *et al.* measure dissimilarity in GDP per capita between partner countries *j* and *k* via the index $INEQGDC^{jk} = 1 + \frac{\left[w^{jk}\ln(w^{jk}) + (1-w^{jk})\ln(1-w^{jk})\right]}{\ln 2}$, where $w^{jk} = GDC^j/(GDC^j + GDC^k)$, and $INEQGDC^{jk}$ varies over the range 0 to 1. The larger is $INEQGDC^{jk}$, the smaller the level of intra-industry trade.

[14] Prior to Helpman's (1987) work, a body of empirical work had evolved analyzing factors affecting intra-industry trade. Typically these studies estimated an industry cross-section regression, with an index of intra-industry trade as the dependent variable, and the explanatory variables consisting of proxies for the level of scale economies and product differentiation in specific industries, e.g., Loertscher and Wolter (1980). This work has met with fairly trenchant criticism on the grounds that, "...the linkage of the theory and the data analyses of necessity is often casual..." (Leamer, 1992, p.33)

[15] Under these assumptions, goods X_1 and X_2 are 'perfectly intra-industry', i.e., for all factor price ratios, they are produced under identical factor intensity.

trade where country k imports goods X1 and X2 from j in exchange for exports of good Z (j is capital abundant); (ii) partial inter-industry trade where country k is self-sufficient in X2, and exports Z to j in exchange for X1 (j is capital-abundant); (iii) pure intra-industry trade where country j exports X1 to k in exchange for X2, and each country is self-sufficient in Z (identical capital-labor ratios); (iv) heterogeneous trade where country k produces only X2 which it trades in exchange for its entire consumption of X1 and Z (j is labor-abundant). The key to this model then is the interaction between technology differences and factor endowments in explaining the structure of trade.

There are also models that assume small numbers of firms: Brander (1981) and Brander and Krugman (1983) show that where the free trade market structure is Cournot-Nash duopoly, cross-hauling of homogeneous goods can occur, a phenomenon they describe as "reciprocal dumping". Shaked and Sutton (1994), develop a model where under autarky, the equilibrium number of firms producing vertically differentiated goods in a Nash-Bertrand oligopoly is a function of the extent of fixed costs of increasing product quality and the distribution of income. They then show that if countries trade with each other, firms will have to exit, and depending on the location of the remaining firms, there may be intra-industry trade in goods of differing quality. The problem with the latter types of model is that they lack a general equilibrium context.

Gravity and Monopolistic Competition

Volume of Trade and Country Size

Perhaps the most fundamental prediction that comes out of the work of Helpman and Krugman (1985) concerns the relationship between relative country size and the volume of trade. Suppose in the model outlined earlier that goods X and Z are both differentiated and produced under increasing returns, monopolistic competition prevails, all trade between the two countries being intra-industry. In this set up, a key result is that as countries become more similar in size, the volume of trade between them as a proportion of their aggregate GDP should increase (Helpman, 1987; Hummels and Levinsohn). Specifically, Helpman (1987) shows that if countries have identical homothetic preferences and trade is balanced, then the following structural equation holds:

$$\frac{V^A}{Y^A} = e_A\left[1 - \sum_{j\in A}(e_A^j)^2\right] \qquad (19)$$

where V^A is the volume of trade between a group of countries A, Y^A is the aggregate GDP of the group of countries, e^A is the share of group A in world GDP, and e_A^j is the share of country j's GDP in group GDP. The right-hand side of (19) is a measure of size dispersion that increases as countries become more similar in size.

Helpman (1987) defined A to be a group of 14 OECD countries, computing the left and right-hand sides of (19) for every year from 1956 to 1981. When graphed, these data points showed a strong positive correlation between the two variables, Helpman (1999) concluding that, "...This co-movement is consistent with models of product differentiation in which specialization in production is driven by brand proliferation..." (p. 137) [16]

Hummels and Levinsohn re-examined this result using data for the same 14 OECD countries over the period 1962 to 1983, but focusing instead on bilateral trade flows, and also using panel data econometric methods to estimate (19). Rearranging (19), and taking logs, Hummels and Levinsohn estimated:

$$\ln(V_t^{jk}) = \alpha^{jk} + \beta_1 \ln[Y_t^{jk}(1-(e_t^j)^2 - (e_t^k)^2)] + \mu_t^{jk}, \tag{20}$$

where the superscript jk denotes a country-pair, and α^{jk} is a country-pair fixed effect that includes the country-pair's share of world GDP, e^{jk}, assumed constant over time. Their results confirm Helpman's (1987) original finding. However, when they estimate the same equation in levels for a sample of 14 non-OECD countries over the period 1962 to 1977, they found the same relationship performed well, even though bilateral trade in this sample is unlikely to be characterized by differentiated goods.

More recently, Debaere (2005) has revisited this issue for the period 1970 to 1989, using Helpman's (1987) original sample of 14 OECD countries, and 12 of Hummels and Levinsohn's sample of non-OECD countries. Debaere (2005) estimates the following equation:

$$\ln(V_t^{jk}) - \ln Y_t^{jk} = \alpha^{jk} + \beta_1 \ln e_t^{jk} + \beta_2 \ln[(1-(e_t^j)^2 - (e_t^k)^2] + \mu_t^{jk}, \tag{21}$$

arguing that Hummels and Levinsohn's transformation of (19) is not "innocuous", multiplication of the joint GDPs, Y_t^{jk}, and the size dispersion index, $[(1-(e_t^j)^2 - (e_t^k)^2]$, allowing size to impact the estimation due to the fact that the covariance between them is positive. In addition, the share of world GDP, e_t^{jk} is allowed to vary over time, and is evaluated separately from the size dispersion index, $[(1-(e_t^j)^2 - (e_t^k)^2]$. Debaere's (2005) results indicate that for the OECD sample of countries, increased trade to GDP ratios for this sample of countries are positively related to their share of world GDP and to their similarity in terms of size, confirming Helpman's (1987) previous result. In contrast, for the non-OECD sample, while the sign on share of world GDP is positive, the sign on the index of size dispersion is negative. Consequently, these results, along with those of Hummels and Levinsohn, would seem to raise significant doubts about the ability of the monopolistic competition model to consistently explain trade patterns at the country-level.

The Gravity Equation

As both Helpman (1987) and Hummels and Levisohn note, (19) fits the general form of the gravity equation. However, based on Evenett and Keller's (2002) observation, there appears to be a model identification problem: the gravity equation works well empirically for both

[16] As noted by Leamer (1992), and later Leamer and Levinsohn (1995), equation (19) can also be derived in a setting where each good is produced in one country under an Armington assumption about preferences.

differentiated and homogeneous goods. In addition, Feenstra (2004) argues that maybe one should not be too surprised by Debaere's (2005) results, due to the fact non-OECD countries are less likely to trade differentiated goods. The empirical issue then becomes one of determining which theoretical model generates 'gravity-like' trade volumes in a given sample of data (Evenett and Keller, 1998, p.1).

The so-called gravity equation of trade predicts that the volume of trade between two countries will be proportional to their GDPs and inversely related to any trade barriers between them. Typically, bilateral trade flows between country *j* and country *k* have been explained by the following specification:

$$V^{jk} = \beta_0 (Y^j)^{\beta_1} (Y^k)^{\beta_2} (D^{jk})^{\beta_3} (A^{jk})^{\beta_4} u^{jk} \tag{22}$$

where V^{jk} is the value of exports (imports) by country *j* to *k* (*j* from *k*) Y^j (Y^k) is the value of nominal GDP in *j*(*k*), D^{jk} is the distance from *j* to *k*, A^{jk} is a vector of other factors that may positively or negatively impact trade between *j* and *k*, and u^{jk} is a log-normally distributed error term with $E(\ln u_{jk}) = 0$. This particular specification was originally used by Tinbergen (1962). The gravity equation, in fact, is probably one of the great success stories in economics, many studies being able to account for variation in the volume of trade across country pairs and over time (Leamer and Levinsohn, 1995). However, until fairly recently, the theoretical foundations for the gravity model were considerably less well understood.

Feenstra *et al.* (2001) note the gravity equation is not implied by the many-country, H-O model. However, with perfect specialization an equation of this sort does arise, and can be derived from quite different theoretical models. This specialization can be due to an Armington demand structure (Anderson, 1979; Bergstrand 1985), increasing returns (Helpman, 1987; Bergstrand, 1989), technological and geographical differences (Davis; Eaton and Kortum, 2002), and factor endowment differences (Deardorff, 1998; Evenett and Keller, 2002). Grossman (1998) notes, "...Specialization – and not new trade theory or old trade theory – generates the force of gravity..." (p. 29)

Due to the emergence of a theoretical literature developing the micro-foundations for the gravity model, its application to explaining bilateral trade patterns has become popular again in recent years. It has been used extensively in analysis of the effects of exchange rate uncertainty in country panel data sets, e.g., Rose (2000), De Grauwe and Skudelny (2000), Dell'Ariccia (2000), Rose and Wincoop (2001), and Glick and Rose (2001). In addition, tests of the different theoretical models underlying the gravity equation have become quite common, e.g., Helpman, 1987, Hummels and Levinsohn, Rauch (1999), Head and Ries (2001), Baier and Bergstrand (2001), Feenstra *et al.* (2001), Chen (2002), Evenett and Keller (2002), and Rose (2004).

Derivation of the Gravity Equation

The results presented in Feenstra *et al.* (2001) and Evenett and Keller (1998; 2002) are probably the most developed in terms of attempting to embed different theories of international trade into the gravity equation, and as a result generating restrictions on the country income parameter(s) that form the basis for hypothesis testing. In order to derive these restrictions, Evenett and Keller (1998; 2002), are followed to initially derive the gravity equation in the case where there is perfect good specialization, based on increasing returns/product differentiation.

Similar to the Helpman and Krugman (1985) model outlined previously, suppose there are two countries, j and k, two goods, X and Z, and two factors of production, K and L. The goods X and Z come in many varieties, and are produced by the same increasing returns to scale technology. The two countries have identical, homothetic preferences, consumers having CES utility functions where all varieties of each good enter symmetrically. Due to increasing returns, each variety is produced by only one firm in equilibrium, the equilibrium number of varieties being determined by free entry and firms behaving monopolistically competitively. n_g^c is the number varieties, $g = X,Z$, produced in country $c = j, k$, s^c is country c's share of world spending, and x^c (z^c) is the equilibrium quantity of a variety of good $X(Z)$. Let Y^c be a country's GDP, and world GDP is $Y^w = Y^j + Y^k$. Also assume good Z is the *numeraire*, i.e., p_y=1, and p_x is the relative price of a variety of good X.

Assuming balanced trade, where $s^c = Y^c / Y^w$, $\forall c$, and there are zero transport costs, then in an increasing returns/product differentiation world, both countries will demand all varieties according to the countries' GDP as a share of world GDP. As a result, any variety produced in country k and consumed in j must be imported. As a result, country j's (k's) imports from country $k(j)$ are given as:

$$M^{jk} = s^j[p_x n_x^k x^k + n_z^k z^k], \tag{23}$$

$$M^{kj} = s^k[p_x n_x^j x^j + n_z^j z^j]. \tag{24}$$

The terms in brackets in (23) and (24) are equal to the GDP of country k and country j respectively, so by substituting Y^j and Y^k into (23) and (24) yields:

$$M^{jk} = s^j Y^k = \frac{Y^j Y^k}{Y^w} = s^k Y^j = M^{kj}. \tag{25}$$

Equation (25) is the gravity equation, based on an increasing returns/product differentiation structure, where imports M^{jk} (M^{kj}) are strictly proportional to GDPs.

Following Helpman and Krugman (1985), it is easy to show that (25) holds whenever there is perfect product specialization, all consumers are faced with the same goods prices and have identical homothetic preferences, and trade balances. Suppose that goods X and Z are both homogeneous and produced under constant returns to scale. Assume that good X is capital-intensive in production, while good Z is labor-intensive, and also that country $j(k)$ is sufficiently relatively well-endowed in capital (labor) that country $j(k)$ specializes in producing good $X(Z)$. If X^c is production of good X, and Z^c is production of good Z, then $X^j = X^w$, and $Z^k = Z^w$, the value of production of good X equals country j's GDP, $p_x X^j = Y^j$, and the value of production of good Z equals country k's GDP, $Z^k = Y^k$. As a result, the following can be written:

(26) $$M^{jk} = s^j Z^k = s^j Y^k = \frac{Y^j Y^k}{Y^w}, \text{ and } M^{kj} = s^k p_x X^j = s^k Y^j = \frac{Y^j Y^k}{Y^w},$$

This is identical to the gravity equation (25), and is termed the multi-cone H-O model (Feenstra). Again imports M^{jk} (M^{kj}) are strictly proportional to GDPs.

These two versions of the gravity model are illustrated in figure 2, constructed in the same fashion as figure 1. Suppose country *j* is evaluated from the *O* origin, and country *k* from the *O** origin, and that the endowment for the increasing returns/product differentiation case is given by point *E* on the diagonal vector *OO**, i.e., relative factor endowments are the same in both countries, so product specialization is based entirely on increasing returns to scale. Country *j*(*k*) will devote resources to producing n_x^j (n_x^k) varieties of good *X* and resources to producing n_z^j (n_z^k)varieties of good *Z*. In turn, the consumption level of country *j*(*k*) is OC_X (O^*C_X) for varieties of *X*, and OC_Z (O^*C_Z)for varieties of *Z*. This results in a pattern of trade that is pure intra-industry, i.e., country *j*(*k*) specializes in producing specific varieties $n_x^j(n_x^k)$ of good *X* and specific varieties $n_z^j(n_z^k)$ of good *Z* which are then consumed in both countries.

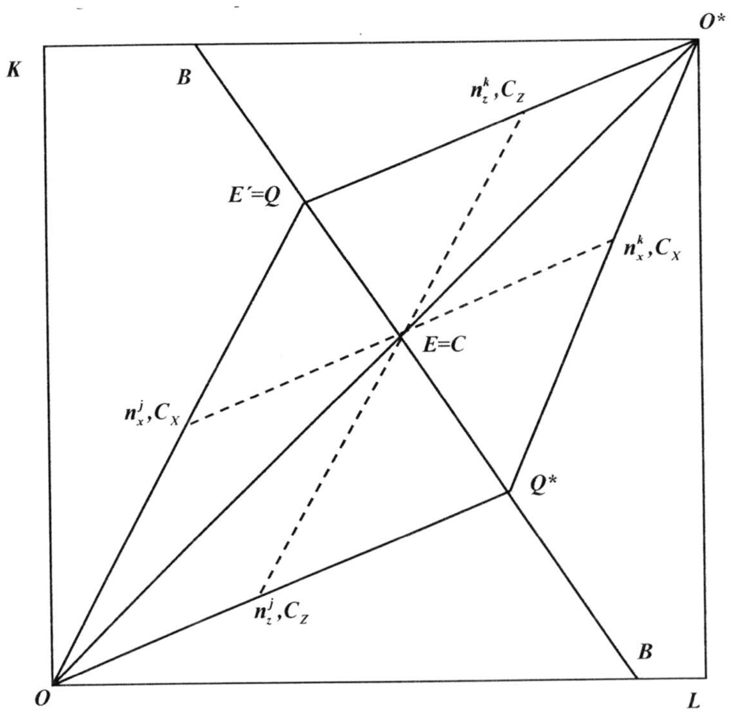

Figure 2. Perfect Specialization.

Suppose instead for the multi-cone H-O model that the endowment of factors is given by point *E′*=*Q*. Now country *j*(*k*) specializes in producing homogeneous good *X* (*Z*) at point *Q*, while the pattern of consumption is still given by the parallelogram drawn from point *C* on the diagonal *OO**. The pattern of trade is now pure inter-industry, with country *j*(*k*) exporting (importing) good *X* and importing (exporting) good *Z*.

The gravity equation(s) derived above is overly restrictive as it relies on perfect specialization, in terms of either increasing returns/differentiated goods or constant returns/homogeneous goods. Evenett and Keller (1998; 2002) also allow for the possibility of imperfect specialization. Suppose X is a differentiated goods sector, with increasing returns and a technology that is capital-intensive, while Z is a homogeneous good sector with constant returns and a technology that is labor-intensive, known as the increasing returns/uni-cone H-O model. For endowments inside the factor price equalization set, the volume of bilateral trade is given as:

(27) $$T^{jk} = s^k p_x X^j + s^j p_x X^k + (Z^k - s^k Z^w),$$

where the first term on the right hand side of (27) is country j's exports (country k's imports M^{kj}), and the other two terms are its imports of other varieties of X and good Z (M^{jk}). Suppose then that $\gamma^j = \dfrac{Z^j}{p_x X^j + Z^j}$ is the share of good Z in country j's GDP, $(1-\gamma^j)$ being the share of good X in country j's GDP. With balanced trade, $M^{jk} = M^{kj}$, so that $M^{kj} = s^k p_x X^j$, and given the definition of γ^j, then $M^{kj} = s^k(1-\gamma^j)Y^j$, the following adjusted gravity equation can be written[17]:

(28) $$M^{jk} = (1-\gamma^j)\frac{Y^j Y^k}{Y^w}.$$

In comparison to (25), this gravity equation implies that for any value of $\gamma^j > 0$, the level of bilateral imports is lower than the case where both X and Z are differentiated. In addition, as the share of Z in GDP declines, the level of imports rises, and in the limit, as $\gamma^j \rightarrow 0$, then (28) reverts back to (25). Therefore, the volume of trade is higher the lower is the share of the homogeneous good in GDP.

Suppose now that there is imperfect specialization in the case where both goods X and Z are homogeneous and produced under constant returns, a case known as the uni-cone H-O model (Feenstra). The volume of bilateral trade is given by:

(29) $$T^{jk} = p_x(X^j - s^j X^w) + (Z^k - s^k Z^w).$$

Country j's exports are given by the first term $p_x(X^j - s^j X^w)$, country j's imports, M^{jk}, are given by the second term $(Z^k - s^k Z^w)$, and with balanced trade, $M^{jk} = M^{kj}$. From the H-O theorem, if country j is relatively capital-abundant it exports the relatively capital-intensive good X, and imports the relatively labor-intensive good Z, and vice-versa for country k. Given $X^w = (X^j + X^k)$, and the definition of γ, then M^{jk} can be written as $M^{jk} = (1-\gamma^j)Y^j - s^j(1-\gamma^j)Y^j - s^j(1-\gamma^k)Y^k$. In turn, as $s^k = (1-s^j)$, this expression can

[17] See Keller (1998) for the derivation of equation (28).

be re-written as, $M^{jk} = s^k(1-\gamma^j)Y^j - s^j(1-\gamma^k)Y^j$. From this, the following gravity equation can be written[18]:

$$M^{jk} = (\gamma^k - \gamma^j)\frac{Y^j Y^k}{Y^w}. \tag{30}$$

As the capital-labor ratios of the two countries converge, so $\gamma^k \to \gamma^j$, and in the limit when $\gamma^k = \gamma^j$, there is no trade. In addition, the multi-cone H-O model is a special case of (30) when $\gamma^j = 0$ and $\gamma^k = 1$.

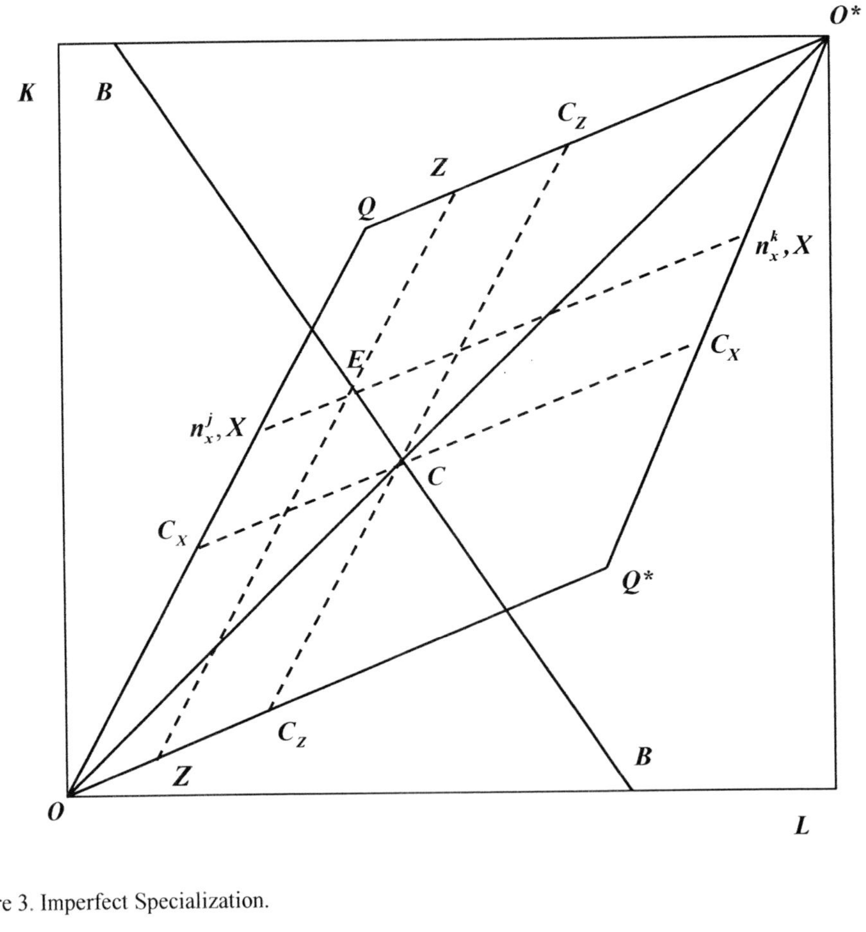

Figure 3. Imperfect Specialization.

These two cases of imperfect specialization are illustrated in figure 3. For an endowment point *E*, in the increasing returns/uni-cone H-O model, country *j* produces n_x^j and consumes C_X varieties of the differentiated good *X*, and produces *Z* and consumes C_Z of the homogeneous good *Z*, and vice-versa for country *k*. The pattern of trade, therefore, is simultaneous intra-industry trade in varieties of good *X*, and inter-industry trade in goods *X* and *Z*, country *j*(*k*) being a net exporter (importer) of varieties of *X* and an importer (exporter)

[18] See Keller for the derivation of equation (30).

of Z. Likewise in the uni-cone H-O model, country j produces OX and consumes C_X of good X, and produces Z and consumes C_Z of good Z, and vice-versa for country k. The pattern of trade, therefore, is inter-industry trade in goods X and Z, country $j(k)$ being an exporter(importer) of X and an importer (exporter) of Z.

Empirical Analysis of the Gravity Equation

Given this analysis, it is useful to outline the recent empirical work by Evenett and Keller (2002) and Feenstra *et al.* (2001), which presents a potential strategy for analyzing trade in the food and agricultural sector, and a means for addressing the empirical puzzle noted by Cho *et al.* concerning the differential effect of income on bilateral food and agricultural trade for EMS versus non-EMS countries.

Perfect Versus Imperfect Specialization

Focusing first on Evenett and Keller (2002), they work with a cross-sectional data set for 58 countries in 1985, generating a possible 3,306 bilateral import relations. To test the gravity models outlined in the previous section, they first calculated the GL^{jk} index for each country pair using 4-digit SITC data on all goods trade, creating a sample of 2,870 observations, some country pairs having no positive amounts of trade between them. They then split this sample into two sub-samples based on an arbitrarily chosen level of the GL^{jk} index, $\overline{GL} = 0.05$ where, if $GL^{jk} > \overline{GL}$, it is expected that trade would be more likely based on product differentiation and scale economies. This resulted in 630 observations in the high GL^{jk} sample, which was then split into V=5 classes, where GL^{jk} increases by class, $v=1,\ldots,V$. For each v, the following version of (25) was estimated:

$$M_v^{jk} = \alpha_v \frac{Y_v^j Y_v^k}{Y^w} + \mu_v^{jk}, \tag{31}$$

where for perfect specialization based on increasing returns, the predicted value of $\alpha_v = 1$. The results show the estimated values of α_v range from 0.016 to 0.139, which falls well short of the predicted value, and when the whole sample is used, $\alpha_v = 0.087$. This model clearly over-predicts the level of bilateral trade between countries.

Turning to the 2,240 observations where $GL^{jk} < \overline{GL}$, Evenett and Keller (2002) split this sample into V=5 classes, where factor proportions increase by class, $v=1,\ldots,V$. For each v, the following version of (25) was estimated:

$$M_v^{jk} = \alpha_v \frac{Y_v^j Y_v^k}{Y^w} + \mu_v^{jk}, \tag{32}$$

where in the multi-cone H-O model, with perfect specialization in homogeneous products, the predicted value of $\alpha_v = 1$. The results show the estimated values of α_v range from 0.039 to 0.111, which again falls well short of the predicted value, and when the whole sample is used, $\alpha_v = 0.052$. Again, this model over-predicts the level of bilateral trade between countries.

Given these results, Evenett and Keller (2002) also allow for imperfect specialization. Focusing first on the increasing returns/uni-cone H-O model, and assuming X is capital-intensive, they re-estimate (31) as:

$$M_v^{jk} = (1-\gamma_v^j)\frac{Y_v^j Y_v^k}{Y^w} + \mu_v^{jk}, \tag{33}$$

if country j is relatively capital-abundant, and as:

$$M_v^{jk} = (1-\gamma_v^k)\frac{Y_v^j Y_v^k}{Y^w} + \mu_v^{jk}, \tag{34}$$

if country k is relatively capital-abundant, where the predicted values of $(1-\gamma_v^j)$ and $(1-\gamma_v^k) < 1$. Given the number of estimated values of $(1-\gamma_v^j)$ and $(1-\gamma_v^k)$ varies by and within each class v, the median estimated values range from 0.053 to 0.128, increasing non-monotonically in the level of GL^{jk}, and the median estimated value for the whole sample is 0.086. In addition, the simple correlation between $(1-\gamma_v^j)$ and K^j / L^j, is found to be negative, i.e., the share of differentiated products in GDP does not increase with the relative abundance of capital to labor.[19] From this, Evenett and Keller (2002) conclude that these results provide mixed support for the increasing returns/uni-cone H-O model, i.e., it correctly predicts more production of differentiated goods with higher intra-industry trade, but the link to factor proportions is weak.

Finally, Evenett and Keller (2002) analyzed the uni-cone H-O model by re-estimating (32) as:

$$M_v^{jk} = (\gamma_v^k - \gamma_v^j)\frac{Y_v^j Y_v^k}{Y^w} + \mu_v^{jk}, \tag{35}$$

if country j is relatively capital-abundant, and as:

$$M_v^{jk} = (\gamma_v^j - \gamma_v^k)\frac{Y_v^j Y_v^k}{Y^w} + \mu_v^{jk}, \tag{36}$$

if country k is relatively capital-abundant, where the predicted values of $(\gamma_v^k - \gamma_v^j)$ and $(\gamma_v^j - \gamma_v^k) < 1$. The median estimated values range from 0.021 to 0.080, increasing non-

[19] Testing the model under the assumption that the homogeneous good is capital-intensive also fails to provide support for the increasing returns/uni-cone H-O model.

monotonically with differences in factor proportions, and the median estimated value for the whole sample is 0.04. In addition, the simple correlation between γ_v^j and K^j / L^j is found to be negative, i.e., the share of the labor-intensive good *Z* in GDP does not increase with the relative abundance of capital to labor. Evenett and Keller (2002) conclude that the uni-cone H-O model works well, even when factor proportion differences are large. Overall, they conclude that both factor endowments and scale economies can explain different components of variations in production and trade. [20]

'Home-Market' Effect

Turning to the Feenstra *et al.* (2001) study, a key feature of their work is that they focus explicitly on using the gravity equation to test for the 'home-market' effect. As noted in the introduction, it is possible that if countries differ in their relative size as measured by GDP, then there may be a 'home-market' effect which is expected to result in a larger income elasticity effect on bilateral trade for the home country (Krugman, 1980; Feenstra *et al.*, 2001). In the increasing returns/uni-cone H-O model, the 'home market' effect occurs if the relative size of, say country *j*, is increased, resulting in an increase in the net exports of varieties of good *X*. As country *j*'s GDP increases with size, demand for varieties of good *X* in *j* increases, this raises profits of existing firms in country *j*, causing entry of new firms, so that in equilibrium, country *j* specializes in and exports more varieties of the differentiated good, i.e., there is more than a one-for-one relationship between the increase in demand share of the larger country and the change in its output share.

As noted by Feenstra *et al.* (2001), the 'home-market' effect is actually quite sensitive to the extent of free entry into the differentiated goods sector, so that there might be a reverse 'home market' effect if there are barriers to entry to producing new varieties. Therefore, to provide an alternative to the monopolistic competition model with free entry, Feenstra *et al.* (2001) follow Head and Ries (2001) by assuming an Armington-type structure. In this case, there is perfect competition, goods are differentiated by country of origin, and the number of goods is fixed at one in each country. As each country produces its good in proportion to its size, the price of country *j*'s good is the same as the price of country *k*'s good, and each country will demand the two varieties in the same ratio. If country *j* is larger than country *k*, then country *j*'s exports of the good are lower than its imports, i.e., there is a reverse 'home-market' effect. Essentially, this structure assumes that location of production is exogenous, so that an increase in income, and hence demand, in one country, is met by additional output by firms in both countries, so that there is a less than one-for-one relationship between the increase in demand share of the larger country and the change in its output share.[21,22]

---

[20] Evenett and Keller (2002) also evaluated the robustness of their results by lowering the critical value of $\overline{GL}$ to 0.033. Essentially they found a similar pattern of results for both the perfect and imperfect specialization models. In addition, their results prove to be robust to allowing for the effects of distance.

[21] Head and Ries note that the Armington structure is also consistent with a short-run version of the monopolistic competition model where the number of firms is fixed. In addition, in reference to Davis's model of intra-industry trade, they argue that the Armington model, "...may be viewed as representative of a broader class of models where a larger market does not induce reallocation of the location of firms and product varieties..." (pp. 859-860)

Feenstra *et al.* (1998; 2001) also propose a setting where goods are homogeneous rather than differentiated, drawing on the 'reciprocal dumping' model of Brander, and Brander and Krugman noted earlier. Given Cournot-Nash behavior and free entry, if country j is larger than country k, the zero profit condition implies that more firms enter the market in j, resulting in prices being lower in j than k, so that j is a net exporter of the homogeneous good, despite the increase in demand in j, i.e., there is a 'home-market' effect. Alternatively, given a Cournot-Nash duopoly in homogeneous goods, the model predicts that the relative shares of the two firms are the same in both export markets. Consequently, if country j is larger than country k, given constant relative export market shares, then the smaller country k will have larger exports than the larger country j. In other words there will be a reverse 'home-market' effect.

Re-writing the basic gravity equation in logarithmic form,

$$\ln M^{kj} = -\beta_0 \ln Y^w + \beta_1 \ln Y^j + \beta_2 \ln Y^k , \tag{37}$$

where M^{kj} is the value of imports by country k from j, and the income elasticity parameters for countries j and k are β_1 and β_2 respectively. In the case of perfect specialization and zero transport costs, the term $-\beta_0 \ln Y^w$ is a constant in a cross-sectional regression, while $\beta_1 = \beta_2 = 1$. If initially both countries are of the same size, and then there is a small transfer of GDP from k to j, this can result in the 'home market' effect whereby $\beta_1 > \beta_2$, i.e., a country's net exports of the differentiated good are more sensitive to own income than their partner's income. Depending on the specific data set, this result is consistent either with the monopolistic competition story or the 'reciprocal dumping' story with free entry. In contrast, if initially both countries are of the same size, and again there is small transfer of GDP from k to j, this can result in the reverse 'home market' effect whereby $\beta_1 < \beta_2$, i.e., a country's net exports are more sensitive to their partner's income than their own income. Again, depending on the specific data set, this result is consistent either with the Armington story or the 'reciprocal dumping' story with no entry.

Feenstra *et al.* (2001) work with a 110 country data set for five cross-sections: 1970, 1975, 1980, 1985, and 1990, and rather than use the *GL* index, they separate goods into differentiated and homogeneous following Rauch's (1999) classification based on 5-digit level SITC data aggregated to the 4-digit level. Rauch defines homogeneous goods as those traded in an organized exchange, while differentiated goods are neither traded in an organized exchange, and nor do they have a reference price. The version of (37) they estimate allows for other control variables such as distance, common language, and membership of a free trade customs union/agreement that are typically included in a gravity equation, e.g., see Cho *et al.* The results for the complete sample of countries show that in the case of differentiated goods, the average estimated value of β_1 is 1.09, and for β_2 it is 0.65, while in the case of homogeneous goods, the average estimated value of β_1 is 0.51, and for β_2 it is 0.82. Feenstra *et al.* (2001) conclude that these results are consistent with there being a 'home market' effect

[22] Head and Ries' empirical results for tariff reductions following implementation of the 1988 US-Canadian free trade agreement indicate support for the Armington structure as opposed to the monopolistic competition model.

in the case of differentiated goods under monopolistic competition, and a reverse 'home market' in the case of homogeneous goods with duopoly and 'reciprocal dumping'. They also find these results hold when they split the sample into OECD countries and OPEC to non-OPEC countries. Their overall conclusion is that, "...the theoretical foundations for the gravity equation are actually quite general, but the empirical performance is quite specific..." (p.446)

Application to Food and Agricultural Trade

The previous discussion leads to one basic prediction: depending on whether goods in a particular sample are differentiated or homogeneous, one type of model is expected to do a better job of explaining trade in that sample than another. All this suggests that using the appropriate data and econometric methods, it ought to be possible to test which trade theories best explain bilateral trade in food and agricultural products. As noted earlier, observed intra-industry trade in this sector appears to differ substantially between agricultural commodities and processed food products and by country (McCorriston and Sheldon), and some success has already been had in applying gravity-type models to the sector (Hirschberg *et al*; Cho *et al.*). By separating bilateral trade flows into differentiated and homogeneous goods, using either of the classification schemes outlined above, it should be possible to identify whether the increasing returns/product differentiation story can explain processed food trade, and whether the homogeneous goods/relative factor abundance story can explain trade in agricultural commodities.

Table 1. Summary of Parameter Restrictions on Gravity Model

Trade model	Income parameter restriction	Good type
Increasing returns/ Multi-cone H-O model	$\beta_1 = \beta_2 = 1$	Differentiated/homogeneous
Increasing returns/ Uni-cone H-O model	$\beta_1 = \beta_2 = (1 - \gamma^i) < 1$	Differentiated/homogeneous
Uni-cone H-O model	$\beta_1 = \beta_2 = (\gamma^j - \gamma^i) < 1$	Homogeneous
Increasing returns/ 'Home-market'	$1 \geq \beta_1 > \beta_2$	Differentiated
Armington/ Reverse 'home-market'	$\beta_2 > \beta_1$	Differentiated
Oligopoly/ 'Home-market'	$\beta_1 > \beta_2$	Homogeneous
Duopoly Reverse 'home-market'	$\beta_2 > \beta_1$	Homogeneous

On balance, the Feenstra *et al.* (2001) approach seems most attractive in several respects. First, adaptation of Rauch's approach to classifying food and agricultural goods into homogeneous and differentiated groups is quite appealing given his definition of homogenous goods, and avoids the type of problems associated with measuring intra-industry trade. Second, in estimating (37), the Evenett and Keller (2002) approach can be nested by appropriate restrictions being placed on the parameters β_1 and β_2. Third, other models of trade can be captured through restrictions on these same parameters implied by the 'home market' effect. Table 1 contains a summary of these parameter restrictions that might be tested for in food and agricultural trade data.

SUMMARY

This paper has focused on what is recognized as the most commonly used, theoretical alternative to the neoclassical trade model – one based on product differentiation, scale economies, and monopolistic competition. The evolution of this model came out of the empirical challenge that observed intra-industry trade presented to the way international economists think about trade. Even though there are some well-known problems associated with measuring intra-industry trade, the monopolistic competition model has become the dominant theoretical alternative to the neoclassical model, and has also become very popular in computable general equilibrium approaches to trade modeling. So does the theory carry any empirical weight?

While Helpman's (1987) initial work seemed to present fairly strong evidence for the theory, the later empirical analysis of Hummels and Levinsohn did raise significant doubts about its validity. However, the follow-up work by Gebaere (2005) on the original Helpman (1987) structural equation, and the recent theoretical and empirical work using the gravity model, suggests that evidence for the increasing returns/product differentiation story may be found in the appropriate trade data sets. Given that intra-industry trade has been found to exist in the food and agricultural sector, there is no obvious reason why the type of methodology developed by Evenett and Keller (2002), and Feenstra *et al.* (2001) should not be adapted and applied to the sector.

ACKNOWLEDGEMENTS

Paper prepared for presentation at the theme day, "New Dimensions in Modeling Food and Agricultural Markets", Winter Meeting of the International Agricultural Trade Research Consortium, San Diego, CA, December 4-6, 2005. Ian Sheldon is Professor in the Department of Agricultural, Environmental and Development Economics, The Ohio State University. Address for correspondence: Department of Agricultural, Environmental, and Development Economics, 2120 Fyffe Road, The Ohio State University, Columbus, OH 43210, e-mail: sheldon.1@osu.edu.

REFERENCES

Anderson, J. "A Theoretical Foundation for the Gravity Equation." *American Economic Review* 69(1979): 106-116.

Aquino, A. "Intra-Industry Trade and Intra-Industry Specialization as Concurrent Sources of International Trade in Manufactures." *Weltwirtschaftliches Archiv* 114 (1978): 275-295.

Baier, S.L. and Bergstrand, J.H. "The Growth of World Trade: Tariffs, Transport Costs, and Income Similarity." *Journal of International Economics* 53(2001): 1-27.

Balassa, B. *Economic Development and Integration.* Mexico: Centro Estudios Monetarios Latinamericanos. 1965.

Balassa, B. "Tariff Reductions and Trade in Manufactures among Industrial Countries." *American Economic Review* 56(1966): 466-473.

Balassa, B. and Bauwens, L. "Intra-Industry Specialisation in a Multi-Country and Multi-Industry Framework." *Economic Journal* 97(1987): 923-939.

Bergstrand, J. "The Gravity Equation in International Trade: Some Microeconomic Foundations and Empirical Evidence." *The Review of Economics and Statistics* 67(1985): 474-481.

Bergstrand, J. "The Generalized Gravity Equation, Monopolistic Competition and the Factor-Proportions Theory of International Trade." *Review of Economics and Statistics* 71(1989): 143-153.

Bergstrand, J.H. "The Heckscher-Ohlin-Samuelson Model, the Linder Hypothesis and the Determinants of Bilateral Intra-Industry Trade." *Economic Journal* 100(1990): 1216-1229.

Brander, J. A. "Intra-Industry Trade in Identical Commodities." *Journal of International Economics* 11(1981): 227-242.

Brander, J. A. and Krugman, P.R. (1983) "A Reciprocal Dumping Model of Intra-Industry International Trade." *Journal of International Economics* 13(1983): 313-321.

Brülhart, M. "Marginal Intra-Industry Trade: Measurement and Relevance for the Pattern of Industrial Adjustment." *Weltwirtschaftliches Archiv* 130(1994): 600-613.

Brülhart, M. "Dynamics of Intra-Industry Trade and Labor-Market Adjustment." *Review of International Economics* 8(2000): 420-435.

Carter, C.A. and Yilmaz, A. "Intra-Industry Trade and Foreign Direct Investment in Processed Food as Alternatives to Trade Theory." *Global Markets for Processed Foods: Theoretical and Practical Issues*. D.H. Pick, D.R. Henderson, J.D. Kinsey, and I.M. Sheldon, eds. Boulder, CO: Westview Press. 1998.

Chen, N. "Intra-National versus International Trade in the European Union: Why do Borders Matter?" *CEPR Working Paper* 3407(2002), London: CEPR.

Cho, G., Sheldon, I.M. and McCorriston, S. "Exchange Rate Uncertainty and Agricultural Trade." *American Journal of Agricultural Economics* 84(2002): 931-942.

Christodoulou, M. "Intra-Industry Trade in Agrofood Sectors: The Case of the EEC Meat Market." *Applied Economics* 24(1992): 875-884.

Davis, D.R. "Intra-Industry Trade: A Heckscher-Ohlin-Ricardo Approach." *Journal of International Economics* 39(1995): 201-226.

Davis, D.R. and Weinstein, D.E. "What Role for Empirics in International Trade." *NBER Working Paper* 8543 (2001a), Cambridge, MA: NBER.

Davis, D.R. and Weinstein, D.E. "An Account of Global Factor Trade." *American Economic Review* 91(2001b): 1423-1453.

De Grauwe, P. and Skudelny, F. "The Impact of EMU on Trade Flows." *Weltwirtschaftliches Archiv* 136 (2000): 383-402.

Deardorff, A. V. "Determinants of Bilateral Trade: Does Gravity Work in a Neoclassical World?" *The Regionalization of the World Economy*. J.A. Frankel, ed. Chicago, IL: Chicago University Press. 1998.

Debaere, P. "*Relative* Factor Abundance and Trade." *Journal of Political Economy* 91(2003): 589-612.

Debaere, P. "Monopolistic Competition and Trade, Revisted: Testing the Model without Testing for Gravity." *Journal of International Economics* 66(2005): 249-266.

Dell'Arricia, G. "Exchange Rate Fluctuations and Trade Flows." *IMF Staff Papers* 46 (2000): 293-314.

Dixit, A. and Norman, V. *Theory of International Trade*. Cambridge University Press: Cambridge. 1980.

Dixit, A. and Stiglitz, J. "Monopolistic Competition and Optimum Product Diversity." *American Economic Review* 67(1977): 297-308.

Drèze, J. "Quelques Refléxions Sereines sur l'Adaptation de l'Industrie Belge au Marché Common." *Comptes Rendus des Travaux de la Societé Royale d'Economique de Belgique* 275 (1960).

Drèze, J. "Les Exportations Intra-CEE en 1958 et la Position Belge." *Recherches Economiques de Louvain* (1961): 717-738.

Eaton, J. and Kortum, S. "Technology, Geography and Trade." *Econometrica* 70(2002): 1741-1779.

Evenett, S.J. and Keller, W. "On Theories Explaining the Success of the Gravity Equation." *NBER Working Paper* 6529 (1998), Cambridge, MA: NBER.

Evenett, S.J. and Keller, W. "On Theories Explaining the Success of the Gravity Equation." *Journal of Political Economy* 110(2002): 281-316.

Feenstra, R.C. *Advanced International Trade: Theory and Evidence*. Princeton, NJ: Princeton University Press. 2004.

Feenstra, R.C., Markusen, J.R. and Rose, A.K. "Understanding the Home Market Effect and the Gravity Equation: The Role of Differentiated Goods." *NBER Working Paper* 6804 (1998), Cambridge, MA: NBER.

Feenstra, R.C., Markusen, J.R. and Rose, A.K. "Using the Gravity Equation to Differentiate Among Alternative Theories of Trade." *Canadian Journal of Economics* 34 (2001): 430-447.

Finger, J.M. "Trade and Intra-Industry Trade." *Economic Inquiry* 13(1975): 581-589.

Francois, J., van Meijl, H. and van Tongeren, F. "Trade Liberalization in the Doha Development Round." *Economic Policy* 42(2005): 349-391.

Fujita, M., Krugman, P.R. and Venables, A.J. *The Spatial Economy: Cities, Regions and International Trade*. Cambridge, MA: MIT Press. 1999.

Glejser, H., Goosens, K. and Vanden Eede, M. "Inter-Industry and Intra-Industry Specialization in Exports and Imports (1959-1970-1973)", *Journal of International Economics* 12 (1982): 353-369.

Glick, R. and Rose, A. K. "Does a Currency Union Affect Trade? The Time Series Evidence." *NBER Working Paper* 8396 (2001), Cambridge, MA: NBER.

Greenaway, D. and Milner, C. R. "Trade Imbalance Effects and the Measurement of Intra-Industry Trade." *Weltwirtschaftliches Archiv* 117(1981): 756-62.

Greenaway, D. and Milner, C. R. "On the Measurement of Intra-Industry Trade." *Economic Journal* 93 (1983): 900-908.

Greenaway, D. and Milner, C. R. "Categorical Aggregation and International Trade: A Reply." Economic Journal, 95 (1985): 486-487.

Greenaway, D. and Milner, C. *The Economics of Intra-Industry Trade*. Oxford: Basil Blackwell. 1986.

Grossman, G.M. "Comment." *The Regionalization of the World Economy*. J.A. Frankel, ed. Chicago, IL: Chicago University Press. 1998.

Grossman, G.M. and Helpman, E. *Innovation and Growth in the Global Economy*. Cambridge, MA: MIT Press. 1992.

Grubel, H.G. and Lloyd, P.J. *Intra-Industry Trade: The Theory and Measurement of Trade in Differentiated Products*. London: Macmillan. 1975.

Hamilton, C. and Kniest, P. "Trade Liberalization, Structural Adjustment and Intra-Industry Trade: A Note." *Weltwirtschaftliches Archiv* 127(1991): 356-367.

Hart, T. and McDonald, B.J. *Intra-Industry Trade Indexes for Canada, Mexico and the United States, 1962-87*. Agriculture and Trade Analysis Division, Economic Research Service, U.S. Department of Agriculture, Staff Report No. AGES 9206 (1992).

Head, K. and Ries, J. "Increasing Returns versus National Product Differentiation as an Explanation for the Pattern of US-Canada Trade." *American Economic Review* 90(2001): 858-876.

Helpman, E. "International Trade in the Presence of Product Differentiation, Economies of Scale and Monopolistic Competition." *Journal of International Economics* 11(1981): 305-40.

Helpman, E. "Imperfect Competition and International Trade: Evidence from Fourteen Industrial Countries." *Journal of the Japanese and International Economies* 1(1987): 62-81.

Helpman, E. "The Structure of Foreign Trade." *Journal of Economic Perspectives* 13(1999): 121-144.

Helpman, E. and Krugman, P.R. *Market Structure and Foreign Trade: Increasing Returns, Imperfect Competition and the International Economy*. Cambridge, MA: MIT Press. 1985.

Hirschberg, J.D. and Dayton, J.R. "Detailed Patterns of Intra-industry Trade in Processed Food." *Industrial Organization and Trade in the Food Industries*. I. M. Sheldon and P. C. Abbott, eds. Boulder, CO: Westview Press. 1996.

Hirschberg, J.D., Sheldon, I.M. and Dayton, J.R. "An Analysis of Bilateral Intra-Industry Trade in the Food Processing Sector." *Applied Economics* 26(1994): 159-167.

Hummels, D. and Levinsohn, J. "Monopolistic Competition and International Trade: Reconsidering the Evidence." *Quarterly Journal of Economics* 110(1995): 799-836.

Keller, W. "Gravity Models of Trade without Specialization of Production: A Note." Mimeo, University of Wisconsin, 1998.

Kol, J. and Mennes, L.B.M. "Intra-Industry Specialization: Some Observations on Concepts and Measurement." *Journal of International Economics* 21(1986): 173-181.

Krugman, P.R. "Increasing Returns, Monopolistic Competition, and International Trade." *Journal of International Economics* 9(1979): 469-479.

Krugman, P.R. "Scale Economies, Product Differentiation, and the Pattern of Trade." *American Economic Review* 70(1980): 950-959.

Krugman, P.R. "Intra-Industry Specialization and the Gains from Trade." *Journal of Political Economy*, 95(1981): 959-973.

Krugman, P.R. "Increasing Returns, Imperfect Competition and the Positive Theory of International Trade." *Handbook of International Economics*. G.M. Grossman and K. Rogoff, eds. Amsterdam: Elsevier. 1995.

Lancaster, K. "Intra-Industry Trade under Perfect Monopolistic Competition." *Journal of International Economics* 10 (1980): 151-176.

Leamer, E.E. "Testing Trade Theory." *NBER Working Paper* 3957 (1992), Cambridge, MA: NBER.

Leamer, E.E. and Levinsohn, J. "International Trade Theory: The Evidence." *Handbook of International Economics*. G.M. Grossman and K. Rogoff, eds. Amsterdam: Elsevier. 1995.

Leontief, W. "Domestic Production and Foreign Trade: The American Capital Position Re-examined." *Readings in International Economics* R. E. Caves and H. G. Johnson, eds. London: Allen and Unwin. 1968.

Loertscher, R. and Wolter, F. "Determinants of Intra-Industry Trade: Among Countries and Across Industries." *Weltwirtschaftliches Archiv* 116(1980): 281-93.

Lovely, M. and Nelson, D. "Marginal Intra-Industry Trade and Labor Adjustment." *Review of International Economics* 8(2000): 436-447.

McCorriston, S. and Sheldon, I.M. "Intra-Industry Trade and Specialization in Processed Agricultural Products: The Case of the US and EC." *Review of Agricultural Economics* 13(1991): 173-184.

Noland, M. "Econometric Estimation of International Intra-Industry Trade." Unpublished working paper (1989), Washington DC: Institute for International Economics.

Rauch, J.E. "Networks versus Markets in International Trade." *Journal of International Economics* 48(1999): 7-35.

Rose, A. K. "One Money, One Market: The Effect of Common Currencies on Trade." *Economic Policy* 30 (2000): 7-46.

Rose, A.K. "Do We Really Know That the WTO Increases Trade?" *American Economic Review* 94(2004):

Rose, A. K. and van Wincoop, E. "National Money as a Barrier to International Trade: The Real Case for Currency Union." *American Economic Review, Papers and Proceedings* 91(2001): 386-390.

Shaked, A. and Sutton, J. "Natural Oligopolies and International Trade." *Monopolistic Competition and International Trade* H. Kierzkowski, ed. Oxford: Clarendon. 1984.

Tharakan, P. K. M. "The Economics of Intra-Industry Trade: A Survey." *Intra-Industry Trade: Empirical and Methodological Aspects* P. K. M. Tharakan, ed. Amsterdam: North Holland. 1983.

Tharakan, P.K.M. "Empirical Analysis of the Commodity Composition of Trade." *Current Issues in International Trade: Theory and Policy*. D. Greenaway, ed. London: Macmillan. 1985.

Tinbergen, J. *Shaping the World Economy: Suggestions for and International Economic Policy*. New York: The Twentieth Century Fund. 1962.

Trefler, D. "The Case of Missing Trade and Other Mysteries." *American Economic Review* 85(1995): 1029-1046.

Verdoorn, P.J. "The Intra-Bloc Trade of Benelux." *Economic Consequences of the Size of Nations*. E.A.G. Robinson, ed. London: Macmillan. 1960.

In: International Agricultural Trade and Development
Editor: Dragan Miljkovic, pp. 33-38
ISBN: 978-1-60021-965-8

Chapter 3

COMMENTS BY PHILIP ABBOTT[1] ON: "MONOPOLISTIC COMPETITION AND TRADE: DOES THEORY CARRY ANY WEIGHT?" BY IAN SHELDON, SEPTEMBER 2005

Philip Abbott

There has been a resurgence of empirical work by general economists specializing in international trade over the last ten to fifteen years. Advanced econometric techniques have been used to investigate the several empirical puzzles evident in data on international trade patterns. For example, much of that work has focused on resolving the Leontief paradox and so examining under what condition, and with what modifications, can Heckscher-Ohlin theory rationalize observed data. Much emphasis is put on evaluating received theory and assessing its consistency with market observations. A hallmark of this work has been development of rigorous theoretical underpinnings to models estimated.

Sheldon's paper starts from two of those puzzling empirical regularities in trade patterns which challenge neoclassical orthodoxy, and examines the theoretical underpinnings of models addressing those regularities. The first is the finding based on the Grubel-Lloyd index that there is substantial intra-industry trade. Much of Sheldon's prior work on imperfect competition and trade is motivated by this evident characteristic of both general and agricultural trade, which he and others have gone to great lengths to verify. Even casual observation of supermarket shelves would corroborate this point, that cross-hauling is substantial and important, and must be accommodated in whatever theory underlies our models. The second is that the gravity model, a seemingly ad hoc explanation of bilateral trade patterns, has been extremely successful in "explaining" trade patterns. That is, contrary

[1] Discussant comments on a Theme Day Presentation, "New Dimensions in Modeling Food and Agricultural Markets", Winter Meeting of the International Agricultural Trade Research Consortium, San Diego, CA, December 4, 2005.

to both Heckscher-Ohlin and Riccardo, it appears that similar countries (in terms of income levels at least) trade more with each other than with different countries. The gravity results also suggest that neighboring countries tend to trade more with one another, as distance seems to proxy well for trade costs. The basis for specialization is not always apparent in the success of the gravity model, however. One is uncertain as to the underlying mechanisms giving rise to observed behavior, and to correlations in trade data. A link between these two findings has been drawn in work that suggests the success of the gravity model may be because it captures increasing returns to scale, and so one of the reasons behind imperfect competition critical to New Trade Theory outcomes.

It is also useful to put into context work motivating this paper, an earlier analysis by Cho, Sheldon and McCorriston investigating impacts of exchange rate uncertainty on international trade. In order to econometrically test for these impacts a base model explaining bilateral trade patterns was required. Therefore, Cho, Sheldon and McCorriston begin with a gravity model specification as their theoretical underpinning, and added variables describing exchange rate uncertainty to assess their marginal impact on trade flows. This approach has also been extensively used in econometric investigations of bilateral trade agreements (e.g. NAFTA) by both agricultural economists and general economists. There dummy variables explain deviations due to the trade agreements from predictions of a gravity model. The problem is always that a base model which explains bilateral trade flows is required as the starting point for analysis, one of the most important problems in my view still confronting international trade specialists. But the gravity model, or alternatives like the Armington model, may be only ad hoc correlations not well grounded in underlying theories derivable from plausible economic behavior. Then collinearity with these compounding factors (exchange rates, trade agreements) may also cloud empirical tests. Estimated parameters may be biased and, more likely, empirical tests may be imprecise. Both problems are evident in the perplexing income effects of the Cho, Sheldon and McCorriston paper, which Sheldon hopes here can be explained by distinctions between models of differentiated and homogeneous good trade.

To follow the theoretical underpinnings of work in this literature, Sheldon does us all a great service in this paper by carefully developing models which underlie the key theories to be investigated. He first examines the Grubel-Lloyd index of intra-industry trade, including in his derivations more recent critiques identifying potential shortcomings of this index. While it is not clear which of the corrections must be applied, work with any form of this index demonstrates the importance of intra-industry trade, and that carries over to agricultural and especially processed food trade. Sheldon also carefully develops the classic Helpman and Krugman model of monopolistic competition and shows how it may be incorporated into a general equilibrium trade model. That theory is at the heart of the debate on theoretical underpinnings of the gravity model.

Much recent work has been done to establish those theoretical underpinnings for the gravity model, in order to address this concern with its potential ad hoc nature, and more importantly to interpret results and assess exactly what theory underlies observed trade patterns. But as Sheldon notes, several competing explanations can give rise to the gravity

Abbott is Visiting Professor, DERG, Department of Economics, University of Copenhagen, Studiestræde 6, DK-1455 Copenhagen K, Denmark. He is on sabbatical leave from the Department of Agricultural Economics, Purdue University, West Lafayette, IN 47907. Email: abbottpc@purdue.edu

model specification – scale economies and increasing returns, Armington demand structure, technological and empirical differences, and factor endowment differences. Correspondence between investigations of the theoretical underpinnings of the gravity model and on other empirical puzzles, and so other threads of empirical work on international trade, remain entangled. Work by some of the same people on the Leontief paradox emphasize Riccardian explanations based on technological differences (Reimer), trade costs (Anderson and van Wincoop) and heterogeneous demand (Cranfield, Eales, Hertel and Preckel), issues assumed away in the underlying theoretical models of the thread followed by Sheldon.

Sheldon relies heavily on recent papers by Evenett and Keller and by Feenstra, Markusen and Rose to uncover the relevant underlying theory rationalizing a particular international trade dataset. Two aspects of those models emerge as devices to identify what theory is consistent with empirical results of modified gravity model specifications. Feenstra, Markusen and Rose emphasize entry barriers, showing that another of the empirical puzzles, the "home market effect", and the income effects that drive it, differ depending on whether the underlying model and market correspond with free entry or a fixed number of firms over the time frame of observations. Evenett and Keller separate the two income terms of the "mass variable" of the gravity equation (Yi * Yj), and suggest the now differing coefficients on each income term can be used to identify whether observed behavior is consistent with complete or incomplete specialization, and more importantly whether the appropriate model is for differentiated goods as in monopolistic competition models or better fits a world of homogeneous goods. In their empirical work on manufacturing trade, Evenett and Keller reject the complete specialization models and suggest that actual trade is likely to include a varying mixture of homogenous and differentiated goods depending on where one is looking.

On the one hand, these results should be appealing to agricultural trade economists, as empirical conditions will lead to differing applicable models and so different trade patterns. And in his Table 1 Sheldon delineates the outcomes which should allow us to differentiate between competing explanations of trade patterns. But there may be identification problems in the model identification strategies of this line of work.

In the case of the entry barrier assessment, the predictions of the models depend on two extreme assumptions – either free entry or a fixed number or firms. If in reality firm numbers sluggishly adjust to market conditions in a systematic way and partially over the period of observation, neither assumption will be fully appropriate. If the speed of adjustment varies among firms or among goods in an aggregate, that will make this assessment imprecise. So explanations of the rate of adjustment of firm entry may confound this method of model assessment.

In the case of income effects, Evenett and Keller investigate aggregate manufacturing so have the luxury of assuming homogeneous demand (and unitary income elasticties) without doing great violence to the data. But for agricultural goods recent work has shown not only that income elasticities of demand differ from one, but also that they can vary with income (Cranfield, Eales, Hertel and Preckel). In poor societies likely to export homogeneous commodities, income elasticities of demand for food may approach one, but in more developed economies and when processed food trade becomes important income elasticities of demand may be lower, and certainly differ by product. Hence, there may be a systematic correlation between income effects and the nature of trade (homogenous or differentiated goods) explained by varying income levels due to the stage of development, and not whether the underlying model is monopolistic competition or Armington.

A persistent, remaining concern is that aggregation bias could continue to plague this work, even when looking at agricultural commodities or processed food, a problem noted by Sheldon. In the work most prevalent among international trade economists now, CGE simulation modeling, this approach to partially address product differentiation and so imperfect competition is implicitly assumed, and might be justified due to either categorical aggregation or product differentiation. Assumed Armington elasticities are key to typical CGE model results. This work suggests that may not be the right (or the only) story, and helps to explain why estimation of Armington elasticties is so difficult. After all, the driving force for including the Armington specification in CGE models is to accommodate the observed diverse pattern of trade and not to incorporate imperfect competition theory. In some work by general economists, disaggregation to 3 digit SITC level is pursued, and little benefit to using finer trade classification data is found, but stories abound on cross hauling of what amount to differentiated agricultural goods or foods which are not captured even at the 5 digit level in trade statistics. In my work on bilateral trade flows, more disaggregated models with technical (agronomic or engineering) underpinnings are more easily estimated and yield plausible results, but don't lead to general explanations of trade. One of the problems for economists has been that New Trade Theory suggests specific, not general, explanations of trade behavior.

I couldn't help but think about other factors which could explain observed trade patterns and so empirical difficulties related to the fundamental issues in the Cho, Sheldon and McCorriston paper. In the papers of Evenett and Keller and by Feenstra, Markusen and Rose, as well, in their theoretical world the alternative to monopolistically competitive trade is autarky. But foreign direct investment (FDI) may be the key alternative internationalization strategy, especially in the face of exchange rate uncertainty. In earlier work by Sheldon and colleagues it has been recognized that FDI is a more prevalent mode for firms to go overseas than is trade, yet this avenue is assumed away in the theoretical underpinnings of these models. They noted that sales by foreign affiliates of U.S. firms can exceed three times trade flows for processed food products. In work with Juan Solana in the mid 1990s, we observed that this ratio of foreign affiliate sales to exports varied systematically by good, being greater for food - where transactions costs would be higher - than for manufactured goods or more homogeneous agricultural commodities. One distinction to be made by this model identification strategy is systematically related to the choice between FDI and trade as an internationalization strategy. We also observed that this ratio varied over time in ways systematically related at least to the levels of exchange rates – when highly valued exchange rates dissuaded exports from the U.S. in the mid 1980s, even greater dependence on FDI rather than trade was observed. And it is difficult to disentangle exchange rate variability from the large movements in actual exchange rate levels. This leads me to question whether the theoretical models of this literature which ignore FDI as a behavioral mechanism will disentangle the problematic income results of the Cho, Sheldon and McCorriston paper.

The disappointment of this paper was that Sheldon did not try the proposed strategy for testing the increasing returns/product differentiation story, the punch line of this paper, on his earlier data set. Relatively minor modifications to the specification in the Cho, Sheldon and McCorriston gravity model could have accommodated this test. But he may have been wise not to do so, as, the existing results demonstrated a high degree of collinearity between income and exchange rate uncertainty effects, and the evident imprecision in estimating income effects would likely have precluded definitive tests along the lines laid out by Sheldon and by Evenett and Keller.

In conclusion, while I applaud Sheldon's efforts in this paper, as in his earlier work, to establish rigorous theoretical underpinnings for some of the more complex theories explaining trade patterns, I remain skeptical that the gravity model is a theoretically sound basis for doing this. Now the problem is too many competing theories rather than a lack of theory, but based on very rigid assumptions. Too many mechanisms must be assumed away for rigorous theoretical models to be derived in estimable form. This is an especially difficult problem for sector specific work in food and agriculture, where factors like differing income elasticities of demand for different countries or the importance of FDI as an alternative to trade, come into play. But understanding and utilizing the models of imperfect competition to explain observed bilateral trade patterns seems to me to be a sound strategy, if requiring that we go back to the basics of those models and not rely on something as general as the gravity model, which may nest several of those theories but in ways which will be quite difficult to test empirically. Thus, the bridge between theory and empirical work will remain treacherous and difficult, but is a path worth taking if better understanding of bilateral trade patterns is to be found.

REFERENCES

Abbott, P.C. and J.B. Solana-Rossilo, "International Firms in the Manufacture and Distribution of Processed Foods," *Global Markets for Processed Foods: Theoretical and Practical Issues*, D.H. Pick, D.R. Henderson, J.D. Kinsey and I.M. Sheldon, eds., Westview Press, Boulder, CO, 1998.

Anderson, J.E. and E. van Wincoop, "Trade Costs." *Journal of Economic Literature*, 42 (2004): 691-751.

Cho, G., Sheldon, I.M. and McCorriston, S. "Exchange Rate Uncertainty and Agricultural Trade." *American Journal of Agricultural Economics* 84 (2002): 931-942.

Cranfield, J., J. Eales, T.W. Hertel and P. Preckel, "Changes in the Structure of Global Food Demand," *GTAP Working Papers* 295, Center for Global Trade Analysis, Department of Agricultural Economics, Purdue University, 1998.

Evenett, S.J. and Keller, W. "On Theories Explaining the Success of the Gravity Equation." *Journal of Political Economy* 110 (2002): 281-316.

Feenstra, R.C., Markusen, J.R. and Rose, A.K. "Using the Gravity Equation to Differentiate Among Alternative Theories of Trade." *Canadian Journal of Economics* 34 (2001): 430-447.

Grubel, H.G. and Lloyd, P.J. *Intra-Industry Trade: The Theory and Measurement of Trade in Differentiated Products*. London: Macmillan. 1975.

Helpman, E. and Krugman, P.R. *Market Structure and Foreign Trade: Increasing Returns, Imperfect Competition and the International Economy*. Cambridge, MA: MIT Press. 1985.

Reimer, J.J. "Global Production Sharing and Trade in the Services of Factors." *Journal of International Economics,* forthcoming in 2005.

Sheldon, I.M. "Monopolistic Competition and Trade: Does Theory Carry Any Weight?" Theme Day Presentation, "New Dimensions in Modeling Food and Agricultural Markets", *Winter Meeting of the International Agricultural Trade Research Consortium,* San Diego, CA, December 4, 2005.

In: International Agricultural Trade and Development
Editor: Dragan Miljkovic, pp. 39-80
ISBN: 978-1-60021-965-8

Chapter 4

Product Differentiation and Trade in Agri-Food Products: Taking Stock and Looking Forward*

Rakhal Sarker [1] ***and Yves Surry*** [2]
[1] Department of Agricultural Economics and Business; University of Guelph; Guelph, Ontario; CANADA
[2] Department of Economics; Swedish University of Agricultural Sciences; Uppsala, SWEDEN

Abstract

The Heckscher-Ohlin-Samuelson trade model focuses mainly on the supply side of the economy and assumes that trade takes place in homogeneous goods. According to this model, specialization of production and trade among countries are shaped by factor endowments and factor intensities. While this is a simple, logical and powerful prediction, the H-O-S model is ill equipped to explain trade in differentiated products. Similarly, it cannot explain the existence and growing importance of intra-industry trade in agri-food products. The "New Trade Theory" developed by Helpman and Krugman (1985) focuses on economies of scale, product differentiation and imperfect competition and offers persuasive explanation of IIT. An attempt is made in this paper to provide an overview of this literature, highlight major developments since the mid 1980s and assess the overall status of product differentiation models used to analyze trade in agri-food products. While notable progress has been made since the early 1990s, a lot more needs to be done in this area. Some thoughts on future refinements of empirical product differentiation models and their applications to trade in agri-food products are provided.

---

* An Invited Paper Presented on the Theme Day, "*Modeling Food and Agricultural Markets*" at the 2005 Annual Meeting of the *International Agricultural Trade Research Consortium* in San Diego California, December 4-6, 2005.
We would like to thank Julian Alston and Philip Abbott for their thoughtful comments on our paper at the IATRC Meeting in San Diego. The usual disclaimer applies

Key words: Trade theory, Intra-industry trade, Product differentiation, Agri-food trade, Trade policy

INTRODUCTION

In determining comparative advantage and gains from trade, traditional trade models focused primarily on the production side of the economy. While the oversimplification of the consumption side allowed trade theorists to derive a set of simple but powerful predictions about why countries engage in specialization and trade, the consequences of overly simplified trade models have been brought to the forefront since the 1970s.

The theory of comparative advantage developed by David Ricardo at the beginning of the 19th Century has played an important role in shaping modern thinking about trade. Ricardian trade model assumes that labor is the only input used in a fixed proportion to produce an output in each country. It predicts that a country will export products in which it has higher labor productivity relative to its labor productivity in other products (i.e., it has a comparative advantage). Except for a few early attempts such MacDougall (1952) and Stern (1962), there is hardly any empirical study of trade flows that relies exclusively on the Ricardian trade model. This is perhaps due to its exclusive focus on labor productivity and neglect of the contributions of other factors of production as well as its inability to explain what causes labor productivity to vary across countries. However, despite its empirical weaknesses, the Ricardian model remains useful for thinking about the effects of technological changes on specialization, patterns of trade and the distribution of trade benefits (Davis, 1995; Eaton and Kortum,1997).

The framework of trade proposed by Heckscher (1919) and Ohlin (1924) departs from the Ricardian model in that it emphasizes the roles of land, labor and capital in both agricultural and industrial production and attempts to explain how variations in the availability of these factors of production determine a country's nature of specialization and patterns of trade. Paul Samuelson added elegance to this framework by developing a two-factor, two-sector and two-country version of the Heckscher-Ohlin model that became the cornerstone of modern theory of international trade. According to the Heckscher-Ohlin-Samuelson (H-O-S) theory of trade, a country should specialize in and export a product that uses more intensively the factor of production with which the country is well endowed. Therefore, a capital-rich country like the United States should export the capital-intensive products while a labor-rich country like Bangladesh should export various labor-intensive products. While this theory offers a more logical way to think about trade among nations than the Ricardian approach, it too exclusively focuses on the supply side of the economy and suggests that differences in factor endowments can explain specialization patterns and the volume of trade between countries. The demand side is muted through the assumptions of *identical and homothetic preferences* of consumers and that countries trade in *homogeneous products*. The refinement of the H-O-S trade model continues along with the development of empirical implications of the factor content of net trade flows (Helpman, 1999).

While the assumption that international trade takes place in *homogeneous* goods is an important element of the H-O-S trade model, it is quite restrictive in view of the fact that as countries progress economically wide varieties of new products emerge on the market and old products disappear over time. While some countries produce the new products first, other countries end up producing them after a time lag and in some cases, with minor modifications. As a result, many countries, particularly, in the developed world, engage in trade of mostly differentiated products and less so in homogeneous goods. A casual observation would reveal that many products traded among countries today are differentiated by brand such as computers, medical equipments, breakfast cereals, baby formulas, toothpaste, clothing etc. Moreover, it was observed during the 1960s and 1970s in the European Economic Community (EEC) that large volumes of trade flow between members of the EEC with similar factor endowments and that within some industries, trade overlap exists. The latter, in fact, has grown significantly over time in the European Union (EU). According to the H-O-S model of trade, such overlaps should not exist. The existence and growth of trade overlaps in certain industries suggest that a considerable share of trade among developed countries may not be driven by differences in factor endowments as predicted by the H-O-S model. Note that trade among developed OECD countries account for more that 50% of total merchandise trade flows while about 30% of total trade flows between developed and developing countries. The bulk of trade between developed and developing countries consist of inter-industry trade while trade among developed countries consists mostly of intra-industry trade (IIT). The first comprehensive measurement of the extent of trade overlap by Grubel and Lloyd (1975) attracted considerable research interests in this area (Greenaway *et al.*, 1995). The results from these studies cast serious doubt on the relevance of the H-O-S model of trade and may have provided impetus for the development of the "New Trade Theory" by Helpman and Krugman in the 1980s. Product differentiation is at the centre of the "New Trade Theory" which attempts to explain the prevalence of intra-industry trade that currently dominates bulk of commodity trade among the OECD countries.

While the treatment of an agricultural commodity such as wheat, rice, beef, wool, cheese, maize and wine as a homogeneous good appears to be reasonable in theory, in practice differences in production practices, seeds, geographical locations of production, sanitary and phyto-sanitary (SPS) measures and food safety requirements make the quality of these commodities (at least, as they are perceived by consumers) different. Moreover, the processed agri-food commodities have become the most important type of agricultural commodities traded internationally, particularly among developed OECD countries. The processed agri-food commodities vary considerably in terms of their factor contents, quality attributes and marketing features. Thus, differences in brand, quality and other aspects of heterogeneity make these products differentiated in international trade. Since the pioneering attempt by Armington (1969) to model trade in agricultural products differentiated by the country of origin, a number of researchers used this model to explain trade in major agri-food commodities (Thursby *et al.*, 1986; Goddard, 1988; Alston *et al.*, 1990). While the Armington's approach to model trade in agricultural product differentiated by country of origin is the first attempt to relax the assumption of homogeneous good in international trade, it implicitly imposes a set of rather untenable restrictions such as: (i) import shares respond only to changes in relative prices and not to changes in income, and (ii) that the income elasticities of demand for imports of the good from all sources are equal to one. It has also been demonstrated that empirical data do not support either the homotheticity or the separability assumptions often maintained in Armington's framework (Slesnick, 1998; Alston *et al.*, 1990). Furthermore, the nature of product differentiation entertained in an Armington model is not related to variations in product quality and hence can be considered exogenous to consumers' decision calculus related to their *'love for variety'* or quality as argued by Lancaster (1979). Nevertheless, this approach has been quite popular among agricultural economists for the last three decades.

The most prominent forms of product differentiation in international trade in recent years have been horizontal and vertical product differentiations which are related to differences in product attributes and quality not just perceived by consumers but also due to differences in factor contents in each product. While significant progress has been made during the 1980s in terms of developing the theoretical framework to guide empirical research aimed at explaining intra-industry trade, the progress in applying these models in international trade in agri-food products has been slow. The purpose of this paper is to provide a survey of the literature on product differentiation and international trade in agricultural products, critically assess what has been done, how and why. It is hoped that such a synthesis will open up new avenues for stimulating analytical and empirical research in this area.

The paper proceeds as follows. Section two deals with the theoretical framework relevant for IIT and highlight major developments since the 1990s. Section three concentrates on how IIT is classified and measured. This section also highlights some of the challenges researchers face in measuring intra-industry trade in agri-food products. Section four is devoted to gain a better understanding of the determinants of IIT in agri-food products. This section focuses on econometric studies and highlights some of the modeling challenges faced by empirical researchers in this area. Section five concentrates on how various product differentiation models have been applied to agri-food trade during last fifteen years. Despite the dominance of national product differentiation models during this period, other types of product differentiation models emerged since the 1980s and have been employed to analyze various agricultural trade policies. Due emphasis is given to the new type of product differentiation models in this section. Issues to be considered for future modeling endeavors in this area are discussed in Section six. The final section concludes the paper.

Trade Theory and Intra-Industry Trade

As indicated earlier, neither the Ricardian model nor the H-O-S model of trade is adequate to explain extensive IIT. Indeed, the development of various indices to measure the extent of intra-industry trade predates the development of a relevant trade theory and many early attempts tried to identify some patterns of trade overlaps. For example, Loertscher and Wolton (1980) found that the share of intra-industry is high when the trading partners are highly developed and at comparable level of development. They also noted that the share of intra-industry is high when the trading partners are large and their sizes are similar. Also during the late 1970s, several industrial organization (IO) theorists, particularly, Dixit and Stiglitz (1977) and Lancaster (1975) developed microeconomic foundations for the traditional Chamberlinian monopolistic competition and successfully embedded monopolistic competition in differentiated products in general equilibrium models. While these models relied on restrictive assumptions about tastes and technology, they offered fresh and innovative ways to think about trade based on economies of scale rather than on comparative advantage, factor endowments and factor intensity (Krugman, 1995a). Thanks to the contributions of Dixit and Stiglitz (1977) and Lancaster (1975), the theoretical literature on product differentiation, imperfect competition and IIT grew rapidly in the early 1980s through the works of Krugman (1979, 1980), Helpman (1981), Lancaster (1980), Shaked and Sutton (1984), Brander (1981) and Brander and Krugman (1983). At the early stage of development, various trade models with monopolistic competition seemed inconsistent with the H-O-S model of trade and also with each other. However, by thinking in terms of an integrated-economy approach, it is possible to embed trade in differentiated products within a factor proportions model. Thus, the H-O-S trade model and the "New Trade Theory" are complementary in nature; inter-industry trade results from factor endowments and specialization while the intra-industry trade can be explained by product differentiation and scale economies. This is the essence of the remarkable synthesis advanced in Helpman and Krugman (1985). It is no surprise that even after two decades, Helpman and Krugman (1985) remains the most influential text for the "New Trade Theory". What follows next is a non-technical elaboration of this theory and the testable predictions it generates.

The integrative view of international trade developed by Helpman and Krugman (1985) relaxes the neoclassical assumptions of homogeneous products, constant returns to scale and perfect competition and allows for an interplay among economies of scale, product differentiation and factor proportions by embracing Chamberlinian monopolistic competition in trade. Since many intermediate and final consumer goods are differentiated by brand or by other means, to explain extensive IIT, Helpman and Krugman (1985) introduced sectors with differentiated products into the trade theory and argued that product differentiation typically involves economies of scale. The prevalence of scale economies motivates firms in a country to produce differentiated products that enhance foreign trade. Furthermore, the existence of economies of scale motivates countries to invest in research and development so that new techniques of production can be developed and employed to exploit the benefits of scale economies over time. Due to the benefits of learning-by-doing or of prudent investments in research and development (R&D), some companies in some countries will have access to certain technologies (note such technological races in the electronics and pharmaceutical industries which are not available to their rivals). As a result, a company developing a differentiated product gains some monopoly power because there is no perfect substitute for its unique brand in the market. Finally, the economies of scale limit the range of differentiated products that can be supported by the market. The smaller the economies of scale, the larger the number of profitable brands that become available on the market. This results in each country specializing in the production of some differentiated products and trading them with other countries. On the demand side, due to variations in income, tastes and preferences among its people, each country demands a wide variety of differentiated products. When trade takes place among these countries, brand-specific economies of scale lead to *intra-industry* trade. Helpman and Krugman (1985) also demonstrated that economies of scale, product differentiation and various forms of competition are compatible with factor price equalization and with the factor content of trade.

Since, the vast majority of empirical research in intra-industry trade, either in agri-food or in manufacturing sectors, is based on this theory, it is important to bring out the key predictions of this theory. The key predictions generated by Helpman and Krugman (1985) trade theory are as follows:

- The share of *intra-industry* trade (IIT) is larger between two countries that are similar in composition of factor endowments and in size. In a generalized framework with multi-country trade, this theory suggests that relatively more IIT will take place between a pair of countries with similar factor compositions than between a pair of countries with dissimilar factor compositions. The difference in factor composition across countries can be measured by cross-country differences in income per capita. Therefore, the most important testable hypothesis in this case is that "*the share of intra-industry trade in bilateral trade flows is larger for countries with similar per capita income*". It is also possible to develop another hypothesis related to relative sizes of trading partners and the share of IIT in bilateral trade flows. These hypotheses are related to the composition of bilateral trade flows.

- Economies of scale and product differentiation drive firms and countries to specialize and specialization encourages larger volumes of international trade. Assuming that consumers in all countries have identical and homothetic preferences for traded goods and trade is balanced, spending levels on each good are proportional to levels of Gross Domestic Product (GDP). Thus, it implies that *a given percentage increase in the GDP of a country will expand its trade volume with another country by the same amount*. This idea is also at the heart of a "Gravity Equation" which has a long and rich history in empirical analysis of trade flows between countries and has been a workhorse in empirical trade studies for almost half a century (see Timbergen, 1962; Linnemann, 1966; Anderson, 1979; Bergstrand, 1985 & 1989; Deardorff, 1998; Baier and Bergstrand, 2001; Anderson and Wincoop, 2003; Feenstra, 2002 & 2004).
- Finally, for a group of countries, the share of IIT in the within-group trade volume should be larger when within-group dispersion of per capita income (proxy for factor composition) is smaller. This hypothesis deals with the composition of within-group trade flows.

Although there has been no major development in trade theory during the last two decades following the publication of Helpman and Krugman (1985), a number of authors made attempts to test the hypotheses from the “New Trade Theory” using different data sets. In addition to examining the consistency of the above hypotheses with data, these studies also develop insightful empirical implications of the “New Trade Theory”. It is useful to recap the findings in this literature before examining how the theory has been applied to explain trade flows in agri-food commodities.

Since empirical measurement of the extent of intra-industry trade predates formal articulation of the “New Trade Theory” by Helpman and Krugman (1985), many early attempts deal with elaboration and explanation of trade-overlaps rather than rigorous testing of any theoretical prediction. Of many attempts to empirically examine IIT since 1985, Helpman (1987) is particularly noteworthy. Drawing on Helpman and Krugman (1985), Helpman (1987) developed two simple models of monopolistic competition, which yield three testable hypotheses. He used data on trade flows for 14 OECD countries from 1956 to 1981 to investigate the consistency of theoretical predictions with data. Helpman used the absolute difference in GDP per capita to capture the differences in the composition of factor endowments and the level of each country's GDP to measure the size variable. Using graphs and simple regression analysis, Helpman found that the extent of IIT was larger the more similar were the income per capita in trading nations. He also found that the size of a smaller country had a positive effect while that of a larger country had a negative effect on the share of IIT among the OECD countries in his sample. Finally, he used the ratio of the standard deviation of income per capita to its mean (dispersion index) to examine the relationship between the within-group share of IIT and the degree on dispersion in per capita income. Based on a scattered plot of 26 data points (and not a standard hypothesis test), he observed that they are negatively correlated. Based on these results, Helpman (1987) argued that empirical results are more consistent with the predictions of the "New Trade Theory" in which scale economies and product differentiation drive specialization in production and trade than they are with factor endowments based explanations.

Hummels and Levinsohn (1995) reexamined Helpman's (1987) evidence employing different data sets and rigorous econometric analysis. Starting with a simple model in which all trade take place in differentiated products produced by countries employing increasing returns to scale technologies and consumers in all trading nations have identical homothetic preferences, Hummels and Levinsohn were able to reproduce Helpman's (1987) results. They used OECD data from 1962-83 and treated each country-pair in each year as an observation to generate a sample of 2002 observations and estimated a gravity equation with fixed and random effects (with and without detrending). They found that even after controlling for deterministic trends in data and country-pair fixed effects, about 98 percent of the variation in trade volume is explained by the model and Helpman's size dispersion index was highly significant. Therefore, the results strongly support one of the predictions of the "New Trade Theory" and corroborate the findings of Helpman (1987). To test the robustness of these results, Hummels and Levinsohn then set out to develop a counterfactual, arguing that if product differentiation is the main reason for the remarkable fit, the equation should not perform well in a mixed sample of developed and developing countries since trade between these countries are based more on differences in factor endowments (i.e., inter-industry) and less on similar but differentiated products (i.e., intra-industry). While the model did not fit as well when they applied it to a group of developed and developing countries, as it did in the OECD sample (the goodness-of-fit declined from 0.98 to 0.67), it was nevertheless significant. Hummels and Levinsohn also demonstrated that Helpman's (1987) results continue to hold if one uses income per worker or absolute differences in capital-labor ratios or land-labor ratios instead of using differences in per capita income to capture differences in factor endowments. However, when they introduced country-pair dummy variables into the equation, these dummies could explain most of the variation in the share of IIT. This finding implies that unspecified characteristics of country-pairs explain IIT more than the variables emphasized by the "New Trade Theory". They concluded that the evidence does not support the view that product differentiation with scale economies is the main reason why IIT flows have grown among countries with similar sizes and that the theory needs refinement to better fit the data.

Durkin and Krygier (2000) employed the method developed by Greenaway *et al.* (1994) to examine the relationship between differences in per capita income and the share of intra-industry trade in bilateral trade flows. Based on the 5-digit Standard International Trade Classification (SITC), they used data on bilateral trade flows for 20 OECD countries from 1989 to 1992. They distinguished between horizontally and vertically differentiated trade and found that about 70% of the US IIT with other OECD countries is vertically differentiated and that variation in income distribution has a significant effect on vertically differentiated products trade but not on trade of horizontally differentiated goods. Thus, for vertically differentiated goods, difference in per capita income has a positive effect on the share of intra-industry trade while for horizontally differentiated goods the relationship is negative.

This finding calls into question some of the results from studies not differentiating trade in vertically and horizontally differentiated products.

While it is well known that the gravity equation performs well in explaining variation in bilateral trade flows, there is little agreement in the literature about which theory or theories, the H-O-S trade model or the "New Trade Theory" can account for its empirical success. Evenett and Keller (2002) made an attempt to address this issue. Since both theories can predict the gravity equation, Evenett and Keller developed an estimation procedure to discriminate between two models and determine in a transparent manner whether product differentiation with increasing returns to scale or differences in factor endowments can explain the relationships between trade volumes and the size distributions of trading countries. They used a data set consisting of 58 countries that include almost all developed countries and a few developing countries with GDPs above $1.0 billion US in 1985. They divided 2,870 observations of country-pairs with positive amounts of trade into two sub-samples; one group with less than 5 percent of intra-industry trade measured by the Grubel-Lloyd (G-L) index (a total of 2240 observations) and the other group having more than 5 percent IIT (a total of 630 observations). They assumed that countries in the first group trade in homogeneous goods while those in the second group trade in differentiated products. The results of their empirical investigation show that the size of the differentiated goods sector and the share of IIT trade move together, which implies that scale economies and product differentiation are important in explaining the volume of bilateral trade among developed countries. They did not find evidence to support the hypothesis that differences in factor endowments between countries in the first group drive specialization and trade among them. While these findings support the view that product differentiation and increasing returns to scale are empirically relevant factors in helping to explain changes in trade volumes, they do not represent full endorsement of the "New Trade Theory" for two reasons. First, data for the first group of countries appear to contain noise that might have tainted the results. Second, there is little support for trade models that predict perfect specialization. Moreover, trade between developing and developed countries are well explained by an imperfect specialization H-O-S model of trade in homogeneous goods. Taken together, these results highlight the importance of both relative factor endowments and increasing returns to scale as determinants of the extent of specialization and trade. Of course, the relative importance of the traditional and "New Trade Theory" depend on the particular sample in question.

The above finding resonates well with the results of Antweiler and Trefler (2000) who developed a methodology for estimating the size of returns to scale (very important for addressing a wide variety of welfare-related questions) at the sectoral level from international data. They assembled a data set for 71 countries with 37 industries and 11 factors from 1972 to 1992. They looked at the factor content of exports and imports separately for each trade partner that essentially allows all countries to have different techniques of production. Then they compared these results to difference between total factors in an economy and factors used in domestic consumption. Based on their estimation, Antweiler and Trefler find that, while a majority of the industries appear to be characterized by constant returns to scale, there is evidence of increasing returns to scale in a number of sectors. These results highlight the empirical relevance of both the H-O-S model of trade and the trade model based on increasing returns to scale and product differentiation.

Since specialization and trade can occur due to an Armington structure of demand (Anderson, 1979; Bergstrand, 1985), economies of scale and product differentiation

(Helpman and Krugman, 1985; Helpman, 1987), technological differences (Davis, 1995), and differences in factor endowments (Deardorf, 1998), the gravity equation can be consistent with a wide range of trade theories. Grossman (1998) argued that specialization drives the gravity type model rather than the traditional or the "New Trade" theories, and Evenett and Keller (2002) argued that specialization need not be complete to derive a gravity model of bilateral trade flows. Feenstra *et al.*. (2001) show that a gravity model to explain IIT can be generated by a trade model with homogeneous goods if there is imperfect competition and the markets are segmented due to restricted entry (also known as the reciprocal dumping model of trade following Brander, 1981; Brander and Krugman, 1983; and Venables, 1985). Feenstra *et al.* (2001) used bilateral trade flows among 110 countries for five different years (1970, 1975, 1980, 1985, and 1990), and a set of covariates such as GDP, distance, geographical contiguity, language, free trade agreement and remoteness to estimate their model. Following Rauch (1999), they divided their sample of 5-digit SITC products into three groups: homogeneous goods, differentiated goods and an in-between category and then estimated gravity equations for bilateral exports in each of the three groups. The results suggest that the elasticity of exports is significantly higher for differentiated products than for homogeneous goods. This is consistent with the predictions of the "New Trade Theory". They also show that a *home market effect* whereby an increase in exporter's income has a more than proportionate effect on exports shows up in the results for differentiated goods. However, for the homogeneous goods, the home market effect is nonexistent and the empirical results are consistent with a reciprocal dumping model with entry barriers. Despite the differences in methodology, these results are broadly consistent with those of Evenett and Keller (2002): (i) a gravity model is consistent with both increasing returns to scale and product differentiation, and with a conventional H-O-S trade model, and (ii) empirical results are consistent with the predictions of both models when care is taken to classify trade flows before econometric estimation.

Debaere (2005) makes an attempt to test predictions from the "New Trade Theory" employing aggregate data on bilateral trade flows for 14 OECD and 14 non-OECD countries from 1970 to 1992 compiled by Feenstra *et al.* (1997). Using some of the recent developments in the gravity literature and panel estimation, he finds that for the 14 OECD countries, increased trade to GDP ratios are positively related to their share in the world trade and to a similarity in size index. However, for the group of non-OECD countries, while trade to GDP ratios were positively related to the world economy, these were not related to their similarity in size index. Finally, contrary to the prediction of the "New Trade Theory", all the estimated parameters were less than one. Thus, while the results for the OECD countries lend empirical support to some of the predictions of the "New Trade Theory", the non-OECD results are clearly at odds with the theoretical predictions and call into question the general applicability of the "New Trade Theory".

The 25th anniversary issue of the *Brookings Papers on Economic Activity* has been devoted to international economic issues. In an influential article, *Growing World Trade: Causes and Consequences*, published in this issue, Krugman (1995b) asked two fundamental questions: why has world trade grown and what are the consequences of that growth?. Regarding the first question, he noted that while the journalistic discussions view the growth in world trade being driven by ever declining costs of transportation and communication due to improvements in technology, economists argue that much of the growth in world trade since World War II can be attributed to policy-induced progress in tariff reductions which enhanced bilateral and multilateral trade liberalization. Therefore, the question remains disputed. In the spirit of Krugman's article, Feenstra (1998) suggested four possible factors contributing to the growth in world trade: (i) trade liberalization, (ii) falling transportation costs, (iii) convergence in economic sizes, increasing returns to scale and product differentiation, and (iv) increased outsourcing due to vertical specialization of multinational firms and disintegration of national production process both of which can cause intermediate goods to cross national borders multiple times. Baier and Bergstrand (2001) measured the relative contributions of reductions in transportation cost, trade liberalization, income convergence and income growth to the expansion of world trade in the post World War II period. Assuming that a consumer in each country maximizes a constant-elasticity-of-substitution (CES) utility function subject to a budget constraint where the prices of the imported products reflect "iceberg" transportation costs and *ad valorem* tariffs and a firm in each country maximizes profits subject to two technological constraints, Baier and Bergstrand developed a generalized gravity equation which incorporates tariff barriers, transportation costs and distribution costs explicitly and highlight the importance of output-expenditure constraints emphasized by Anderson (1979), market structure emphasized by Helpman and Krugman (1985), and distribution costs emphasized by Bergstrand (1985). It also incorporates the notion that larger markets will have relatively higher price and wage levels than smaller markets (Krugman, 1980) explicitly into the gravity model. Using bilateral trade flow data for 16 OECD countries for 1958-60 and 1986-88 periods, they estimated a generalized gravity model and measured the relative contributions of income growth, income convergence, tariff reductions and declines in transportation cost. The results suggest that trade grew by about 148 percents between the 1960s and the 1980s and that about 67-69% of this growth could be attributed to growth in real GDP, 23-26% to tariff-rate reductions, 8-9% to transport cost declines and none to real GDP convergence. The results also suggest that exports are imperfectly substitutable across national markets, which are consistent with the findings of Engel and Rogers (1998) who noted that consumers markets are essentially national markets and that distribution efforts are organized nationally.

To recap, the developments since the 1990s suggest that there is limited empirical evidence to support all predictions of the "New Trade Theory" and that the theory needs to be broadened to explain trade flows among developing countries and between developed and developing countries. What follows next is a brief description of alternative indices used to measure intra-industry trade flows between countries.

Intra-Industry Trade: Definition and Measurement

The large volume of IIT, particularly among developed countries in the post World War II period is often cited as one of the key empirical reasons for developing the "New Trade Theory" based on increasing returns to scale, product differentiation and imperfect competition (Helpman and Krugman, 1985 & 1989). Similarly, in a recent survey article, Leamer (1995) argued that the importance of IIT highlighted by Grubel and Lloyd (1975) is the most important finding since the Leontief Paradox that had a profound impact on the way economists think about international trade. It has been argued repeatedly by various authors that traditional trade theories neglect the role of economies of scale in trade and hence, cannot explain the large volume of trade in differentiated products between countries which are similar in factor endowments and technology (Lancaster, 1980; Balassa and Bauwens, 1988; Helpman and Krugman ,1985). This section focuses on how IIT is defined and measured. It also deals with some of the challenging aspects of measuring IIT with available data.

According to Grubel and Lloyd (1975), IIT can be defined as the value of exports of an 'industry' which can be matched exactly by the value of imports of the same 'industry'. Clearly, the definition of an industry is very important in deriving intra-industry measures of trade. If there are 'n' industries in an economy so that $i=1,2,\ldots,n$ and X_i is the aggregate value of exports of the ith industry and M_i is the aggregate value of imports of that industry, then intra-industry trade can be expressed as:

$$R_i = (X_i + M_i) - |X_i - M_i|$$

Note that the measure of inter-industry trade is $|X_i - M_i|$ which has been widely used in empirical studies of international trade prior to the recognition of IIT. Thus, IIT is simply the complement of inter-industry trade as specified in the above equation. The value of IIT can be normalized by dividing R_i by the total industry trade so that:

$$B_i = R_i / (X_i + M_i) = \{(X_i + M_i) - |X_i - M_i|\} / (X_i + M_i) = 1 - |X_i - M_i| / (X_i + M_i)$$

This is the proportion of total trade that is intra-industry in nature. This is also known as the G-L index of IIT which has been used by Helpman (1987), Helpman and Krugman (1989), Hummels and Levinsohn (1995), and many others studying international trade in differentiated products. The economy-wide measure of IIT can be obtained as a weighted average of B_i for all n industries using the relative shares of total trade for each industry as weights.

Instead of matching the values of exports and imports in a particular industry, one could match the proportions of exports and imports in that industry. This would lead to an alternative measure of IIT. When it is weighted by the average share of the exports and imports of the industry in total trade (exports plus imports), an alternative measure of economy-wide IIT can be obtained (see Lloyd, 2002 for details).

Note that this alternative is essentially a measure of the extent to which industry exports as a share of total exports match industry imports as a proportion of total imports. When the proportions of the volume of imports and export in this measure are replaced by their values, it becomes the G-L index. This measure was developed and popularized by Finger and Kreinen (1979), and Kol and Mennes (1986). It has been used to measure the similarity of distributions of exports by commodity and imports by commodity by Finger and Kreinen (1979). More recently, Glick and Rose (1998) used this index to measure the similarity of distribution of exports of two countries to a third country. Which measure is more appropriate for an empirical study? This depends on the purpose of the study. If, for example, the purpose of a study is to explain the nature of specialization and comparative advantage, the G-L index is more suitable than others. If, however, the main purpose of a study is to measure the similarity between two industries, one needs to match the proportions of exports and imports and not the values.

While the G-L index became the standard to measure IIT in empirical trade studies, the question of whether it should be adjusted to reflect persistent trade imbalance has perplexed empirical researchers. In the presence of trade imbalance, the G-L index would be downward biased and it would capture both IIT and trade imbalance. Aquino (1978) demonstrated that the adjustment suggested by Grubel and Lloyd (1975) applies to aggregate trade and not to an industry or commodity level trade and he suggested an alternative equiproportionate adjustment in each industry. The adjustment proposed by Aquino was applied by Helpman (1987), and Hummels and Levinsohn (1995) but they could not find any perceptible differences in the results. Greenaway and Milner (1981) argued that the Aquino adjustment is inappropriate because it focuses only on manufacturing trade and suggested that it may be best not to make an adjustment to the G-L index. Similar view has also been expressed by Kol (1988). It should also be noted that all empirical trade studies so far deal with trade in goods only but not trade in services because comparable data for trade in services are not available. If comparable data for trade in services become available in the near future and trade in services is included in the analysis, it would reduce aggregate trade imbalance in goods and hence the importance of adjusting the G-L index (Lloyd 2002). However, in an increasingly interdependent world of nations characterized by inter-country borrowing and lending, trade imbalances may persist over many years even after accounting for trade in services. The literature is yet to focus on how such persistent national trade imbalance can be treated in IIT analysis.

To enhance the usefulness of the G-L index for analyzing adjustment issues following a trade agreement, Hamilton and Kniest (1991) introduced a concept called 'marginal intra-industry trade' (MIIT) in which the proportion of the increase in imports and exports are matched rather than the share of exports and imports of total trade. This index will be equal to one when all additional trade is matched and zero when there is no matching at all. The view implicit in this formulation is that one needs to focus on changes in IIT rather than on the level of IIT to evaluate the relationship between IIT and structural adjustment. However, as shown by Greenaway *et al.* (1994), the MIIT suggested by Hamilton and Kniest (1991) can be defined only for non-negative values of changes in exports and imports. Moreover, the index is not scaled and it cannot tell us anything about the initial level of trade or the amount of new trade or even the value of production in the industry under investigation. These issues are very important for evaluating the consequences of structural adjustments originating from a free trade agreement.

The empirical anomaly reported by Hummels and Levinsohn (1995) questioned the adequacy of the Helpman and Krugman (1985) model to guide empirical analysis of IIT. This inspired researchers to further investigate the issues paying closer attention to identification, definition and choice of measurement indicators of relevant variables. Among other things, this led to the recognition of horizontal and vertical product differentiation and measurement, and brought to the forefront some key issues relevant for modeling of vertical IIT and horizontal IIT. The contributions to the theoretical literature by Falvey (1981), Falvey and Kierzkowski (1987) and Falm and Helpman (1987) suggest that vertical IIT is determined by differences in relative factor endowments between trading partners. Note that this prediction is different than the predictions of the Helpman and Krugman (1985) trade model which focuses on horizontal IIT. More recent studies attempt to breakdown total IIT into horizontal IIT (HITT) and vertical IIT (VITT) and use different explanatory variables to investigate the extent of HITT and VITT, and their determinants. The separation of total IIT is based on the assumption that quality is reflected in a product's price and that unit value of export or import can be used for assessing product quality in trade data (Abdel-Rahman,1991; Greenaway *et al.*, 1995; Stigliz 1987). [1] In general, trade flows are considered horizontally differentiated if the spread in unit value of exports relative to the unit value of imports is less than 15% at the five-digit SITC level. When relative unit values are outside this range, the products are considered to be vertically differentiated. Since the determinants of VIIT and HIIT differ, empirical models using total IIT as the dependent variable are likely to be misspecified. Therefore, disentangling VIIT and HIIT, and use of appropriate econometric methods remain a fruitful area of research in IIT (Greenaway and Tortensson, 1997).

There are also some other unresolved issues related to the measurement of IIT. The first issue is called the categorical aggregation problem. Based on the SITC classification, exports and imports are reported at different levels of aggregation (3 digits, four digits etc.). What is the most appropriate level of aggregation in the SITC classification of commodities traded? How to determine which industries are the sequential Dixit and Grossman type (see Dixit and Grossman (1982) for details) and how to aggregate different commodities into exports and imports of the same industry? It becomes even more complex when there is jointness in production and the products produced jointly are used to satisfy very different consumer demand. This phenomenon is particularly relevant for the agri-food sector. Finally, what are the effects of seasonality on trade and their implications for the measurement of IIT? While seasonality does not influence trade in manufacturing, it is likely to have a significant effect on trade in agri-food products. Notwithstanding these issues related to the measurement of IIT, the G-L index has been routinely employed by trade researchers to study the existence, growing importance and drivers of IIT involving agri-food products. The following section is devoted to this literature.

Determinants of Intra-Industry Trade in Agri-Food Products

Despite the growing importance of IIT, only a few attempts have been made to investigate the nature and extent of IIT involving agri-food products. Unlike IIT studies dealing with manufacturing trade, all studies dealing with intra-industry agri-food trade took place after the advancement of the "New Trade Theory" based on the economies of scale and product differentiation in the mid 1980s. While the first few initiatives focused on the determination of the extent of IIT trade in agri-food products, more recent studies have also concentrated on identifying the determinants of IIT through testing relevant hypothesis with both time series and cross sectional data. An attempt is made in this section to provide a brief overview of these studies and a synthesis of the progress made so far in this area.

One of the early studies on IIT in agri-food products is McCorriston and Sheldon (1991) which examined trade in processed meat, cheese products, cereals, processed fruits, processed vegetables, sugar products, alcoholic and non-alcoholic beverages and tobacco to determine the extent of IIT in the European Community (EC) and in the United States. They used an adjusted version of the G-L index to measure the IIT and found that except for exports to

[1] Note that the unit value approach has some limitations. First, the unit values of two bundles which differ in terms of the mix of goods can have different unit values which do not reflect differences in quality. Second, consumers can buy a more expensive product in the short run because of availability or other factors and not

Canada, the US trade in selected processed agri-food products was characterized by inter-industry trade while the bulk of EC trade in processed agri-food products was dominated by IIT. It emphasized the role of proximity to market, distance from foreign markets and economic ties with former colonies as the main factors for explaining differences in specialization and trade in processed agri-food products in the EC and in the United States. Note that these factors are not consistent with those predicted by the "New Trade Theory" and may have been chosen arbitrarily.

Christodoulou (1992) used the unadjusted G-L index to measure IIT in fresh meat and processed meat products (pork and beef) industry in the EC countries in 1988. She used market size, taste overlap, market proximity, stage of processing, scale economies, product differentiation and market structure variables to explain cross country variations in IIT in the EC. The results suggest that taste overlap and imperfect competition were the most important variables for explaining variations in IIT in the EC meat trade. She also noted a rather surprising result that IIT was more significant for both raw and highly processed meats relative to lightly processed meat.

Hirschberg, Sheldon and Dayton (1994) appears to be the first empirical study to analyze IIT in processed food products which closely followed the "New Trade Theory" advanced by Helpman and Krugman to specify relevant variables and the empirical model. They used a panel data set of 30 countries from 1964-1985 and employed a fixed-effect tobit model in their investigation. They used both adjusted and unadjusted versions of the G-L index and used size differences of GDPs, GDP per capita, bilateral inequality between GDP per capita, exchange rate and distance as explanatory variables. They have also used a set of dummy variables to account for common borders, language, and culture among trade partners. The results suggest that IIT incraeses with an increase in GDP per capita and more similar the GDP per capita between two countries. The results also suggest that common border helps the IIT while distance and fluctuating exchange rates do not.

Pieri *et al.* (1997) examined IIT in dairy products among ten European Union (EU) countries from 1988 to 1992 to assess the importance of country-specific and industry-specific factors in dairy products trade. They used EUROSTAT data to compute unadjusted G-L index to measure IIT in dairy products and used a set of theoretically relevant country-specific (reflecting demand conditions such as trade overlaps, market size, proximity to market and trade imbalance etc.) and industry-specific (reflecting supply conditions such product differentiation, scale economies, market concentration etc.) factors to explain variations in IIT involving dairy products among the EU countries. The results suggest that IIT in dairy products is higher the more similar the countries are. The results also suggest that the presence of large farms enhanced IIT in dairy products. However, concentration in the retail sector was found to have a detrimental effect on IIT flows in dairy products among the EU countries during the study period.

Henry de Frahan and Tharakan (1998) examined the importance of horizontal and vertical IIT in the processed food sector in the EU between 1980 and 1990. They used EUROSTAT data for 18 NACE[2] food sub-sectors for eight and eleven EU countries and 39

because of quality considerations. Despite these inadequacies, the unit values are widely used in empirical trade literature, particularly in IIT studies.

2 NACE is the acronym (from the French 'Nomenclature statistique des Activités économiques dans la Communauté Européenne'- Statisitical classification of economic activities) used to designate the various

trade partners in 1980 and 1990. They estimated the levels of horizontal and vertical IIT in the selected commodities and used a set of theoretically relevant variables reflecting country-specific and industry-specific characteristics to explain variations in VIIT and HIIT in processed food products. The results from the Tobit regression suggest that average market size and level of economic development of trade partners and their trade preference and geographical proximity have significant positive impact on the level of horizontal IIT. However, differences in factor endowments, market size and scale economies between pairs of countries have significant negative impacts on horizontal IIT. These results are broadly consistent with the predictions of the "New Trade Theory". The results for the vertical IIT model were not very encouraging as some of the key variables such as factor endowment differences had a wrong sign. Similar results have also been obtained by van Berkum and van Meijl (1999) for the EU agri-food sector. In addition to country-specific and industry-specific variables, the authors included technology variables in their analysis. They used EUROSTAT data for 57 product categories or industries in 1997 and estimated non-linear regressions to explain variations in horizontal and vertical IIT in the EU agri-food sector. While the empirical results for HIIT were consistent with the theory of product differentiation, the results for the VIIT were mixed. They obtained a significant negative coefficient for differences in endowments, which is contrary to the theory. However, differences in technology yielded a positive and significant coefficient only in the VIIT model which is consistent with the "New Trade Theory".

Qasmi and Fausti (2001) made an attempt to evaluate the impact of the North American Free Trade Agreement (NAFTA) on inter- and intra- industry trade in agri-food products in North America and in the rest of the world. They used OECD's SITC Rev. 3 data for 23 agricultural products that include meat, meat products, dairy products, grains and cereal products, processed fruits and vegetables and other related products for 1990 and 1995. They computed adjusted G-L indices to determine the extent of IIT in selected agri-food commodities and how did the IIT change between the two periods. The results show that the proportion of IIT was higher for commodities involving a greater degree of processing while trade in bulk commodities with little or no processing was dominated by inter-industry trade. The results also revealed that the US-Canada bilateral trade is dominated by IIT, while Mexican bilateral trade with either Canada or the United States is dominated by inter-industry trade. The authors also note that the proportion of IIT in agri-food commodities in the US with the rest of the world declined between 1990 and 1995. However, the authors did not make any attempt to explain the IIT using the "New Trade Theory" nor did they provide any explanation of why the US IIT in agri-food products with the rest of the world has declined during the study period.

In an attempt to evaluate the IIT in the US food processing industry, Sun and Koo (2002) used the G-L index to measure the degree of IIT from 1989 to 2001 with particular emphasis on 1997. They used USDA data for 24 sub-industries at the 5-digit NAICS[3] level and trade with 24 trading partners and classified total IIT into vertical and horizontal IIT using 6-digit Harmonized Trade Schedule (HTS) code levels to minimize aggregation problem. The results show that the degree of IIT varies across sub-industries and across different trading partners.

---

statistical classifications of economic activities in the European Community. This system is managed by the statistical office of the EU Commission called 'EUROSTAT'.

[3] NAICS stands for "North American Industry classification System".

Canada is the most important trade partner in processed food products and in 1997 forty one percent of processed food traded between Canada and the US was IIT in nature. Japan, Mexico, France and the United Kingdom are the other important trade partners in this area. While most of the IIT in the US food processing industry is vertical in nature, since 1989 HIIT has been growing faster than the VIIT. However, they do not provide a satisfactory explanation of why this is happening. Sun and Koo (2002) used an identical set of variables to explain HIIT and VIIT in the US food processing sector. The results from their regression analysis suggest that the HIIT model fits data better than the VIIT model and that industry characteristics explain IIT better than the country specific characteristics included in the analysis.

Fertö (2005) investigated the relationship between factor endowment and vertical IIT in agri-food products between Hungary and the EU. He used OECD data on agri-food trade between Hungary and 14 EU countries from 1992 to 1998 and employed three alternative approaches (the G-L index, the approach suggested by Fontagné and Freundenberg (1997) and that suggested by Nilsson 1997) to measure IIT. On the basis of unit value differences, he divided the total IIT into VIIT and HIIT. Using Flam and Helpman (1987) model of trade in vertically differentiated product, Fertö (2005) specified a set of proxy variables and employed panel regression analysis to explain vertical IIT. The results suggest that there is a positive relationship between VIIT and differences in factor endowments, which is consistent with the theory. Note that the author used differences in the endowments of different types of factors such as land, human capital and physical capital in this study, which may have generated theoretically consistent results. The results also suggest that the way IITs are measured may have significant implications for estimates from regression analysis.

To recap, except one all studies used cross-sectional data to measure IIT and the G-L index has been the most popular measure of IIT in agri-food products. While the separation of total IIT into vertical and horizontal IIT has been a useful exercise in agri-food trade, the results from various studies suggest that they are not very encouraging for the vertical IIT model relative to those for the horizontal IIT model. Clearly, much need to be done in refining the empirical analysis of vertical IIT in agri-food products. Following relevant trade theories closely to develop testable hypothesis and focusing alternative specification of proxy variables could help in this regard. Theoretical predictions are often considered to be relevant in the long run but most of the empirical studies conducted so far appear (dealing with both agri-food products and manufacturing) to have produced results that are more relevant in the short run. The issue related to short-run versus long-run relevance of the results has not been entertained in any published IIT study yet. Along the same line, what are the implications of data nonstationarity for the IIT results? Since it is well known that most macroeconomic variables contain unit roots, this issue is particularly relevant for IIT studies employing time series data in their analysis. Since differences in factor endowments is the key driver of specialization and trade according to the H-O-S trade model, what is the threshold difference in factor endowments that changes VIIT into inter-industry trade? Is this threshold commodity-specific or does it vary across countries? Does it vary over time? What factors contribute to changes in the threshold over time, across industries and among different trading partners? All these issues are relevant for future progress in modeling trade is differentiated products.

PRODUCT DIFFERENTIATION MODELS APPLIED TO AGRI-FOOD TRADE

More than fifteen years ago, MacLaren (1990) reviewed various product differentiation models used in modeling agricultural trade with imperfect substitutes and highlighted the need for progress in this area. At that time, with the exception of the Armington model, important product differentiation models developed in the eighties were not applied on a large scale in agricultural trade modeling. Since then, the landscape has changed and various models of product differentiation have been developed and routinely applied by agricultural trade modelers. This section provides an overview of key developments since the 1980s which can be classified into three distinct streams. The first stream is empirical in nature and focuses on econometrically estimating import demand functions for agricultural commodities using the notion of national product differentiation. While most of these studies used a theoretical framework inspired by Armington (1969), the estimated models incorporated some refinements of the original Armington specification. Most of the studies in this group focuses on raw agricultural commodities and only a few deals with processed agri-food products (Surry *et al.*, 2002)[4].

The second stream of agricultural trade-related studies based on product differentiation models focus on the assessment of the impacts of agricultural trade liberalization using calibrated partial equilibrium and applied general equilibrium models. The origin of these studies can be traced back to the mid-1980s when the Uruguay Round of multilateral trade negotiations was initiated. Most of these studies are policy-oriented and are based on the notion of national product differentiation using either the original Armington specification or one of its refinements. It is fair to state that these studies benefited enormously from the development of the Global Trade Analysis Project (GTAP) in the early 1990s at Purdue University under the leadership of Dr. T. Hertel (1997).

The third stream of agri-food trade related studies consider product differentiation not to be exogenous as in national product differentiation models and attempt to endogenize product differentiation at the firm or consumer level by assuming either horizontal or vertical product differentiation. Many of these studies employing econometric analysis have already been reviewed in the previous section. In this section attention is focused primarily on those studies that used calibrated models to study the effects of agricultural trade policies.

Providing a thorough overview of all product differentiation models developed over the last fifteen years and applied to agri-food trade using the former classification would be a monumental task that goes beyond of the scope of this paper. We intend to provide an account of the main *trends* in the application of product differentiation models applied to agri-food trade. Three appendices at the end of this paper summarize notable examples of studies that applied product-differentiated models to agri-food trade. These studies are categorized according to the three types of product differentiation (national, horizontal and vertical)

---

[4] National product differentiation models have been used for the following agricultural commodities: corn, cotton, fruits and vegetables, individual fruits (such as apples, citrus fruit and grapefruits), soybeans, tobacco, wheat, poultry products and red meat. Applications of national product-differentiated models to agri-food processed products have generally been undertaken at a rather aggregate level (three-digit classification of the SITC and were part of a more general empirical work covering a wide range of manufacturing and mining sectors (for examples of such studies, see Brenton, 1989; Reinert and Roland-Host, 1992; and Gallaway *et al.*,2003).

commonly used in the international trade and IO literature[5]. These studies have been selected because they either made some original contributions to agricultural trade modeling or synthesized the state of the arts on this topic[6]. An inspection of the selected studies indicates that agricultural trade models based on national product differentiation are mainly based on the Armington specification (appendix 1). Applications of horizontally differentiated trade models attempt to adapt the Dixit-Stiglitz and Lancaster models to agri-food markets (appendix 2). Finally, notable progress have been made over the last fifteen years concerning the use of vertical product differentiation models to analyze a wide range of old as well as new trade policy issues in agri-food markets such as price discrimination strategies by state trading agencies, labeling foods containing GMOs and the consequences of adopting genetically-modified crops (appendix 3). All these studies are based, in one way or the other, on the vertical product differentiation model developed by Mussa and Rosen (1978).

National Product Differentiation: The Armington Model and its Generalizations

The Armington model has been and continues to be the workhorse of (agri-food) trade modeling. Although it was introduced by Armington (1969) in the late 1960s to explain trade among countries, this model gained popularity during the 1980s and 1990s due to significant growth in applications of computable general equilibrium (CGE) models to study global trade policy issues. The Armington model is based on a weakly separable utility function which assumes a two-stage process in consumers' purchase decisions. First, total quantity of a product to be imported is determined and then it is allocated to competing imports originating from different sources. It is assumed that imports originating from different sources are imperfect substitutes of each other and the model can be characterized by constant elasticity of substitution (CES) demand functions. The existence of a homogeneous and weakly separable utility function also implies that the demand function for import from each source is characterized by a unitary elasticity with respect to total import quantity (expenditures) of the product.

The Armington specification is implemented in the CGE models through a multi-stage process where a representative consumer determines the aggregate demand functions for a basket of goods that are derived from a weakly separable utility function maximization

---

[5] Another dimension of product differentiation based on certain attributes of a good has been adopted to model trade for some agricultural commodities such as wheat (divided into classes defined in terms of protein content, etc.). In this context, various classes are viewed as given and could be considered as many different products of the good under study. It is not our objective to discuss this type of product differentiation. Rather, we refer to those agricultural trade studies that would combine classes of a good with national product differentiation. For an application of such a study, see Haley (1995) for a calibrated model of the world wheat sector combining classes of wheat and a (Armington) national product differentiation dimension (appendix 1). A trade model with similar characteristics but a more general specification than Amington has been developed by Henning and Martin (1989) (see appendix 1).

[6] A detailed description of each of the selected studies is given in three appendices. This is done to foster a good understanding of the product differentiation models used in these studies. These models are so complex that they require stating the underlying assumptions as well as the most important characteristics. Secondly, most of the product-differentiated models could also be a part of a more general and larger framework the characteristics of which need to be known so that it is possible to see how the product differentiation model specification fits into such a global model. This is especially true for theCGE models used to simulate agricultural trade liberalisation scenarios.

problem subject to an income constraint. Then having determined the total demand for each goods, the representative consumer determines how much he will purchase on the domestic market or import from the rest of the world. At the final stage, he decides how total imports must be supplied and allocated between various sources of foreign supplies. Since the fact that the Armington specification rests upon the use of the self-dual CES functional form, it can be implemented either in its dual or primal forms. Another attractive feature of the Armington model is that it could take care of two-way trade and captures the existence of trade policies that affect simultaneously imports and exports of a particular product (van Tongeren *et al.*, 2001).

The Armington specification could also be used in CGE models to represent exports and the various sources of supplies of intermediate inputs consumed by various industries. In the former case, modeling exports with an Armington specification was made possible by allowing firms in a given industry to segment export and domestic markets through the adoption of constant elasticity of transformation (CET) functions. In the latter case, firms are assumed to minimize the costs of intermediate inputs (from domestic and imported sources) subject a technological constraint represented by a CES production function. Such a specification is very helpful for modeling trade in bulk agricultural commodities as they are used as inputs by food and feed manufacturing sectors.

During the second half of the 1980s, when the CGE trade models were gradually implemented to study the economy-wide effects of agricultural policy reforms, some questions were raised about the relevance of the Armington specification in representing agricultural trade (Stoeckel *et al.,* 1989). Many of these questions centered on the notion that agricultural commodities are homogeneous goods and that trade in agricultural commodities represent more of inter-industry trade rather than of intra-industry trade. This view is no longer tenable in light of the growing importance of trade in processed agri-food food products, particularly among the OECD countries. Moreover, there have been several empirical applications showing that raw agricultural products might not be homogeneous (see for instance Larue and Lapan , 1991 for wheat) as it has been argued in the literature.

The Armington model has been used in many empirical (econometrically estimated) agricultural trade modeling exercises[7] but only a few studies have used this approach in calibrated partial equilibrium trade models over the last twenty years[8]. Included in this group are Haley (1995), and Kim and Lin (1990) on wheat, Peterson et Orden (2005) on poultry and Weber (2003) on Russia and Kazakhstan agricultural trade[9]. Recently, an option in the UNCTAD global trade model, ATPSM (Peters and Vanzetti, 2004) allows users to incorporate the Armington specification.

The use of Armington specification in analyzing agricultural trade has raised a number of interrelated issues which mainly deal with its specification and empirical estimation. Concerning the former, extensive recourse of the Armington specification to model trade in CGE models led to the emergence of larger than expected terms of trade effects in trade

[7] See Surry *et al.* (2002) for a review of these studies.

[8] Although this present review of product-differentiated trade model is limited to the last fifteen to twenty years, we should note in passing that the trade modelling works of Grennes *et al.* (1978) on international wheat markets, and the IATRC trade embargo study (USDA, 1986), that have used the Armington modeling approach. In addition, some applications of the USDA SWOPSIM model (Dixit and Roningen, 1986) have been specified with an Armington assumption in the late 1980s.

[9] Haley's, Peterson and Orden's, and Weber's studies are reviewed in appendix 1.

policy simulation exercises, that influence the welfare effects significantly, and in some instances, unexpected ways (Brown, 1987)[10]. Furthermore, the fact that Armington elasticities are assumed constant among different sources of imports has been challenged by several trade modelers who have used more general functional forms (Pogany, 1996).

On the empirical side, most of the studies that have estimated the Armington model econometrically have obtained rather low estimated values of the elasticity of substitution among imported sources of supplies. In their review of the topic, McDaniel and Balisteri (2003) observed that the following robust findings emerge across many reviewed studies: i) long run estimates of the elasticity of substitution are higher than their short run counterparts, ii) the more disaggregated the data sample is, the higher the elasticity of substitution, iii) cross sectional studies generate estimates that are higher than those provided by time series data, and iv) parameter estimates are sensitive to model misspecification (i.e. endogeneity of explanatory variables, underlying theoretical model structure etc.). The above empirical problems associated with the likelihood of obtaining low estimates of Armington elasticities would equally apply for agricultural and processed food commodities.

Most applied economists using the Armington model seemed to have concentrated their efforts on testing and assessing its basic characteristics that are frequently violated (Alston *et al.*, 1990). The assumption that elasticities of substitution among pairs of import sources are constant is not supported by the data in many cases. It has also been revealed that imports from various sources are sensitive to the size of the market, implying that the elasticity of each import source with respect to total imports is not unitary as assumed in this model. Another issue that has been overlooked is the inability of the Armington model to deal with the question of separability between home production and different sources of imports (Surry *et al.*, 2002).

Over the last fifteen to twenty years a wide range of solutions has been implemented to overcome the weaknesses of the Armington model. They led to the development of more refined national product differentiation models with varying elasticities of substitution. Indeed, it has not been a difficult task to develop more general national product differentiation model specifications that could overcome the basic assumptions of the Armington model such as separability and homogeneity. To do so, a two-pronged strategy has been adopted. The first one consisted of relaxing some of the assumptions of the Armington model such as homogeneity or constant elasticity of substitution (see for instance Hjort, 1988; and Ito *et al.*, 1990 for agricultural-related applications). The second approach to refine the Armington model has been to use the more general functional forms and/or models that could account for non-homogeneity, non-separability and varying elasticities of substitution, simultaneously. Hence, following the seminal paper of Winters (1984), a long list of econometric studies was published, dealing with the estimation of import demand models by geographical sources using flexible functional forms such as AIDS, translog, generalized Leontief and normalized symmetric quadratic functional forms[11].

Agricultural trade modelers have been involved in adopting flexible functional forms to study import demand for agricultural commodities by geographical sources of origin. In particular, it is interesting to observe that a large portion of such agricultural-based import

[10] To address this issue more thoroughly, CGE modellers undertake systematic sensitivity analysis of the Armington elasticities when they conduct trade policy simulation scenarios.

[11] Interested readers are encouraged to consult the works of Brenton (1989), Kohli (1991) and Lawrence (1989).

demand studies published during the 1990s was based on the use of the AIDS demand framework or the use of the Barten-Theil differential approach (Rotterdam demand model or some of its variants such as CBS, NBR or AID). Some of these studies even refined the AIDS import demand framework by allowing the possibility to estimate import demand that could be at the same time source-differentiated and differentiated by sources of production (Yang and Koo, 1994; Carew *et al.* 2004). None of these studies, however, entertained the question of separability between home production and different sources of imports perhaps due to the paucity of comparable price data for domestic production and imports from various sources.

The important recurrent question of rather small values of Armington substitution elasticities can be addressed by employing cross-section data within which prices are assumed constant. To obtain such estimates of the elasticities of substitution is undertaken by exploiting the spatial (country) variation of tariffs and trade (transportation) costs that are part of the arguments of the Armington model. This approach has been successfully applied by Hummels (1999) who derived much greater estimates than those "produced" with time series data[12]. Keeney and Hertel (2005) used Hummel's estimates of Armington elasticities in the recent agricultural-specific version of GTAP model (GTAP-AGR) (appendix 1). Panel data as used by Erkel-Rousse and Mirza (2002) could also be another way to generate greater reliable estimates of Armington elasticities.

In calibrated (agricultural) CGE and partial equilibrium models, there have been some attempts to use more general specifications than the Armington model to represent trade. Hence, in a CGE model context, Robinson *et al.* (1991) applied an AIDS model to represent imports by geographical sources. In the same vein, Winter and Frohberg (2004) employed the McFadden flexible functional form to model agricultural trade flows in calibrated policy models. In CGE models characterized by multistage separable structures, economists cannot employ non-homogeneous national product differentiation trade models because price aggregators defined at various stages of the model need to be consistently defined and be independent from the quantities. This is a major challenge which partly explains why non-homogeneous models are hardly applied in calibrated trade models. Given this hurdle, is it possible to use more generalized versions of the Armington specification in calibrated national product differentiation trade models? The answer to this question is yes. There are ways to do so by refining the Armington model through the addition of a new layer consisting of endogenizing the product differentiation through the behavior of national agents. This leads to a new category of trade models based on horizontal and vertical differentiation that are discussed now.

To conclude, the Armington model is still the "workhorse" in agri-food trade modeling. Despite its weaknesses, it has been routinely used in trade policy assessment as well as in empirical trade studies. It is also important to note that the Armington specification has been used to provide a theoretical justification of the empirical gravity models used for more than 40 years to explain bilateral trade flows (see Anderson, 1979; Anderson and van Wincoop, 2003).

[12] An inspection of Armington elasticity estimates obtained by Hummels indicates that they vary from 2.4 to 8 with an average of 4.54 for agricultural commodities and food processing activities.

Horizontal and Vertical Product Differentiation Models (Dixit-Stiglitz, Lancaster, and Mussa and Rosen):

Endogenizing product differentiation in agri-food trade models has been pursued through the use of three horizontal and vertical product differentiation models developed in the 1970s and 1980s. As explained earlier, the first of these three models is the one specified by Dixit and Stiglitz (1977), which assumes horizontal differentiation on the demand side, imperfect competition and increasing returns to scale (that are internal to the firm) on the supply side. The underlying utility function is based on a two-stage structure of the consumer preferences and is assumed to be homothetic. The lower stage is made up of sub-utility functions that depend upon the varieties of each product demanded by the consumer. In general, these sub-utility functions are represented by a CES functional form with constant elasticities of substitution among varieties of the same product, that are greater than one. In a trade context, the Dixit-Stiglitz model is specified in such a way that the demand for each product is first distinguished by domestic and import sources (Armington specification). Then within each source of supplies, various varieties are explicitly introduced as arguments of a CES sub-utility function. Often the imperfect market structure adopted in such a model is monopolistic competition, while other forms of imperfect market structures such Cournot-Nash hypothesis can also be incorporated.

The Dixit-Stiglitz model has been used to conduct both partial and general equilibrium analysis of agri-food trade policies. In the former case, interest stems from the fact that food manufacturing sectors in industrial economies are highly concentrated and face trade impediments when they purchase agricultural inputs and sell differentiated final products. Under such circumstances, the effects of trade policy reform could be ambiguous. Lanclos and Hertel (1995) addressed this issue in the context of five food processing industries. They developed an appropriate two-country partial equilibrium trade model with a horizontally differentiated product produced by a monopolistically competitive food processing sector purchasing a homogenous, traded intermediate (agricultural) input. A description of this model and the main findings are in appendix 2. Lanclos *et al.* (1996) applied this model at a more disaggregated level for 33 food processing sectors. The results show that "the effects of input tariff reform outweigh the effects of output tariff reform in the food manufacturing sector". As a result, food manufacturing firms reduce their production costs and this increases their competitiveness in the world market. By contrast, output tariff reform favours the competitiveness of foreign manufacturers. As the net effects of the two tariff reforms are ambiguous, this requires to be analyzed empirically. Offering interesting insights on the effects of joint tariff reforms in the intermediate and final output markets, this type of trade policy analysis of the food processing sector should be extended to other developed countries (like EU member countries).

It is, however, in a general equilibrium context that the Dixit-Stiglitz framework has been used the most to study the economy-wide effects of agricultural policy reforms. For this purpose, global CGE trade models would generally assume that agricultural sectors are perfectly competitive and characterized by constant returns to scale. On the other hand, imperfect competition, increasing returns to scale and consumer demand for horizontally differentiated products will characterize manufacturing and service sectors. Various forms of imperfect market structures have been adopted, although the most popular one is monopolistic competition. Such global CGE models based on the Dixit-Stiglitz specification began to be implemented in the mid 1990s with studies aimed at quantifying the outcomes the Uruguay round on the world economy. At that time, it was acknowledged that the conventional CGE model based on perfect competition and constant returns to scale was inadequate to capture the imperfect market structures of industrial sectors and the heterogeneity of consumer preferences. Swaminathan and Hertel (1996), Harrison *et al.* (1997) and Francois (1998) among others developed global CGE models that incorporated the Dixit-Stiglitz product-differentiated specification. In doing so, they were able to show that incorporating horizontal product differentiation and increasing returns to scale could explain a major portion of the welfare benefits resulting from the implementation of the Uruguay Round. The CGE models with horizontally differentiated products and imperfect markets structures have been used more recently to analyze the economy-wide effects of the Doha round (see Laborde and Le Cacheux, 2003; and Francois *et al.*, 2005).

The second endogenous product-differentiation model applied to (agri-food) trade has been introduced by Lancaster (1980) who considered that consumers prefer a particular variety, called "ideal" and will choose a variety that is closest to the ideal one, should the latter not be available. In such a model, consumer preferences are asymmetric. The model is implemented by assuming that the differentiated product in the underlying utility function depends upon this ideal variety[13]. When the Lancaster model is adapted to study international trade, it is combined with a partial or general equilibrium model that also assumes imperfect market structures. Unlike the previous Dixit-Stiglitz model, this framework has not been used extensively in agri-food trade. To the best of our knowledge, only Philippidis and Hubbard (2001, 2003) used this framework to analyze the economic costs of the Common Agricultural Policy (CAP). Their basic argument was that negative utility effects associated with the loss of domestic food varieties could offset the potential efficiency gains of reforming the CAP. To address this question, they assumed that consumers have preferences that allow distinguishing between food products according to their domestic and imported varieties. In addition, they assumed imperfect market structures for processed food products (for more details see appendix 2). The results suggest that that consumer preference heterogeneity has a negligible impact on the net cost of the CAP.

---

[13] When such a consumer preference structure is implemented, different functional forms could be adopted to represent the associated (sub-) utility function. For instance, Phillipidis and Hubbard (2001, p. 382) used the following CES sub-utility function for the differentiated products:

$$U_{i,s} = A_{i,s}\left[\sum_{r} \delta_{i,r,s} Q_{i,r,s}^{-\rho_i} Z_{i,r,s}\right]^{-\frac{1}{\rho_i}} \quad \text{for } r \neq s,$$

where $U_{i,s}$ is the level of sub-utility from the consumption of differentiated commodity i in region s, $Q_{i,r,s}$ is the consumer demand in region s for representative variety i from region r, subscripts r and s represent (geographical) varieties, $\delta_{i,r,s}$ is a CES distribution parameter, $A_{i,s}$ is a scale parameter, and ρ_i is a substitution parameter. $Z_{i,r,s}$ which represents a bilateral hierarchical utility associated with the consumption of the representative variety is given by the following expression:

$$Z_{i,r,s} = \left[1 + V_{i,r,s}\right]^{\gamma_{i,s}} \text{ with } \gamma_{i,s} > 0.$$

where $V_{i,r,s}$ is the preference value of the variety measured in relation to the "ideal" and $\gamma_{i,s}$ is the preference heterogeneity parameter. The larger the parameter γ is, the more strongly the consumer identifies with varietal choice. On the other hand, a zero value for the parameter γ implies that all representative varieties have the same hierarchical utility value, which also means preference homogeneity. It can be seen that $Z_{i,r,s}$ is strictly increasing in V. Varieties with higher preference values ($V_{i,r,s}$) result in higher amounts of hierarchical utility ($Z_{i,r,s}$) compared to less favoured varieties.

The third model we refer to in this section is the one developed by Mussa-Rosen (1978) and based on vertical product differentiation[14]. In such a context, consumers would prefer the highest quality variety. Although ideally suited to study the demand for consumer goods by capturing consumers' heterogeneity in purchasing quality good, this model could also be used for intermediate products. In this latter case, what is interesting to study is the heterogeneity of firms' technology and characteristics of their output's (Lavoie, 2001). Appendix 3 summarizes four studies that have adapted the Mussa-Rosen model to address different issues relevant for agri-food trade policy analysis. The work by Bureau *et al.* (1998) showed how it is possible to study the welfare effects of trade liberalisation in the case of a credence consumer good (i.e. the EU-US trade dispute hormone-treated beef). In Cooper *et al.* (1995) and Lavoie (2005), the Mussa-Rosen model is adapted to study intermediate agricultural commodities (sweetener market in the EU and Canadian bread wheat, respectively). Finally, the work by Sobolevsky *et al.* (2005) shows how the Mussa-Rosen framework can be used to study the market repercussions of GM varieties in the international soybean complex through its incorporation into the well-known spatial equilibrium trade model developed by Samuelson (1952), and Takayama and Judge (1971).

To sum up, the applications of various endogenous product differentiation models in agri-food trade area show that when these models are applied properly to address both old and new issues, useful insights can be gained. The studies reviewed in this section suggest that such product differentiation models offer significant potentials for innovation that have not yet been fully exploited in the study of agri-food policy, trade and trade policies.

LOOKING FORWARD

This rather non-technical review of various product differentiation models has shown how they have been applied to agri-food trade. In addition, an attempt was made to show how the "New trade theory" based on product differentiation and imperfect competition can be used to explain the growing importance of IIT in agri-food products. Important questions and issues have been raised in this review. Will all these trade models with product differentiation continue to be relevant in the future to explain trade in agri-food products?

It is more than likely that the "New Trade Theory" will continue to be relevant in agricultural trade and policy analysis. It is our belief that more and more applications of product differentiation models to agricultural trade will occur in light of the evolution experienced by the international agricultural trade complex. Thus, foreign trade in agricultural and food products would be more and more characterized by processed products. In addition, the international agricultural trading system is becoming more globalized with the need for food processing firms to remain competitive internationally. This trend appears to be accelerating with the growing importance of information technology in international trade. International trade disputes in agriculture would likely concern more and more issues dealing with technical regulations and phyto-sanitary questions. Consumer concerns about food safety and the growing role of biotechnology in agriculture are also elements that would influence

[14] More specifically, as explained by MacLaren (p. 118), "vertical product differentiation refers to preferences about the quality of a good, where a quality reflects the absolute amounts of the characteristics contained in the product".

the direction of agricultural policies and trade in agri-food products in the future. Given all these emerging issues, there is no doubt that traditional trade models based on the notion of homogeneous products and preferences will be less and less suited to study trade in agri-food products. By contrast, trade models based on product differentiation would be more appropriate to capture most of the elements appearing in the international agricultural system. As a result, the product- differentiation models will play an increasingly important role in agricultural trade analysis in the future.

The national product differentiation model and its emblematic representative, the Armington model, will continue to be used as a cornerstone in agri-food trade modeling. However, additional efforts need to be directed to enhance its partial equilibrium version to enable researchers to study the impacts of trade policies and assess the trade effects of technical regulations in agri-food markets. Concerning the use of Armington models in calibrated CGE models, further progresses need to be made to tackle the issues of functional form and separability. In this regard, it would be useful to replace the conventional CES functions with more general and flexible functional forms that satisfy global regularity conditions. As far as separability is concerned, further improvements in trade modeling could be made in CGE models by adopting, for instance, the notion of latent separability (see Gohin, 2005 for more details on this question). One of the major problems associated with the Armington model is that econometric estimates of the elasticity of substitution tend to be low. In this area, more empirical studies based on cross-sectional and panel data should occur and apply to trade in agri-food products. If this trend in the use of panel data continues in the future, it could lead to some improvements in the theoretical foundations of the Armington model by adopting a notion of product differentiation that could be grounded either at the firm or at consumer levels.

Turning to the horizontal and vertical differentiation models that have been reviewed, we do not see any reason for a decline in their use. The Dixit-Stiglitz model combined with monopolistic competition market structures will become a standard tool in agricultural trade policy analysis. The important contributions made recently by some analysts adapting the Mussa-Rosen model (vertical differentiation) are good signs that more complicated issues such as food labeling, environmental concerns and food safety issues could be investigated with this type of product differentiation models.

As IIT in agri-food products will continue to expand in the future, the profession should invest additional efforts to explain such trends. The quality and findings of such empirical studies will be enhanced if more elaborate trade data become available enabling researchers to capture different patterns of product differentiation while studying agri-food trade flows across commodities and over time. This is often a neglected and more resources should be provided so that necessary agri-food trade data become available to agricultural economists.

Recently, there has been a revival of the role of trade costs in applied trade analysis (Anderson and van Wincoop, 2004). The renewed focus recognizes the new role of economic geography in economic theory and attempts to use it in explaining trade patterns (Fujita *et al.*, 1999). This area has not been reviewed in this paper because we did not find any emerging trends but potentials to apply such theoretical tools to trade in agri-food products do exist.

CONCLUDING REMARKS

The H-O-S theory of international trade focuses primarily on the supply side of the economy and suggests that the volume and composition of trade between countries are driven by differences in factor endowments across countries. On the demand side this model assumes that consumers in all countries have identical and homothetic preferences and that all countries trade in homogeneous products. A casual observation would reveal that many products (either manufactured or agri-food) traded between countries today are not homogeneous and are, in fact, differentiated by brand names, factor contents or by other forms. Product differentiation is so prevalent today that researchers need to justify the use of models with homogeneous products only. Thanks to Helpman and Krugman (1985), a rich theory now exists to guide the empirical trade research that incorporates product differentiation and scale economies and is capable of explaining the growing importance of IIT. An attempt is made in this paper to provide an overview of this literature, highlight major developments since the mid 1980s and assess the overall status of the application of various product differentiation models to analyze trade in agri-food products.

While the researchers now have at their disposal a number of alternative theoretical models to guide empirical trade research, the developments since the 1990s suggest that there is empirical relevance to both the H-O-S model of trade and trade based on increasing returns to scale and product differentiation. The results also suggest that the "New Trade Theory" needs to be broadened to explain trade flows among developing countries and between developed and developing countries.

Despite the growing importance of product differentiation and IIT in agri-food products, particularly among OECD countries, relatively few attempts have been made to investigate the extent of IIT in agriculture and to determine the factors driving the IIT. A few attempts that have been made did not explicitly model imperfect competition in their empirical model. Instead, they start with the theoretical prediction of Helpman and Krugman model or Falm and Helpman model to identify the variables, specify the proxy variables and conduct standard regression analysis to determine which factors have contributed to the growing importance of horizontal and vertical IIT.

Despite some well known weaknesses, the Armington model is still the "workhorse" in agri-food trade modeling and has been routinely used either in its original form or its refinements to model national product differentiations both in partial equilibrium and CGE frameworks. We have good reasons to believe that the "New Trade Theory" will continue to be relevant in agricultural trade analysis and additional refinements will occur to the Armingtom model so that it becomes more useful in explaining horizontal and vertical IIT involving agri-food products in the future. Our critical assessment of the current state of research in product differentiation and trade also suggests that the Dixit-Stiglitz model combined with monopolistic competition will become a standard tool for agricultural trade policy analysis in the future and that the Mussa-Rosen model could be adapted to address emerging trade policy issues which are ever more complicated.

While some progresses have been made since the mid 1990s in refining empirical analysis, the results of our synthesis suggest that more needs to be done in this area. For example, while the separation of total IIT into vertical and horizontal IIT has been a useful exercise in agri-food trade, the results are disappointing for the VIIT model relative to those for the HIIT model. Following relevant trade theories closely to develop testable hypothesis and focusing alternative specification of proxy variables could help in this regard. Secondly, theoretical predictions are considered to be relevant in the long run but most of the empirical studies conducted so far (dealing with both agri-food products and manufacturing) appear to have produced results that are more relevant in the short run. The issue related to short-run versus long-run relevance of the results has not been entertained in any published IIT study yet. Along the same line, what are the implications of data non-stationarity for the IIT results? Since it is well known that most macroeconomic variables contain unit roots, this issue is particularly relevant for IIT studies employing time series data in their analysis. Finally, since differences in factor endowments is the key driver of specialization and trade according to the H-O-S trade model, what is the threshold differences in factor endowment that changes VIIT into inter-industry trade? Is this threshold commodity specific or does it vary across countries? Does it vary over time? What factors contribute to changes in the threshold over time, across industries and trading partners? Future modeling endeavors to address these issues will enrich the current state of knowledge in product differentiation and trade.

REFERENCES

Abd-el-Rahman, K. (1991), Firms' competitive and national comparative advantage as joint determinations of trade composition. *Weltwirtschaftliches Archiv* 127:83-97.

Alston, J., C. A. Carter, R. Green and D. Pick (1990). Whither Armington trade Models? *American Journal of Agricultural Economics* 72: 455-477.

Anderson J. E. (1979). A Theoretical Foundation for the Gravity Equation, *American Economic Review* 69: 106-16.

Anderson, J. E., and E. van Wincoop (2003) Gravity with Gravitas: a Solution to the Border Puzzle. *American Economic Review* 93: 170-92.

Anderson, J. and E. van Wincoop (2004). Trade Costs. *Journal of Economic Literature* 42: 691-751.

Antweiler, W. and D. Trefler (2000). Increasing Returns and All That: A View from Trade" *NBER working paper No 7941.*

Aquino, A. (1978) Intra-industry trade and inter-industry trade specialization as concurrent sources of international trade in manufactures. . *Weltwirtschaftliches Archiv* 114:275-296.

Armington, P. S. (1969). A theory for demand of products distinguished by place of production. *IMF Staff Papers* 16: 159.178

Baier, S. and J. H. Bergrstrand (2001) The growth of world trade: tariffs, transport costs and income similarity. *Journal of International Economics* 53: 1-27.

Balassa, B. and L. Bauwens (1988). *Changing Trade Patterns in Manufactured Goods : an Econometric Investigation.* Amsterdam, North-Holland, 1988.

Bergstrand, J. (1985). The generalised gravity equation, monopolistic competition and the factor-proportions theory in international trade. *Review of Economics and Statistics* 67(3): 474-481.

Bergstrand, J. (1989). The gravity equation in international trade: Some microeconomic foundations and empirical evidence. *Review of Economics and Statistics* 71(1): 143-153.

Brander, J. A. (1981). Intra-industry trade in identical commodities. *Journal of International Economics* 15:1-14.

Brander, J. A. and P. R. Krugman (1983). A 'reciprocal dumping' model of international trade. *Journal of International Economics* 15: 313-321.

Brenton, P. A. (1989). The allocation approach to trade modelling: Some tests of separability between imports and domestic production and between different imported commodity groups. *Weltwirtschafliches Archiv* 125: 230-252.

Brown, D. (1987). Tariffs, terms of trade and national product differentiation. *Journal of Policy Modeling* 9(3): 503-526.

Bureau J-C, S. Marette and A. Schiavina (1998). Non-tariff barriers and consumers' information: The case of EU-US trade dispute in beef. *European Review of Agricultural Economics* 25:437-462.

Carew, R.W., W.J. Florkowski, and S. He. 2004. Demand for Domestic and Imported Table Wine in British Columbia: An Almost Ideal Demand System Approach. *Canadian Journal of Agricultural Economics* 52:183-199.

Christodoulou M. (1992). Intra-industry in agrofood sectors: the case of the EEC market. *Appplied Economics* 24: 875-884.

Cooper J. C., E. Giraud-Héraud and V. Réquillart (1995). Economic impacts of isoglucose deregulation on the European sweetener market. *European Review of Agricultural Economics* 22:435-445.

Davis, D. R. (1995). Intra-industry trade: a Hecksher-Ohlin-Ricardo approach. *Journal of International Economics* 39(3-4): 201-226.

Debaere, P. (2005). Monopolistic competition and trade, revisited: testing the model without testing for gravity. *Journal of International Economics,* 66: 249-266.

Deardorff, A. (1998). Determinants of bilateral trade: does gravity work in a neoclassical world? in: Frankel, J. A.(ed.). *The regionalization of the world economy.* Chicago, University of Chicago Press, pp 7-28.

Dixit, A. K., and G.M. Grossman (1982). Trade and protection with multistage production. *Review of Economic Studies*, 49: 583-594.

Dixit, P. and V. O. Roningen (1986). Modeling bilateral trade flows with the SWOPSIM modeling framework. *Staff report No AGES861124.* USDA, ERS. Washington. December 1986. 61 pages.

Dixit A. K. and J. E. Stiglitz (1977). Monopolistic competition and optimum product diversity. *American Economic review* 67: 297-308.

Durkin, J. and M. Krygier (2000). Differences in GDP Per Capita and the Share of Intra-Industry Trade: The Role of Vertically Differentiated Trade. *Review of International Economics* 8(4): 760-774.

Eaton, J. and S. Kortum (1997). Technology and Bilateral Trade. *NBER Working Paper No.* 6253.

Engel, C. and J. Rogers (1998). Relative Price Volatility: What Role does the Border Play? *International Finance Discussion Paper* No. 623, Board of Governors of the Federal Reserve System.

Erkel-Rousse, H. and D. Mirza (2002). Import price elasticities: reconsidering the evidence. *Canadian Journal of Economics* 35: 282-306

Evenett, S. J. and W. Keller (2002). On theories explaining the success of the gravity equation. *Journal of Political Economy* 110: 281-316.

Falvey, R. (1981). Commercial policy and intra-industry. *Journal of International Economics* 11(4): 495-511.

Falvey R. and H., Kierzkowski (1987). Product, quality, intra-indiustry trade and (im)perfect competition. in Kierzkowski, H. (ed.). *Protection and Competition in International trade.* Oxford, Blackwell.

Feenstra, R.C. (1998) Integration of trade and disintegration of production in the global economy. *Journal of Economic Perspectives* 12(4): 31-50.

Feenstra, R. C. (2002). Border effects and the gravity equation: Consistent methods for estimation. *Scottish Journal of Political Economy* 49:491-506.

Feenstra, R.C.(2004) *Advanced international trade. Theory and evidence.* Princeton, Princeton University Press.

Feenstra, R.C., J. R. Markusen and A. K. Rose (1998). Using the gravity equation to differentiate among alternative theories of trade. *Canadian Journal of Economics*, Vol 34: 430-447.

Feernstra, R. C, R. Lipsey, H. P. Bowen (1997). World trade flows, 1970-1992, with production and tariff data. *National Bureau of Economic Research. Working paper* No 5910. CD-ROM.

Fertö, I. (2005). Vertically-differentiated trade and differences in factor endowment. The case of Agri-food products between Hungary and the EU. *Journal of Agricultural Economics* 56(1): 117-134.

Finger, J. M. and M. E. Kreinen (1979). A measure of "export similarity" and its possible uses. *Economic Journal* 89: 905-912.

Flam, H. and E. Helpman (1987). Vertical product differentiation and North-South trade. *American Economic Review* 76(5): 810-822

Fontagné, Lionel and Michael Freudenberg (1997). Intra-indutry trade: methodological issues reconsidered. *CEPII working paper* #97-01. Paris, 32 pages.

Francois, J. (1998). Scale economies and imperfect competition in the GTAP model. *GTAP technical paper* No 14. September 1998. Purdue University.

Francois, J., H. van Meijl and F. van Tongeren (2005). Trade liberalization in the Doha development round. *Economic Policy* 20: 349-391.

Fujita, M., P. Krugman and A. J. Venables (1999). *The spatial economy. cities, regions and international trade*. Cambridge: The MIT Press.

Gallaway P. M., McDaniel C. A. and S. A. Rivera (2003). Short-run and long-run industry-level estimates of Armington elasticities. *North American Journal of Economics and Finance* 14: 49-68.

Glick, R. and A. K. Rose (1998). Contagion and trade: Why are currency crises regional? *NBER working group Paper* series No 6806.

Goddard (1988). Export Demand Elasticity in the World Market for Beef. In Colin Carter and Walter Gardiner (eds.) *Elasticities in International Agricultural Trade*, Chapter 8, pp. 225-253, Boulder: Wesview Press.

Gohin A. (2005). The specification of price and income elasticities in computable general equilibrium models: An application of latent separability. *Economic Modelling* . 22(5): 905-925.

Greenaway, D., R. C. Hine and C. R. Milner (1994). Country-specific factors and the pattern of horizontal and vertical intra-industry trade in the UK. *Weltwirtschafliches Archiv* 130(1): 77-100.

Greenaway, D., R. C. Hine and C. R. Milner (1995). Vertical and horizontal intra-industry trade: a cross-industry analysis for the United Kingdom. *Economic Journal* 105: 1505-1518.

Greenaway, D. and C. R. Milner (1981). Trade imbalances effects in the measurement of intra-industry trade. . *Weltwirtschaftliches Archiv* 117:756-762

Greenaway, D. and J. Tortensson (1997). Back to the future: Taking Stock on Intra-Industry Trade. *Weltwirtschafliches Archiv* 133(2): 249-269.

Grennes, T., P. R. Johnson and M. Thursby (1978). *The Economics of world grain trade*. New York: Preager publishers.

Grossman, G. (1998). "Comment", in *The Regionalization of the World Economy*, J.A. Frankel ed. Chicago: The University of Chicago Press.

Grubel, H. G. and P. J. Llyod (1975). *Intra-industry trade: The theory and measurement of international trade in differentiated products*. London, MacMillan Press.

Haley, S. (1995) Product differentiation in wheat trade modelling. *Technical bulletin* No 1838. ERS, USDA. Washington. June 1995. 25 pages.

Hamilton, C. and P. Kniest (1991). Trade liberalization, structural adjustment and intra-industry trade: A note. *Weltwirtschaftliches Archiv* 112:356-367.

Harrison, G. W., T. F. Rutherford and D. G. Tarr (1997). Quantifying the Uruguay Round. *Economic Journal* 107: 1405-1430

Heckscher, E. (1919). The Effect of Foreign Trade on the Distribution of Income, *Ekonomisk Tidskrift*, 497-512. In Hecksher-Ohlin Trade Theory. Heckscher, E. and B. Ohlin (translated, edited and introduced by H. Flam and M. Flanders). Cambridge, MA: The MIT Press 1991.

Helpman, E. (1981). International trade in the presence of product differentiation, economies of scale and monopolistic competition: A chamberlinian-Heckscher-Ohlin approach. . *Journal of International Economics* 11: 305-340.

Helpman, E. (1987). Imperfect competition and international trade: evidence from fourteen industrial countries. *Journal of the Japanese and International Economies* 1: 62-81

Helpman, E. (1999). The Strucutre of Foreign Trade, *Journal of Economic Perspectives* 13(2): 121-144.

Helpmann, E. and P. R. Krugman (1985). *Market structure and foreign trade: Increasing returns, imperfect competition, and the international economy*. Cambridge, MA: The MIT Press.

Helpmann, E. and P. R. Krugman (1989). *Trade policy and market structure*. Cambridge, MA: The MIT Press.

Henning, J. and L. Martin (1989). An Economic Evaluation of Expanded 3-M Wheat Exports. *Canadian Journal of Agricultural Economics* 37: 445-467.

Henry de Frahan, B. and J. Tharakan (1998). Horizontal and vertical intra-industry trade in the processed food sector. *Slected paper presented for the American Agricultural Economics Association annual meeting*, Salt Lake City, USA, August 2-5, 1998.

Hertel, T. (1997). *Global trade analysis. Modeling and applications*. Cambridge, Cambridge University Press.

Hirschberg, J., I. Sheldon and J. Dayton (1994). An Analysis of Bilateral Intra-Industry Trade in the Food Processing Sector. *Applied Economics* 26(2): 159-167.

Hjort, K. (1988). Class and source substituability in the demand for imported wheat. *Phd thesis*. Purdue University. West Lafayette, IN.

Hummels, D. (2001). Toward a Geography of Trade Costs. *Unpublished paper.* Department of Economics, Purdue University.

Hummels, D. and J. Levinsohn (1995). Monopolisitc competition and international trade: reconsidering the evidence. *Quarterly Journal of Economics* 110: 799-836.

Ito, S., Chen, D. T. and Peterson, W. (1990). Modeling international trade flows and market shares for agricultural commodities: A Modified Armington Procedure for Rice. *Agricultural Economics* 4: 315-333.

Keeney, R. and T. W. Hertel (2005). GTAP-AGR. A framework for assessing the implications of multilateral changes in agricultural policies. *GTAP technical paper* No. 24, 60 pages. Department of Agricultural Economics, Purdue University.

Kim, C. S. and W. Lin (1990). An export-side Armington model and trade liberalization in the world wheat market. *The Journal of Agricultural Economics Research* 42(3): 10-19.

Kohli, U. (1991). *Technology, duality and foreign trade: the GNP function approach to modeling importsd and exports*. New-York: Harvester Wheatleaf.

Kol, J. (1988). The measurement of intra-industry trade. *A Ph.D. Thesis*, Rotterdam: Erasmus University.

Kol, J. and B. M. Mennes (1986). Intra-industry specialization and some observations on concepts and measurement. *Journal of International Economics* 21:1173-1181.

Krugman, P. R. (1979). Increasing returns to scale, monopolistic competition and international trade. *Journal of International Economics* 9:469-479.

Krugman, P. R. (1980). Scale economies, product differentiation and the pattern of trade. *American Economic Review* 70(5):950-959.

Krugman, P. R. (1995a). Increasing Returns, Imperfect Competition and the Positive Theory of International Trade", in *Handbook of International Economics*, Vol. 3. Grossman, G., and K. Rogoff eds. Amsterdam: North Holland.

Krugman, P. R. (1995b). Growing world trade: causes and consequences. *Brookings Papers on Economic Activity*, Vol 1: 327-377.

Laborde, D. and J. Le Cacheux (2003). Price and welfare effects of agricultural liberalization with imperfect competition in food industries and trade. *Contributed paper presented at the GTAP 6th annual Conference*. June 12-14, 2003. The Hague. Netherlands.

Lancaster, K. (1975). Socially optimal product differentiation. *American Economic Review* 65: 567-585.

Lancaster, K. (1979). *Variety, equity and efficiency*. New York, Columbia University Press.

Lancaster, K. (1980). Intra-industry trade under perfect monopolistic competition. *Journal of International Economics* 10:151-175.

Lanclos, D. K. and T. W. Hertel (1995). Endogenous product differentiation and trade policy: implications for the food industry. *American Journal of Agricultural Economics* 77: 591-601.

Lanclos, D. K., T. W. Hertel and S. Devadoss (1996). Assessing the effects of tariff reform on manufacturing industries: the role of imperfect competition and intermediate inputs. *Agricultural Economics*, Vol 14: 201-212.

Larue, B. and H. E. Lapan (1991) Is wheat an homogeneous product? *Canadian Journal of Agricultural Economics*, Vol. 39, No. 1: 103-117.

Lavoie, N. (2001). An empirical Evaluation of ther Canadian wheat board's ability to price discriminate in bread wheat exports. *Contributed paper presented at the AAEA annual meeting.* Long Beach, California. July 28-31, 2002.

Lavoie, N. (2005). Price discrimination in the context of vertical differentiation: An application to the Canadian Wheat Board. *American Journal of Agricultural Economics* 87: 835-855.

Lawrence D. (1989). An Aggregator Model of Canadian Export Supply and Import Demand Responsiveness. *Canadian Journal of Economics* 22: 503-521.

Leamer, E. E. (1995) The Hecksher-Ohlin Model in theory and practice. Princeton Studies in *International Finance* No 77.

Linnemann, H. (1966). *An Econometric Study of International Trade Flows*. Amsterdam: North Holland.

Loetscher, R. and F. Wolton (1980). Determinants of intra-industry trade among countries and across industries. *Weltwirtschaftliches Archiv* 116: 280-293.

Llyod (2002). Controversies Concerning Intra-Industry Trade, in: Lloyd, P. J. and H.-H. Lee (eds), *Frontiers of research in intra-industry trade*. New York, Palgrave MacMillan, pp. 13-32.

MacDougall, G. (1952). British and American Exports : A Study Suggested by the Theory of Comparative Costs, Part II. *Economic Journal*, 62 : 487-521.

MacLaren (1990) Implications of New Trade Theory for Modelling Imperfect Substitution in Agricultural Trade. In Carter, C., A. McCalla and J. Sharples (eds), *Imperfect competition and political economy, The new trade theory in agricultural trade research*. Boulder: Westview Press.

McCorriston, S. and I. M. Sheldon (1991). Intra-Industry Trade and Specialization in Processed Agricultural Products: The Case of the US and the EC. *Review of Agricultural Economics* 13(2): 174-184.

McDaniel C. A. and E. Balistreri (2003). A Review of Armington Trade Substitution Elasticities. *Economie Internationale* 94-95: 301-314.

Nilsson, L. (1997). The Measurement of Intra-Industry Trade between Unequal Partners. *Weltwirtschaftliches Archiv* 133(1): 554-565.

Mussa, M. and S. Rosen (1978). Monopoly and product quality. *Journal of Economic Theory* 18: 301-317.

Ohlin, B. (1924). “The Theory of Trade”, in *Hecksher-Ohlin Trade Theory*. Heckscher, E. and B. Ohlin (translated, edited and introduced by H. Flam and M. Flanders). Cambridge, MA: The MIT Press 1991.

Peters, R. and Vanzetti, D. (2004). User Manual aand Handbook on Agricultural trade Policy Simulation Model (ATPSM). *Policy Issues in International Trade and Commodities Study* Series No 24. Trade analysis branch. UNCTAD. Geneva. 33 pages.

Peterson, E. B. and D. Orden (2005). Effects of Tariffs and Sanitary Barriers on High- and Low-Value Poultry Trade. *Journal of Agricultural and Resource Economics*, 30(1): 109-127.

Philippidis G. and L. Hubbard (2001). The economic cost of the CAP revisited. *Agricultural Economics* 25 : 375-385.

Philippidis G. and L. Hubbard (2003). Varietal utility and patriotic preference: the case of European Agriculture. *Cahiers d’Economie et Sociologie Rurales* 66 :6-25.

Pieri, R., D. Rama and L. Venturini (1997) Intra-industry trade in the European dairy industry. *European Review of Agricultural Economics* 24 (3-4) 411-425.

Pogany, P. (1996). The Almost Ideal Demand System and Applications in General Equilibrium Calculations. *Working Paper* No. 96-05-A. Office of Economics, U.S.I.T.C. Washington. May 2005.

Qasmi, B. A. and S. W. Fausti (2001). NAFTA Intra-Industry Trade in Agricultural and Food Products. *Agribusiness* 17(2): 255-271.

Rauch, J. E. (1999) Networks Versus Markets in International Trade. *Journal of International Economics* 48 : 7-35.

Reinert, K. A. and Roland-Holst, D. W. (1992). Armington Elasticities for the United States Manufacturing Sectors. *Journal of Policy Modeling* 14: 631-639.

Robinson S., Soule M., Weyerbrock S. (1991). *Import demand functions, trade volume, and terms-of-trade effects in multi-country trade models.* Unpublished manuscript, Department of Agricultural and Resource Economics, University of California at Berkeley.

Samuelson, P. A. (1952). Spatial price equilibrium and linear programming. *American economic Review* 42: 283-303.

Shaked, A. and J. Sutton (1984). Natural oligopolies and international trade in Kierzkowski, H. (ed.). *Monopolistic competition and competition in international trade*. Oxford: The Oxford University Press.

Slesnick, D. (1998). Empirical Approaches to the Measurement of Welfare. *Journal of Economic Literature*, 36: 2108-2165.

Sobolevsky A., G. Moschini and H. Lapan (2005). Benetically modified crops and product differentiation: trade and welfare effects in the soybean complex. *American Journal of Agricultural Economics* 87: 621-645.

Stern, R. (1962). British and American Productivity and Comparative Costs in International Trade. *Oxford Economic Papers* . 14:275-296.

Stiglitz, J. E. (1987). The causes and consequences of the dependence of quality on price. *The Journal of Economic Literature* 25: 1-48.

Stoeckel, A. R., D. Vincent, and S. Cuthberston (1989). *Macroeconomic Consequences of Farm Support Policies*. Durham, Duke University Press.

Sun, C.. and W. Koo (2002). Horizontal and vertical Intra-industry trade in the food processing industry. *Agribusiness and Applied Economics Report* No 502. Center fro Agricultural Policy and Trade Studies. Department of Agribusiness and Applied Economics. North Dakota State University. Fargo. December 2002. 20 pages.

Surry, Y, Herrard, N and Y. Leroux (2002). Modelling Trade in Processed Food Products: An Econometric Investigation. *European Review of Agricultural Economics* 29(1): 1-29.

Swaminathan P. and T. Hertel (1996). Introducing monopolistic competition into the GTAP model. *GTAP technical paper* No 6. October 1996. Purdue University.

Takayama, T,. and G.G. Judge (1971). *Spatial and temporal price and allocation models.* Amsterdam. North Holland.

Thursby, M. C., P. R. Johnson and T. J. Grennes (1986). The law of one price and the modelling of disaggregated trade flows. *Economic Modelling* 3(4): 293-302.

Tinbergen, J. (1962). *Shaping the world economy*. New York, Twentieth Century Fund.

United States Depåartment of Agriculture (1986). Embargoes, Surplus disposal and Agriculture. Washington, DC: Department of Agriculture Staff Report No AGES860910, Economic Research Service, November 1986.

Van Berkum S. and H. van Meijl (1999). Horizontal and vertical intra-industry trade in agricultural and food products: an analysis of patterns and explanatory factors for EU countries. *Contributed paper presented at the 1999 European trade study group*. Rotterdam, 24-26 September, 1999.

Van Tongeren F, H. van Meijl and Y. Surry (2001). Global Models Applied to Agricultural and Trade Policies: A Review and Assessment. *Agricultural Economics*, Vol 26(2) : 149-172.

Venables, A. J. (1985) Trade and Trade Policy with Imperfect Competition: The Case of Identical Products and Free Entry. *Journal of International Economics* 19: 1-20.

Venables, A. J. (1987). Trade and trade Policy with differentiated products: A Chamberlinian-Ricardian model. *Economic Journal*. Vol 97: 700-719.

Winters, A. (1984). Separability and Specification of Foreign Trade Functions. *Journal of International Economics* 17: 239-263.

Weber, G. (2003). Russia's and Kazakhstan's agro-food sectors under liberalized agricultural trade: a case for national product differentiation. *Economic Systems* 27: 391-413.

Winter, E. and K. Frohberg (2004). Using flexible McFadden export supply and import demand functions for bilateral trade analysis. *Contributed paper presented at the International Conference on Policy Modeling*. University of Paris I, Paris, June 30-July 2, 2004.

Winters, A. (1984). Separability and Specification of Foreign Trade Functions. *Journal of International Economics* 17: 239-263.

Yang, S-R and W. W. Koo (1994). Japanese Import Demand Estimation with the Source Differentiated AIDS Model. *Journal of Agricultural and Resource Economics* 19(2): 396-408.

Appendix 1. Product-Differentiated Models Applied to Agricultural and Food Processing Commodities: The Case of National Product Differentiation

Authors	Commodity coverage	Study's objectives	Model characteristics	Main findings
Haley (1995)	Wheat	To assess the impact of export subsidy programs in the cases of differentiated and homogeneous wheat trade.	-Wheat differentiated by quality (classes) et geographical sources of origin - Three-stage model: For a given region, the model determines how much wheat to import, then wheat classes and finally the sources of suppliers. -Imperfect substitution among wheat classes and geographical sources of supplies through constant elasticities of substitution (use of CES functions). - Comparative static world model (six exporters, 26 importers and seven classes of wheat) calibrated for the period 1986-1991.	- Need to differentiate wheat by end use and country of origin. - Export Enhancement Program (EEP). policy impacts are dependent upon the extent of differentiation. Thus, removing EEP subsidies over the period 1986-1991 induced an average 16% reduction in export volume for the case where wheat is an homogeneous product while the same effect would be 11% for the differentiated case. - If wheat were homogeneous, the EEP is calculated to have expanded export revenue above the cost of the program by 13% between 1986-1991. This figure would only be 4% in the case of differentiation as assumed in this study.
Weber (2003)	Wheat Coarse grains, Oilseeds, Sugar, Vegetables and potatoes, Fruits, Cotton, Milk, Ruminant meat, Pork, Poultry	To assess the impacts of agricultural trade liberalization if Kazakhstan and Russia form a common agricultural market (CAM) with other Commonwealth Independent States (CIS) and become members of WTO.	- Comparative static, partial equilibrium model of Russia and Kazakhstan agricultural sectors broken down into eleven commodities. The model includes four regions (Russia, Kazakhstan, CIS and non-CIS countries) and is calibrated for 1997. -Product differentiation by sources of origin (imports) and destination (exports) for each agricultural commodity. -Simultaneous determination of agricultural prices in Russia and Kazakhstan. In the other two regions, prices are exogenous. - Multistage model specification for the supply side. At the top level, supply and input demand for each agricultural commodity are derived from a multi-output symmetric Generalised McFadden profit function. At the intermediate stage, imperfect transformation (based on a CET function) between domestic and export supplies is assumed for each agricultural commodity. At the bottom stage, various export supply functions (by destination) are derived assuming a CET transformation function. -Three-stage model specification on the consumer demand side. At the upper stage, demand functions for each agricultural commodity are derived from a normalized quadratic expenditure function.	- The implementation of the CAM scenario results in a modest decline (2%) in net producer revenues and a slight increase (less than 1%) in consumer welfare. As government loses revenues from import tax collection, the overall economic welfare is negligible. -In Kazakhstan, the implementation of the CAM scenario induces a 14% decline in net producer revenues, while consumers experience a modest increase (0.5%) in welfare. Government experiences a modest decline in revenue stemming from import tax collection. Overall, there is a small improvement of overall economic welfare on agricultural markets of Kazakhstan. - Product differentiation seems to matter in analysing the effects of liberalized trade on CIS agro-industries. Stronger national product differentiation would benefit single sectors of the agro-industrial complex in reducing negative impacts on their profits.

Appendix 1. Continued

Authors	Commodity coverage	Study's objectives	Model characteristics	Main findings
			Then, consumers determine the demand for domestically produced and imported products based on a CES aggregator functions. Finally, various import demand by geographical sources are derived at the lowest stage from a CES aggregator function. -Various agricultural policy instruments (import tariffs and subsidies, export subsidies and direct payments) enter the various price transmission equations.	
Peterson and Orden (2005)	Poultry	To evaluate the effects of sanitary barriers to poultry trade in combination with non-technical barriers in the forms of tariffs and tariff-rate quotas (TRQs).	- Distinction between "high-value " (white meat) and "low-value" (dark meat) poultry products. - Joint production of these two categories of poultry products. - Four-stage model: For a given region, the model first determines the total demand for poultry, then the demand for high- and low-values poultry products, then demand for domestically produced and total imports, and then sources of imports. -At the various stages of the model, substitutability patterns are captured by CES (sub)utility functions. -Static world model (eight regions including USA, Brazil, Rest of World exporting region (ROWE), EU, China, Japan, Russia and Rest of World importing region (ROWM)) calibrated for 1998. -Government policies included are the various tariffs, TRQs for the EU and SPS regulations.	-Simulation results tend to show that nontechnical barriers to trade have significant effects on world trade. Hence, removing all these nontechnical barriers to trade would expand global trade by 25%. It is also expected that the USA could gain additional access to the EU market. - When Brazil is assumed to enter low-value poultry markets of Russia and the ROWM region as new markets, effects on production and exports resulting from trade policy reform are reduced for the US and the EU and their exports are diverted to China.

Appendix 1. Continued

Authors	Commodity coverage	Study's objectives	Model characteristics	Main findings
Keeny and Hertel (2005)	-29 sectors highlighting agricultural (12) and food processing (8) sectors -6 other industrial sectors -3 service sectors	To provide a better assessment of multilateral trade liberalization scenarios of agricultural markets, taking into account the specificities of agricultural sectors. This is implemented by introducing in the standard GTAP model additional relationships (behavioural, technical) representative of agricultural sectors. This new agricultural–based version of GTAP is called GTAP-AGR.	- Labor and capital are segmented between agricultural and non-agricultural sectors, while they are perfectly mobile within both groups (agricultural and non-agricultural). To capture this former segmentation, a CET function with fixed factor endowments is specified. Within agriculture, land is also segmented according to final use: This is again implemented using a CET function. - A nested-CES production function is specified for each agricultural sector, the output of which is produced by combining purchased and farm-owned (value-added) inputs. - Explicit modelling of crop-livestock interactions by separating among purchased agricultural inputs feedstuffs from the rest. -The same two-stage consumer structure as in GTAP (based on the use of the 'Constant difference of elasticities' (CDE) specification) is kept in GTAP-AGR. It is however assumed that food and non-food commodities are separable. -Elasticity of substitution among imports in GTAP-AGR that are econometrically estimated and on average greater than those used in GTAP. -Explicit model representation of OECD farm households in GTAP-AGR. This is done by assuming that farm households share the same utility function as the representative GTAP household but they differ in their earnings. -Explicit representation of agricultural policy instruments to reflect their changing nature over time. Thus, special care is given to the representation of decoupled programs (payments) in the EU. -GTAP-AGR is made up of 23 regions and calibrated for 2001.	- In terms of model validation, it was found that GTAP-AGR was doing reasonably well in reproducing the economy-wide and global impacts of weather-induced shocks. Even in some cases, it was performing better than the conventional GTAP model framework. -Concerning policy simulation scenarios on multilateral trade liberalization under the WTO Doha round, GTAP-AGR generates impact results for overall trade, world prices and national welfare aggregates, that are of similar magnitude as those obtained with the conventional GTAP model framework. -Where GTAP-AGR "produces" different impact results from the conventional GTAP model has to do with the repercussions on farm specific variables such as farm labour and farm household welfare. For instance, the fact that imperfect labour mobility is assumed in GTAP-AGR induces moves of unskilled labour out of agriculture such as in Japan, EU and the USA, that are much more moderate that those obtained with the conventional GTAP model.

Appendix 2. Product-Differentiated Models Applied to Agriculture and Food Processing Commodities: The Case of Horizontal Differentiation

Authors	Commodity coverage	Study's objectives	Model characteristics	Main findings
Lanclos and Hertel (1995)	Processed food products in the United States, including fruits and vegetables, milled consumer goods, beverages, confectionary products and other food products.	-To study the effects of tariffs on intermediate inputs and final goods in monopolistically competitive industries. -Theoretical propositions are derived and comparative static results are generated and compared to an Armington-like model based on prefect competition. - The model propositions are then tested and checked on several food industries.	-Adaptation of Venables (1987), two-country, two-product model with a homogeneous, traded, intermediate input produced under perfectly competitive conditions. - The model is of partial equilibrium nature and assumes that the first country applying a tariff is a small importer while country 2 represents Rest of world. - On the consumer side, a two-stage separable, homothetic preference structure is assumed with two products, one being an homogeneous *numeraire*, while the second one is a differentiated (food) product. -A CES sub-utility function *à la* Dixit-Stiglitz is defined for the varieties making the differentiated commodity. - On the producer side, representative firms maximize profits assuming fixed cost of entry, operating under conditions of monopolistic conditions (free entry and zero profit) and subject to the second-stage demand function. - It is assumed that consumers exhibit a preference for domestic varieties. -Variables of interest in this model are the number of firms, the output per firm, sectoral output and unit expenditures.	-The effects of a tariff on intermediate farm and food inputs used by food processing industries induce a decline in output per firm and a decline in firm numbers. -These former results are compared with those obtained under perfect competition. It is found that the decline in total industry output is much larger under monopolistic competition. - The impacts of combined tariff shocks to both intermediate inputs and final goods induce a reduction in output per firm while effects on changes in firm numbers and total sectoral output are ambiguous. The change in total output under perfect competition under perfect competition is also characterized by a similar ambiguity.

APPENDIX 2. CONTINUED

Authors	Commodity coverage	Study's objectives	Model characteristics	Main findings
Philippidis and Hubbard (2001, 2003)	Seventeen sectors highlighting agriculture (9 sectors) and food processing (6 sectors) plus manufacturing and services	-To study the economic inefficiency of the Common Agricultural Policy (CAP) when varietal utility and patriotic preference are taken into consideration explicitly. - A full trade liberalisation of the CAP is implemented.	-The varietal utility and patriotic preference specification is captured through an endogenous hierarchical consumer preference based on the region of origin. An additional layer allowing for food patriotic preference (specification based on the Lancaster model) is added to the exogenous region-of-origin approach maintained under the Armington assumption (see text for more details on this question) -The GTAP model is used and aggregated in two regions (EU and Rest of World) and considers only 17 sectors focusing agriculture and food processing. The food processing, manufacturing and services sectors are imperfectly competitive. Varietal effects occur only for food processing in both regions. Primary factors are perfectly competitive. -CAP instruments refer to the McSharry reform. Most of the instruments are expressed in tariffs equivalent forms. However, all the de-coupled area and headage-payments from the cereal ands and livestock sectors (that were considered as output subsidies) are re-calibrated as input subsidies. Set-aside payments are decoupled and treated as a "fictional payment to agricultural household " and thus viewed as a provision for land owners. - The CGE model is calibrated with the version 4.0 of the GTAP data base (1995)	-The CAP may have a significant effect on increasing varietal diversity in the EU through an expansion in domestic food processing industries. -Removal of the CAP reverses this effect, causing hierarchical losses. These are offset by positive varietal effects in manufacturing and services and stronger allocative effects than under preference homogeneity. -Preference heterogeneity has a marginal impact on the net cost of the CAP (estimated for the EU at 0.19% of GDP.

APPENDIX 3. EXAMPLES OF VERTICALLY-DIFFERENTIATED PRODUCT MODELS APPLIED TO AGRICULTURE AND FOOD PROCESSING COMMODITIES

Authors	Commodity coverage	Study's objectives	Model characteristics	Main findings
Cooper *et al.* (1995)	EU sweetener sector	-To assess the potential magnitude of the penetration of isoglucose into the EU sweetener market and its possible impact. - The study assumes that the EU sugar regime as given and attempts to find the best response of isoglucose producers to sugar prices and to derive the welfare impact of the production of isoglucose. -A demand model of vertical product differentiation is developed.	-Sweeteners are intermediate products that are differentiated according to two parameters: sweetness content and physical form (isoglucose or sugar). In addition, divisibility of the products is allowed. -Food processing manufacturers minimize the cost of sweeteners subject to technological constraints on the levels of sweetness and on bulk content. - Aggregate demand for the two sweeteners are assumed to be price inelastic (zero price elasticity) and the associated demand functions depend upon the various levels of sweetness per unit of sweetener, the maximum quantity of sweetener and a cumulative distribution function associated with the random quality parameter on physical form.	- It is shown that liberalisation of the isoglucose market in the EU could not increase welfare if it is not accompanied by a reduction in the sugar quota. - If production of isoglucose were unrestricted in the EU, it could replace 25% of the industrial use of sugar. -It is shown that sweetness viewed as an index of quality is of crucial importance.
Bureau et al. (1998)	Beef	-To study the welfare effects of trade liberalisation in the case of a credence good, using the case of the EU-US trade dispute hormone-treated beef. - A stylised vertically differentiated product model is developed and used to undertake comparative welfare analysis under three situations: autarky, free trade without identification of the quality of the product and free trade with a quality label.	-The analytical model framework is based on a one-period two-region partial equilibrium model under vertical differentiation with two qualities for a single good. -Quality is referred to a single attribute, i.e hormone-treated or non-treated. Quality of the product could be perceived and/or expected by consumers and this specific feature attributed to this manifestation of quality is incorporated into the model through a relevant specification of the demand functions. A parameter defining perceived quality and taking values over the interval [0 1] is defined. A value closed to zero would indicate that the quality of imported beef is of lower quality than the hormone-free domestic beef. On the other hand, if this parameter is close to 1, consumers perceived no quality differences between imported and domestic beef. - The model is then used to generate welfare results for consumers, producers and the EU as a whole.	-The lack of product diversity limits domestic welfare under an autarky situation. No uncertainty on quality would occur and there will be none of the problems linked to adverse selection. -Under a trade liberalisation situation with no labelling, the parameter defining perceived quality plays a key role in welfare results. Thus, promoting trade liberalization when foreign products are perceived of lower quality than domestic goods could lead to market inefficiencies (adverse selection) and multiple equilibria. -The effects of trade liberalisation with a quality label are ambiguous. Domestic welfare losses could occur, depending upon the cost associated with the label and upon the extent of how consumers perceive a significant difference between the two qualities of beef.

Authors	Commodity coverage	Study's objectives	Model characteristics	Main findings
Sobolevsky *et al.* (2005)	Soybean and byproducts	-To assess the trade, price and market repercussions of introducing genetically modified (GM) varieties on the soybean complex. -To attain this objective, a global, spatial, partial equilibrium model allowing for product differentiation and cost segregation is developed for the world soybeans, soybean oil and soybean meal markets. In addition, this model allows the production of conventional and GM-grown soybeans.	- Four regions (including US, Argentina, Brazil and rest of World (ROW)) are included in this model. Soybeans and soybean oil are made up of two varieties: GM (a variety produced with a herbicide-resistant technology) and conventional. -Only, ROW region is modelled with differentiated demand. The demand for GM products is assumed to be a weakly inferior substitute. This is implemented through the use of the vertical product differentiation model of Mussa and Rosen (with unit demand). Consumers have heterogeneous preferences with respect to GM and conventional food products. Linear forms are adopted for the various demand variables. -The impacts of biotechnology innovation of the GM variety on soybean production and demand for soybeans and soybean products are explicitly represented in the model through an appropriate specification. To capture the segregation costs to maintain identity preservation, it also implies a separation of conventional and GM soybeans and soybean product activities and markets. -Trade is allowed all along the supply chain of the soybean complex but also among regions. This feature of the model "allows to study whether different models are affected differently by the introduction of Roundup Ready (RR) technology and to model region-specific policy actions". -Market clearing conditions requiring that total world soybean demand is equal to the total world supply for each variety. -The model is calibrated for the 1998-1999 marketing year. - support price policies for soybeans are incorporated into the model.	- In a world situation with no feasible segregation technology, the long run equilibrium state of the world after cost-saving RR technology is introduced is that of complete worldwide adoption. This equilibrium is characterised by lower prices for soybeans and by-products and a lead on world soybean exports. – In a situation with free of government intervention and trade regulations and with a segregation technology with positive costs, the US is the only region producing both RR and conventional soybeans. All other regions specialize in RR production. - When the ROW and Brazil prohibit the production of RR products, the ROW would benefit from such a ban relative to the no-ban scenario as long as the segregation costs are not too low. In Brazil only farmers would benefit from such regulation.

Appendix 3. Continued

Authors	Commodity coverage	Study's objectives	Model characteristics	Main findings
Lavoie (2005)	Wheat	-To study the behaviour of state-trading enterprises like the Canadian Wheat Board (CWB) to price discriminate in wheat exports. -A conceptual model based on the assumption of vertical differentiation is first developed, specified and resolved to determine and explain the price discriminating behaviour of the CWB. - The hypothesis of price discrimination is then tested through a reduced-form model using confidential data on monthly price and total quantity of Canadian Wheat Red Spring (CWRS) of grade 1 and 2 over a period November 1982 to July 1994.	The model of Mussa and Rosen is used to represent an importer's wheat market. Wheat is viewed as an intermediate good used by millers to produce a final good (flour) with desired qualities. -The model considers two importer's markets and two exporters (US and Canada) and three qualities of wheat (domestic, Canadian and US). It is assumed that importer's domestic wheat is of lower quality than its US counterpart that in turn is inferior to Canadian wheat. -Demand relationships for the three categories of wheat in each importer's market are derived from a representative miller that minimizes its cost of producing flour by blending qualities of wheat through a Leontief technology. -On the supply side, it is assumed that US wheat producers behave as profit maximizers operating in perfectly competitive environment, while the CWB acts as a monopolist with the objective of maximizing producers' surplus through a price discrimination strategy on its various export destination subject to a constraint that the amount exported cannot exceed the total production of wheat in a given year. Resolution of the first order conditions associated with the CWB's optimised objective function results in the determination of export prices high quality wheat, that depend upon the wheat quality variables, processing costs and "instruments" of price discrimination (such as exchange rates, government policy instruments, etc..) - The resulting empirical model links through a linear regression price differences of Canadian export prices as a function of wheat quality variables, processing costs and instruments of price discrimination.	- The empirical model is tested with Canadian wheat export prices representative of four importers markets including Japan, United Kingdom (UK), Rest of World-West Canadian ports (excluding Japan) and Rest of World-East Coast ports (excluding UK)). -Empirical results seem to indicate that CWB do price discrimination by charging different f.o.b. prices to different countries for the same grade and protein content. - Statistical tests support the hypothesis that the CWB exerts market power resulting from product differentiation and uses it to price discriminate across export markets. -empirical results seem also to show that CWB is not fully using the instruments of price discrimination to pursue its stated objectives (like Canadian wheat producer revenues).

In: International Agricultural Trade and Development
Editor: Dragan Miljkovic, pp. 81-87
ISBN: 978-1-60021-965-8

Chapter 5

PRODUCT DIFFERENTIATION AND TRADE IN AGRI-FOOD PRODUCTS: DISCUSSION

Julian M. Alston
Department of Agricultural and Resource Economics
University of California, Davis

Discussant comments on the Invited Paper "Product Differentiation and Trade in Agri-Food Products: Taking Stock and Looking Forward" presented by Rakhal Sarker and Yves Surry at the Theme Day, *New Dimensions in Modeling Food and Agricultural Markets* at the 2005 Annual Meeting of the *International Agricultural Trade Research Consortium* in San Diego, California, December 4-6, 2005.

INTRODUCTION

The paper by Rakhal Sarker and Yves Surry is quite ambitious in scope and large in size (38 pages single-spaced, and almost 20,000 words). As the authors state (p. 3), the purpose is "to provide a survey of the literature on product differentiation and international trade in agricultural products, critically assess what has been done, how and why." I think it is fair to say that the authors have done that and more. In particular they have also (1) provided a useful discussion of the more general history of economic thought in this area, beyond the applications to agricultural products, and (2) gone beyond documenting what is in the literature and attempted to draw conclusions about what the results mean for how we should approach the subject.

To review a paper like this is challenging, especially for someone who is not a specialist in the area. Although I have been involved in modeling trade in differentiated products, off and on, for more than 25 years, I have not really been following all of the relevant literature closely, especially the more general literature on trade theory or the more general literature on industrial organization. So I am not in a good position to judge the extent to which the survey of literature is comprehensive (i.e., fully representative of all of the relevant literature), balanced, and accurate in its interpretation of what the literature means; other readers can judge these things for themselves better than I. These caveats notwithstanding, I was left with the impression that the authors have done a good job of making sense of the relevant literature and organizing the information, and I learned a lot from reading the paper.

One reasonable question to ask is: what does it all mean for those of us who are engaged in modeling international trade in (perhaps increasingly) heterogeneous agricultural commodities? My comments that follow relate mainly to that question.[1]

A recurring theme in the paper by Sarker and Surry is to contrast the predictions of the Heckscher-Ohlin-Samuelson theory of international trade (what used to be called the "modern" theory) and the so-called "new" theory associated with Helpman and Krugman, especially as they relate to the observed patterns of intra-industry trade. In simple terms, the central question is whether a model based on factor endowments (i.e., the "modern" theory) is sufficient, or is it necessary to augment that model with economies of scale to account for the patterns of product differentiation and specialization. The answer to this question is not just of academic interest, since it may have implications for the nature of competition. The authors' conclusion (p. 24) is somewhat equivocal on this issue— "the developments since the 1990s suggest that there is empirical relevance to both the H-O-S model of trade and trade based on increasing returns to scale and product differentiation" —but they seem to lean in the direction of supporting the "new" theory (i.e., increasing returns to scale) as being necessary to account for significant elements of the observed patterns of intra-industry trade.

In what follows I will use a series of examples to consider the potential relevance of increasing returns to scale as a factor accounting for intra-industry trade. My null hypothesis is that an assumption of constant returns to scale at the industry level, and competition, is reasonable for most agricultural commodities in most places. Economies of scale may be important in the marketing stage for some commodities and products.

AGGREGATION, DIFFERENTIATION, AND INTRA-INDUSTRY TRADE

Reading the paper by Sarker and Surry caused me to think about intra-industry trade and what it means. Some of the resulting thoughts were strange and new to me, though they are simple and obvious to me now, and may seem trivial to you. Specifically, I can imagine a model based on the modern theory, with a multitude of heterogeneous products produced using a multitude of heterogeneous factor inputs, in a multitude of diverse places, and no intra-industry trade at all. However, in the same setting, when I aggregate up to a more manageable number of places, factors, and products, I will create the appearance of intra-industry trade.

I find it interesting and worrisome that the extent to which we observe intra-industry trade is determined wholly by decisions we make about the aggregation of heterogeneous outputs across space, time, and form, and how we define industries. This should give us pause before we make strong inferences about the nature of the economy based on observations about patterns of intra-industry trade alone. To make matters more concrete, let me talk more

[1] My comments are also pertinent to the paper presented in the same session by Ian Sheldon, which refers to much of the same literature and many of the same issues.

specifically about aggregating over space, time, and form characteristics of outputs and inputs using some familiar local examples.

Spatial Aspects: Aggregating Over Space

Both the "modern" and "new" trade theories tend to abstract from the spatial dimension. But geopolitical boundaries are somewhat arbitrary and we use them somewhat arbitrarily in our models in a world increasingly characterized by multinational free trade areas. When we treat the United States as a single geopolitical economic entity, we aggregate across very dissimilar places. For instance, California exports wine to the rest of the world, including the rest of the United States, which also imports a lot of wine from other countries. If we disaggregate to the level of states—or better, regions within states—we find a much greater degree of specialization and a much greater consistency of the patterns of production and trade in wine with the predictions of a model based on endowments alone (in particular, endowments of soil, climate, and other agro-ecological factors that are essentially spatial in nature). On the other hand, if we aggregate across states in the United States (or across countries within the EU) we observe a much greater extent of intra-industry trade (with these larger geopolitical aggregates) and we might draw erroneous inferences about why that trade pattern is so.

A second spatial aspect relates to distance, transport costs, and border trade. For instance, suppose Western Canada exports feeder cattle to Montana and Ontario imports beef from Iowa. If we model the beef industry at the level of nations, then, we will observe intra-industry trade between Canada and the United States that reflects two dimensions of aggregation. First we have aggregated across space. Second, we have aggregated across stages of the production and marketing chain, aggregating intermediate and more-nearly final goods. If we opt to model the meat industry rather than the beef industry, we will create even more such possibilities.

Temporal Aspects: Aggregating Over Time

We tend to model commodities on an annual basis, and for certain types of commodities this creates some problems in the context of intra-industry trade. For instance, California is a large producer and exporter of table grapes to the rest of the United States and other countries. However, table grapes are seasonal. In the North American winter and spring, California imports table grapes from Chile and Mexico. In the winter months California exports navel oranges to Australia among other places, and in the summer months California imports navel oranges from Australia and other places. This pattern of trade is entirely a result of endowments (of climate) that result in complete specialization in production of grapes and navel oranges differentiated according to season, but when we aggregate up to a year as the unit of observation, we observe intra-industry trade. Moreover, typically models include all oranges, not just navels. California and Australia both import frozen concentrated orange juice from Brazil and Florida, made from valencia oranges, whilst exporting navel oranges.

Quality Characteristics: Aggregating Over Products

Agricultural commodities more generally are differentiated for similar types of reasons related to agro-ecological endowments. For instance, wheat is differentiated according to its protein content and other characteristics, and these characteristics of the grain are determined by a combination of agro-ecology, technology, and management. Hence we observe a spatial distribution of differentiated wheat production related to endowments that gives rise to trade in differentiated wheat. For example, France imports hard wheat from North America and exports soft wheat to other places. These different types of wheat are blended in various proportions to produce various types of flour used for different breads and other baked goods in both France and North America and other countries. At the same time, North America exports durum wheat to Italy and imports semolina and pasta.[2] If we aggregate across states within the United States and within Europe, across qualities of wheat (perhaps also including durum), and across the marketing chain, we will find a lot of intra-industry trade in the wheat industry.

The same types of issues arise in other industries that we study a lot.[3] In the beef industry, the United States is the world's biggest exporter and importer. It imports hamburger beef (and sometimes kangaroo) from Australia and exports high quality beef to Japan and other places. Similarly the United States imports low quality tobacco and exports high quality tobacco and cigarettes that contain a blend of high- and low-quality tobacco. Is this inter-industry trade or intra-industry trade?

What Should We Do?

If we are going to learn anything about the nature of competition in these industries, and the role of economies of scale and product differentiation as an element of intra-industry trade, we have to be conscious of the role of aggregation of goods and factors over space, time, and form. It seems desirable to treat commodities explicitly as being differentiated according to their space, form, and time dimensions in any such work, and to minimize the extent to which we aggregate across these dimensions. My general impression is that much of the literature discussed in the survey by Sarker and Surry has used relatively aggregative definitions of industries, and this raises issues in my mind about the interpretation of the results.

What about Armington?

In several places in their paper, Sarker and Surry lament what they perceive as an under-utilization of the Armington approach in partial equilibrium models of agricultural commodity trade. I disagree on two grounds. First, my impression is that the authors are not

---

[2] See Alston, Carter, Gray, and Sumner (1997), Alston, Gray, and Sumner (1994), and Alston and James (2002) for some discussion of these aspects of wheat markets and trade.

[3] For instance, see Alston, Carter, and Jarvis (1990) for an application to beef, Alston and Scobie (1987) for an application to chicken meat, James and Alston (2002) for an application to wine, and Sumner and Alston (1987) for an application to tobacco and cigarettes.

aware of numerous studies of this type over the past 20 years, in response to which one could just as well argue that the model has been over-used in partial equilibrium models of agricultural commodity trade. Second, I have some serious misgivings about the use of the Armington approach to proxy for goods differentiated physically and not simply in terms of country of origin.

Markets for Characteristics

My comments so far, like the paper by Sarker and Surry, refer to markets for differentiated products per se. One option may be to model the markets for the less-differentiated characteristics of products, such as protein in wheat. This is increasingly how some of the trade operates and may be helpful from the perspective of modeling as well. For instance, in some recent work (Alston, Balagtas, Brunke, and Sumner, 2005) we modeled the possible impact of a free trade agreement between Australia and the United States for dairy products. The dairy industry is an interesting case because the number of products and the extent to which they are differentiated is so large. Setting aside fluid milk and other "soft" products, we still have several basic classes of dairy products such as skim milk powder, butter, and cheese. But within these classes there is much further differentiation, especially in cheese. Our initial challenge was to find a way to model this industry, globally. We were not content to use an Armington approach to reflect more than country of origin per se, we could not contemplate modeling the full range of differentiated products, yet we did not feel comfortable about aggregating French Camembert and California Cheddar along with all the others into a single commodity, cheese. Our solution was to model the supply and demand for two essentially homogeneous components of milk and dairy products, dairy fat and protein. This type of approach may be helpful in other contexts, though it does involve a loss of information about the markets for the specific products, which may be undesirable in some contexts.

Economies of Scale in Processing and Marketing

I have raised a number of commodities as examples, including wheat, wine, fresh fruit, beef, tobacco and dairy, I am fairly convinced that the industries that produce these products (at least in those countries where I have studied them) are generally competitive and can be characterized as having constant returns at the industry level. However, in several instances there is evidence of significant concentration beyond the farm gate, and this and other evidence is consistent with increasing returns to scale at the next stage of production—such as meat packing, cigarette manufacturing, wheat marketing, and international marketing of wine. But it is not clear to me how much influence the concentration of the downstream agribusiness sector has had on the characteristics of the commodities that they use as inputs, which I would suggest are determined more by endowments. These matters are made more complicated by the fact that the firms that market wine and wheat are multinational and in many cases are elements of much larger firms that trade in other things as well.

Domestic and Border Policy

As a further complication, sometimes domestic or border policies create incentives for product quality, with implications for intra-industry trade (e.g., James and Alston 2002). One good example is the U.S. tobacco industry in which the acreage controls introduced in the 1930s caused U.S. producers to increase yield at the expense of quality. Later, when acreage allotments were replaced with poundage quotas in the 1960s and 1970s, the U.S. industry increased its production share and exports of higher quality tobacco and switched to imports of lower quality tobacco. The U.S. policy influenced the distribution of tobacco quality production around the world, and thus the trade patterns (e.g., Sumner and Alston 1987). Similarly, EU wheat policy has encouraged French farmers to grow higher yielding, lower quality wheat with implications for the quality mix produced in other countries and in trade (e.g., Alston and James 2002). The U.S. sweetener market is another good example. Studies of intra-industry trade that do not take these policy influences into account might mistakenly attribute the phenomena to some other cause.

Conclusion

Agricultural commodities are mostly produced under competitive conditions with constant returns to scale (but still highly differentiated in space, time, and form because of differences in endowments). The appearance of intra-industry trade is mostly a reflection of aggregation of these heterogeneous commodities, and not a reflection of returns to scale or imperfect competition.

In some cases these commodities are used to produce heterogeneous products where part of the marketing chain is characterized by economies of scale and potential departures from competition. The challenge is to determine the extent to which the differentiation in final products is also a result of competition, and a reflection of the differentiation of the commodities, and what role may be played by departures from competition as a determinant of the mix of commodities and products, produced and traded, country by country.

As someone who wants to model the markets for farm commodities and the products they are used to produce, I am left wondering how to deal with this type of situation. In some cases I think I know something, and learned some of it from Sarker and Surry, but I think we have a way to go yet, perhaps especially in applications to agricultural commodities.

References

Alston, J.M, J.V. Balagtas, H. Brunke, and D.A. Sumner. "Supply and Demand for Commodity Components: Implications of Free Trade versus the AUSFTA for the U.S. Dairy Industry." *Australian Journal of Agricultural and Resource Economics* 2006 (second round review)

Alston, J.M., C.A. Carter, R. Gray, and D.A. Sumner. "Third-Country Effects and Second-Best Grain Trade Policies: Export Subsidies and Bilateral Liberalization." *American Journal of Agricultural Economics* 79(November 1997):1300-1310.

Alston, J.M., R. Gray and D.A. Sumner. "The Wheat War of 1994." *Canadian Journal of Agricultural Economics* 42(1994):231-251.

Alston, J.M., and J.S. James. "Price Policies and the Domestic and International Distribution of Commodity Quality: Theory and Application to EU Wheat," in B. Krissoff, M. Bohman, and J.A. Caswell, eds, *Global Food Trade and Consumer Demand for Quality*. Boston: Kluwer Academic Publishers, 2002.

Alston, J.M. and G.M. Scobie. "A Differentiated Goods Model of the Effects of European Policies in International Poultry Markets" *Southern Journal of Agricultural Economics* (1987):59-68.

James, J.S. and J.M. Alston. "Taxes and Quality: A Market-Level Analysis." *Australian Journal of Agricultural and Resource Economics* 46(3)(September 2002): 417-445.

Sumner, D.A. and J.M. Alston. "Substitutability for Farm Commodities: The Demand for U.S. Tobacco in Cigarette Manufacturing" *American Journal of Agricultural Economics* 69(1987):258-265.

In: International Agricultural Trade and Development
Editor: Dragan Miljkovic, pp. 89-109
ISBN: 978-1-60021-965-8

Chapter 6

When Point Estimates Miss the Point: Stochastic Modeling of WTO Restrictions*

Patrick Westhoff*†, *Scott Brown* and *Chad Hart
Food and Agricultural Policy Research Institute
University of Missouri/Iowa State University
westhoffp@missouri.edu
browndo@missouri.edu
chart@iastate.edu

Abstract

Point estimates of agricultural and trade policy impacts often paint an incomplete or even misleading picture. For many purposes it is important to estimate a distribution of outcomes. Stochastic modeling can be especially important when policies have asymmetric effects or when there is interest in the tails of distributions. Both of these factors are important in evaluating World Trade Organization (WTO) commitments on internal support measures. Point estimates based on a continuation of 2005 U.S. agricultural policies and average values for external factors indicate that U.S. support would remain well below agreed commitments under the Uruguay Round Agreement on Agriculture (URAA). Stochastic estimates indicate that the mean value of the U.S. Aggregate Measure of Support (AMS) is substantially greater than the deterministic point estimate. In 41.8 percent of 500 stochastic outcomes, the URAA AMS limit is exceeded at least once between 2006 and 2014.

---

* Paper presented at the meeting of the International Agricultural Trade Research Consortium held in San Diego, CA, December 4-6, 2005. The authors would like to thank John Kruse, Seth Meyer, and Daniel Madison of the University of Missouri, and Gary Adams, formerly of the University of Missouri and now with the National Cotton Council for their work in developing the model used for the analysis, and William Meyers, Joseph Glauber, and Wyatt Thompson for useful comments on an earlier draft.
† Contact author: Patrick Westhoff; Food and Agricultural Policy Research Institute; University of Missouri; 101 Park DeVille Drive, Suite E; Columbia, Missouri 65203 USA; Phone +1 573 882 4647; Fax +1 573 884 4688; westhoffp@missouri.edu

Key words: Agricultural policy, World Trade Organization, stochastic modeling, Aggregate Measure of Support, Doha Development Agenda

A traditional deterministic model of agricultural markets is not always the right tool to use in examining policy issues. Point estimates of policy impacts often fail to tell the whole story and sometimes may lead to inappropriate conclusions. At least for some questions, a stochastic model can be a more useful tool. Stochastic analysis can be particularly useful when policies have asymmetric consequences or when there is intrinsic interest in the tails of distributions.

U.S. agricultural policies provide many examples of asymmetries that increase the value of stochastic analysis. Consider, for example, the operation of the marketing loan program for U.S. grains, oilseeds, and cotton. Producers qualify for loan program benefits when market price indicators (posted county prices in the case of grains and soybeans, adjusted world prices for cotton and rice) fall below the government-specified loan rate.

Suppose that deterministic analysis generates point estimates of future prices that slightly exceed the levels that would trigger marketing loan benefits. Estimated government expenditures on the marketing loan program would be zero. Stochastic analysis, in contrast, would recognize that supply and demand uncertainty makes it more appropriate to consider a distribution of market prices rather than just a point estimate. In most of the possible market outcomes, prices would exceed the level triggering loan program benefits and marketing loan expenditures would be zero, but in some outcomes, prices would be low enough to result in marketing loan benefits. The average value of marketing loan benefits over all the stochastic outcomes, therefore, can be greater than zero even when marketing loan benefits at the average value of market prices would be zero.

The asymmetry of U.S. government farm programs has important implications when estimating taxpayer costs. Projections prepared in early 2005 by the Food and Agricultural Policy Research Institute (FAPRI) indicate that the deterministic estimate for U.S. government farm program expenditures is more than $3 billion per year lower than the mean of 500 possible outcomes from stochastic analysis of the same baseline (FAPRI 2005b). The deterministic and stochastic estimates differ primarily because of large differences in the estimated cost of the marketing loan program, and not because of any significant difference between deterministic point estimates of prices and the mean prices estimated in the stochastic analysis.

From a policy perspective, sometimes the interesting part of a distribution is not the mean, median, or mode, but rather one of the tails. Policy makers may be more concerned with how a policy impacts farm income or government spending in a "bad" year than they are with effects under "normal" conditions. For example, analysis that considers the effects of crop insurance programs assuming average levels of yields and prices is likely to miss the true market and policy significance of the program.

Current World Trade Organization (WTO) rules also create a situation where it is important to focus on tails of distributions. Under the Uruguay Round Agreement on Agriculture (URAA), countries agreed to limit their total current Aggregate Measure of Support (AMS), an indicator of government support that is coupled to production decisions (WTO 1994). In the case of the United States, marketing loan expenditures account for much of the AMS. Because marketing loan expenditures depend on market prices, they are inherently variable. As a result, a given set of farm policies may leave the United States in compliance with its WTO commitments when prices are at average or above-average levels, but might put the country out of compliance when prices are sufficiently low.

The paper will discuss the development of stochastic estimates of the U.S. current AMS. Both deterministic and stochastic analyses will indicate that U.S. support to producers is expected to be considerably below the current AMS limit established by the URAA under the reporting practices that have been followed by the U.S. government. However, examination of the stochastic results indicates that there is some non-zero probability that the United States could breach the URAA limits.

These analytical issues have important implications for evaluation of a possible Doha Development Agenda (DDA) agreement. Anderson, Martin, and van der Mensbrugge (2005) indicated that they generally had to assume large reductions in bound levels of AMS before the hypothetical commitments would become binding and affect estimated market outcomes. Such an assumption was necessary because their deterministic analysis started from a baseline where actual AMS levels in the United States and most other countries were well within their URAA obligations. This paper will show that even when point estimates suggest that existing limits are not binding, reductions in AMS limits increase the probability that limits will be reached or exceeded.

The remaining sections of the paper provide a brief description of the stochastic model equations, the process used to generate stochastic estimates, a discussion of the results, and some concluding remarks.

The Stochastic Model

The FAPRI stochastic model of the U.S. agricultural economy represents an outgrowth of FAPRI's deterministic model of world agricultural markets. The FAPRI deterministic world model is a multimarket, nonspatial, partial equilibrium model that has increased in scope and complexity since the early 1980s. The deterministic model covers markets for major grains (wheat, corn, rice, sorghum, barley, and oats), oilseeds, (soybeans, rapeseed, sunflowerseed, peanuts, and palm oil), cotton, sugar, beef, pork, poultry, and dairy products. Country coverage varies by commodity, but generally includes the United States, the European Union, China, India, Japan, Brazil, Argentina, Canada, Australia, and other major exporters and importers of each commodity. The deterministic model is used to generate annual 10-year baseline projections (e.g., FAPRI 2005a) and analyze a wide range of domestic and trade policy questions (e.g., Fabiosa et al. 2005).

As it became clear that a deterministic model was inadequate for addressing some of the questions posed by policy makers, work began in 2000 on a stochastic version of the model. To keep the scale of the effort manageable, the stochastic model focuses on U.S. markets and is less detailed than its deterministic counterpart. World markets are represented by single reduced form equations, and some of the regional detail included in the U.S. portion of the deterministic model is replaced by national supply equations. Even so, the stochastic model has approximately 1,000 equations representing U.S. crop and livestock supply, demand, trade, and prices, as well as aggregate indicators such as government farm program costs, net farm income, agricultural land values, and consumer food price indices (FAPRI 2005e).

The crop portion of the model includes behavioral equations that determine crop acreage planted, domestic feed, food and industrial uses, trade, and ending stocks. On the livestock side of the model, behavioral equations determine animal inventories, meat, milk and dairy product production, consumption, and, where appropriate, ending stocks and trade. The model solves for the set of prices that brings annual supply and demand into balance in all markets.

Of particular interest to the present study are the equations that determine crop supply. The national planted area equations in the stochastic model approximate the aggregate behavior of the regional crop supply equations in the deterministic model. Planted area (APL) for each crop depends on per-acre expected supply-inducing net returns (ESINR) for the crop in question and competing crops, a weighted average of per-acre decoupled payments for all crops (DECP) and conservation reserve program acreage (CRP):

$$APL_i = f(ESINR_1, ESINR_2, ESINR_3 \ldots ESINR_{10}, DECP, CRP). \quad (1)$$

The synthetic parameters of the model reflect standard relationships between supply and expected returns. Acreage increases with own expected returns, declines when there is an increase in expected competing crop returns, and the own-return elasticity is generally slightly larger than the absolute value of the sum of competing crop return elasticities. Given model parameters, a 1 percent increase in expected supply-inducing net returns for all modeled crops would increase the total land planted to modeled crops by 0.06 percent. Decoupled payments, defined as the weighted sum of direct payments and expected counter-cyclical payments (CCPs) for all crops, have only a small effect on planted area, with elasticities less than 0.02. In a survey of empirical work, Abler and Blandford (2004) found that estimated acreage impacts of production flexibility contract payments and market loss assistance payments (the precursors to direct payments and CCPs) were generally modest. The coefficients on the CRP variable in each equation suggest that a 1 acre increase in CRP area would reduce the area planted to the modeled crops by less than half an acre.

Expected supply-inducing net returns are a function of trend yields (TYLD), expected prices (EPR), expected variable production expenses per acre (VEX), expected marketing loan program benefits (EMLB), and expected CCPs (ECCP):

$$ESINR = EPR*TYLD - VEX + EMLB + 0.25*ECCP. \quad (2)$$

The specification includes both market returns and marketing loan benefits that can only be earned by producing a crop, and assumes that producers value a dollar of expected returns from the market the same as a dollar of expected marketing loan benefits. Also included are 25 percent of expected CCPs. Because CCPs are made on a fixed base, they can be considered at least partially decoupled from production decisions (thus their inclusion in the decoupled payment term in the area equations). However, CCPs do depend on prices, and risk-averse producers may have a positive supply response to the price insurance offered by the program. The 0.25 parameter is based on analyst judgment, reflecting the notion that the crop-specific effect of CCPs on production is likely to be positive, but modest. Because expected CCPs are included in the definition of expected supply-inducing net returns for all crops, an across-the-board increase or decrease in CCPs would have only a small impact on production, given both the 0.25 parameter and the small response of total crop area to proportional changes in all crop returns. A disproportionate decrease in expected CCPs for any one crop, however, would have more noticeable impacts, decreasing acreage for the crop in question but generally increasing acreage for competing crops, given model parameters.

Expected prices depend on the lagged price (PR_{t-1}) and the ratio of lagged yields (YLD_{t-1}) to the trend yield:

$$EPR = f(PR_{t-1}, YLD_{t-1}/TYLD). \qquad (3)$$

The equation parameters are based on an estimation of the proportional year-over-year change in prices as a function of the change in yields. When yields in t-1 were unusually high (low), farmers are assumed to expect that prices in t will be higher (lower) than they were in t-1. While this is only a minor step toward a model assuming more rational expectations, it has important implications for how the model behaves in abnormal years. For example, in 2003 corn yields were at then-record levels while soybean yields were well below normal. Relative to 2002/03 levels, soybean prices increased sharply in 2003/04, while corn prices remained near the previous year's level. A naïve expectations approach would have generated a large increase in soybean acreage in 2004 at the expense of corn, given the change in relative prices in 2003/04. However, given the expected price formulation used in the model, the below-average soybean yield in 2003 offset part of the increase in 2003/04 prices, so the model expected soybean price for 2004/05 was noticeably lower than the 2003/04 actual price. The net result was a model estimate that both corn and soybean acreage would increase in 2004, consistent with observed market results.

Expected marketing loan benefits depend on the loan rate (LR), expected prices, an assumed wedge (MLBW), and the trend yield:

$$EMLB = \max(0, LR - EPR + MLBW) * TYLD. \qquad (4)$$

The wedge variable reflects observed historical differences in per-unit marketing loan benefits (loan deficiency payments and marketing loan gains divided by production) and a simple comparison of loan rates and market prices. For example, corn marketing loan benefits averaged \$0.20 per bushel more than the difference between the corn loan rate and the corn market price between 1998/99 and 2001/02, the last extended period when loan program benefits were available (calculations based on USDA reported production and loan program data). The corn EMLB equation, therefore, assumes MLBW is equal to \$0.20 per bushel. Two factors contributing to the positive wedge are seasonality in prices (producers may take their marketing loan benefits when prices are below season average levels and payment rates are high), and the observed fact that the average of posted county prices used to calculate loan program benefits tends to be lower than the national average market price. While the actual relationship between marketing loan benefits and market prices may be more complicated than suggested by the model specification, it is clear that marketing loan benefits can and do occur when season-average market prices exceed the loan rate.

Finally, the expected CCP depends on the target price (TP), the direct payment rate (DP), expected price, loan rate, fixed CCP program yield (CCPY), and a 0.85 factor established by law:

$$ECCP = \max(0, TP - DP - \max(EPR, LR)) * CCPY * 0.85. \qquad (5)$$

Considering the set of model supply equations, supply response can be very different depending on the level of market prices. Model supply elasticities with respect to expected market prices are zero when prices are below the loan rate, and they reach their maximum value only when expected market prices exceed the target price minus the direct payment rate (i.e., the level where an increase in prices no longer has a negative effect on government payments).

Asymmetries of government policies and the resulting differences in model supply response at different prices have proven important in analyses of various policy scenarios. Tighter limitations on payments available to any one producer were found to have little effect on crop supplies, government costs, or farm income when prices were above average, but much larger impacts at lower price levels (FAPRI 2003). Likewise, the limitation on marketing loan program benefits proposed in the President's budget for fiscal year 2006 was found to have much larger effects on production, government costs, and farm income when prices were low than when prices were high (FAPRI 2005c). Finally, an analysis of the impacts of increased ethanol production indicated that at low baseline levels of U.S. corn prices, increased corn demand would increase prices and reduce government payments to corn producers, but would have little impact on corn production or farm income. At higher baseline corn prices, there would be no government payment offset when increased demand results in higher market prices, and the result would be increased corn producer income and a much larger increase in corn production (FAPRI 2005d).

Space constraints do not permit a full description of the other behavioral equations in the model. Per-capita human consumption equations are generally functions of prices and income levels. Processing industry demand for raw commodities (e.g., soybean crush, corn processing for ethanol and high-fructose corn syrup) depends on endogenous processing margins. Derived demand for feed is a function of livestock sector indicators and feed prices. Beef and pork production depends in part on animal inventories, which in turn depend on dynamic investment behavior. Productivity measures such as milk per cow and livestock slaughter weights depend on output prices, production costs, and technological change. Stock demand equations reflect speculative and other motives for holding stocks, and incorporate provisions of government price support programs as appropriate.

The representation of U.S. agricultural commodity trade in the stochastic model is greatly simplified relative to the large non-spatial model FAPRI utilizes to generate deterministic projections. Single reduced-form equations take the place of the thousands of equations underlying the world models. For example, U.S. corn exports (COREX) are a function of a lagged dependent variable, current prices of corn (CORPR), wheat (WHEPR), sorghum (SORPR), barley (BARPR), and soybean meal (SOMPR), lagged prices of soybeans (SOYPR), and the level of oats net imports (OATIM):

$$\text{COREX} = f(\text{lag}(\text{COREX}), \text{CORPR}, \text{WHEPR}, \text{SORPR}, \text{BARPR}, \text{SOMPR}, \text{lag}(\text{SOYPR}), \text{OATIM}). \qquad (6)$$

Coefficients for the reduced form trade equations are set so that the equations generally mimic the behavior of a global system. In the case of corn, for example, the reduced form equation suggests an own-price elasticity of U.S. export demand of about -1.03 in the short run and about -2.58 in the long run, with positive elasticities with respect to the other crop prices. This approach to modeling trade may be satisfactory when modeling U.S. policy changes, but it does not lend itself to analysis of multilateral policy changes. For example, the current U.S. stochastic framework would require significant modification before it could be used to analyze the impact of an international trade agreement that might systematically change the price responsiveness of export demand.

The model includes a large set of equations that permit estimation of fiscal year government farm program outlays and calendar year net farm income. While it is easy to dismiss these portions of the model as mere accounting, a number of challenges are faced in reconciling crop, calendar, and fiscal year data and in reproducing the detail expected by policy makers in the appropriate format.

Added to the model for the present analysis is a series of equations to estimate the current AMS and other indicators related to WTO internal support issues. The equations are intended to reflect the accounting practices used by the United States in preparing its WTO submissions (the most recent available at the time of this writing covers the 2001 marketing year), but can easily be modified to reflect other rules and practices. Because the focus is on amber box support subject to limitation under the WTO agreement, no effort is made to estimate support the United States has treated as green box support in its submissions. For example, the current AMS estimates to do not include payments made under the U.S. direct payment program, even though the WTO status of those payments is in question at the time of this writing because of the WTO appellate body report on the Brazilian cotton case (WTO Appellate Body 2005).

Most of the accounting to generate AMS estimates is straightforward, given estimates generated by other model equations. For example, the main components of the calculated AMS for most major field crops are various benefits available under the marketing loan program. For most crops, the calculated AMS (CALCAMS) is simply the sum of crop year LDPs (CYLDP) and marketing loan gains (CYMLG) and a proxy for interest rate subsidies on commodity loans (an assumed subsidy rate multiplied by the value of loans made, (LOANSUB*VALLOAN):

$$\text{CALCAMS} = \text{CYLDP} + \text{CYMLG} + (\text{LOANSUB}*\text{VALLOAN}). \quad (7)$$

A different set of calculations are required for sugar and dairy, where the calculated AMS is primarily comprised of the calculated value to producers of a price support program that maintains domestic prices above those that prevailed in world markets between 1986 and 1988. The price support component of the AMS for these two commodities is equal to the product of the quantity produced (PROD) and the difference between the price support level (PRISUP) and the fixed 1986-1988 world reference price (PRIREF). The calculated AMS also includes any coupled direct payments (COUPAY), such as those under the Milk Income Loss Contract (MILC) program:

$$\text{CALCAMS} = (\text{PRISUP-PRIREF}) * \text{PROD} + \text{COUPAY}. \quad (8)$$

The current AMS for each commodity (CURRAMS) is equal to the calculated AMS unless the calculated AMS is less than 5 percent of the value of production (price multiplied by production). If the calculated AMS for a given commodity is less than 5 percent of its value of production, the current AMS for that commodity is set equal to zero, as allowed by the *de minimis* rule in the URAA.

In its WTO submissions through crop year 2001, the United States classified crop insurance and market loss assistance payments as nonproduct-specific support (Economic Research Service 2005). Although the Brazilian cotton case raises questions about the appropriate classification of these programs, the analysis here assumes that crop insurance and counter-cyclical payments (which some consider a successor to market loss assistance payments, although the payment rules differ in several aspects) are classified as nonproduct-specific amber box support measures.

Estimates of counter-cyclical payments are generated by existing model equations. New to the system are equations used to estimate the contribution of crop insurance to AMS measures. Crop insurance net indemnities depend on the mix of crop insurance policies in force, actual and projected market prices, and crop yields at the unit level (farms are often divided into multiple units for crop insurance purposes). As such, it is very difficult to project crop insurance activity based solely on the aggregate U.S. variables estimated in other components of the stochastic model.

The crop insurance stochastic estimates are derived from the results of the FAPRI deterministic crop insurance baseline and the ratios of stochastic draws to the deterministic FAPRI baseline figures for crop acreage, crop yields, and crop prices. For the analysis, estimates for both yield and revenue insurance policies are developed for corn, soybeans, wheat, cotton, rice, sorghum, barley, and oats, and all other commodities are handled as a single aggregate.

Insurance premiums and premium subsidies vary with crop acreage. Loss ratios (the ratio of insurance indemnities to insurance premiums) are computed for the various crops and insurance policies. For yield insurance, the loss ratios depend on the ratio of the stochastic yield draw to the deterministic yield; low stochastic yield draws translate into high yield insurance loss ratios and higher than average yield insurance indemnities. For revenue insurance, the loss ratios depend on the ratio of the stochastic yield draw to the deterministic yield and the ratio of the stochastic price draw to the expected price. For the crop insurance simulations, the expected price is defined as the average of the stochastic price draw for the previous year and the deterministic price for the current year. The combination of low stochastic yield and/or price draws translates into higher revenue insurance loss ratios. As with actual revenue insurance, the simulation structure for revenue insurance allows the impact of a low yield (price) draw to be offset by a higher than average price (yield) draw, mitigating the size of any potential crop insurance payment.

The loss ratio for crop insurance on the commodities not explicitly included in the analysis is derived from its historical relationship with the combined loss ratio for crop insurance on corn, soybeans, wheat, cotton, rice, sorghum, barley, and oats. Indemnities are then calculated as the product of the premiums and the loss ratios. Crop insurance net indemnities equal the sum of indemnities and premium subsidies less insurance premiums.

Nonproduct-specific support is only included in the total current AMS if the sum of all nonproduct-specific support is greater than the *de minimis* level of 5 percent of the value of total agricultural production. For most of the commodities included in the model, the value of production is simply defined as price multiplied by production. For beef and pork, the indicator prices in the model are multiplied by carcass-weight meat production and then by a calibration factor that generates 2001 estimates equal to those reported in the U.S. submission. For many other commodities, the model follows the practice used in the U.S. submission, where calendar year cash receipts for products such as fruits, vegetables, and nursery products are used in lieu of a true value of production measure. One case where this choice is particularly important is hay, where only a small portion of total production is marketed. The hay cash receipts used in the value of production calculation are therefore much less than the result of multiplying the USDA-reported levels of hay production and prices.

The total current AMS includes a number of minor components not endogenous in the stochastic model. For example, the U.S. submission indicates the value of irrigation subsidies in 2001 was $300 million, and this was considered part of nonproduct-specific support. The model treats these components as exogenous variables that are included in the AMS calculations.

THE STOCHASTIC PROCESS

The stochastic baseline process begins with the generation of a deterministic baseline. Each November, FAPRI analysts construct a set of preliminary global baseline projections using the deterministic model. Based on reviewer comments and other new information, a revised deterministic baseline is prepared in January.

As discussed, some of the equations in the stochastic model are different than the corresponding equations in the deterministic model. The stochastic model is calibrated so that it generates precisely the deterministic estimates when all exogenous variables are set at the levels assumed for the deterministic baseline. Thus, when the means of the stochastic baseline differ from the deterministic results, it is because there are non-linearities in the models, asymmetries in the policies, or because of the luck of the random draws, not because the models generate different results for the same set of baseline assumptions.

Considering all the factors that make commodity market outcomes uncertain, there is a very large set of variables one could draw from in conducting stochastic analysis. The FAPRI stochastic model draws from a relatively narrow set of exogenous variables. The process involves both "science" and "art." Rather than sampling all possible sources of uncertainty, an attempt is made to draw from a sufficient number of factors to reflect both supply- and demand-side uncertainty so that resulting price and quantity distributions appear reasonably consistent with historical observations and analyst judgments.

In general, the approach is to make correlated random draws from empirical distributions of selected exogenous variables and solve the model for each of the 500 sets of exogenous variables to generate 500 alternative outcomes for the endogenous variables. Each of the exogenous sets of assumptions and endogenous sets of results are preserved, so that it is possible to decompose any given solution, and so that alternative policy scenarios can effectively be run against 500 different, but related, baselines.

Supply-side exogenous variables used to drive the stochastic analysis include crop yields, the share of planted area which is harvested, production expenses, and error terms from state milk production per cow equations. Demand-side variables include error terms from key domestic consumption, stock, and trade equations. While it is possible to imagine a wide range of other sources of variability (macroeconomic variables, model coefficients, etc.), experience has shown that this subset of factors is sufficient to generate plausible distributions of prices and quantities.

In general, the statistical distributions of exogenous variables are based on about 22 years of annual time series data. Crop yield distributions, for example, are based on deviations from trend yields during the 1983-2004 period. These deviations and corresponding deviations from trend shares of planted area that is harvested are correlated across all modeled crops. For example, drawing a positive deviation from trend corn yields means one is likely, but not certain, to also draw a positive deviation from trend soybean yields. Likewise, error terms from demand equations are also correlated. Results indicate, for example, that error terms from the reduced-form export demand equations for major crops are positively correlated with one another.

The stochastic draws of exogenous variables are made with SIMETAR, software developed by Dr. James Richardson at Texas A&M University. SIMETAR is capable of handling large matrices, but with limited historical observations it is not possible to develop reliable estimates of the correlations of all the selected exogenous variables together. Instead, the exogenous variables are grouped on the basis of similarity or observed correlation, and the correlation across groups is assumed to be zero; e.g., no correlation is assumed between the group containing all crop yield deviations and the group of error terms from meat consumer demand equations.

Given 500 sets of correlated random draws of the selected exogenous variables, the stochastic solution is derived by solving the model for each of the 500 sets. The model simulates in SAS, and results are maintained in SAS data sets and written to an Excel spreadsheet. With 500 solutions for 10 years for approximately 1,000 variables, the file size of the solution spreadsheet exceeds 100 megabytes.

It should be stressed that the stochastic process involves significant analyst judgment in deciding what variables to consider, methods used to detrend or otherwise adjust data, etc. To get a model to generate 500 sets of "reasonable" outcomes requires a robust model and frequent model upkeep and revision. While many of the model parameters are based strictly on econometric results of time series estimations, other parameters are based at least in part on analyst judgment. As argued by Just (2001), it is not reasonable to expect time series data to provide all the information needed to build models appropriate for policy analysis.

RESULTS AND DISCUSSION

Baseline projections prepared in early 2005 indicated modest increases in nominal prices for major U.S. field crops between 2006 and 2014 (Table 1). For all the major crops, deterministic baseline prices rise to levels where marketing loan program benefits would be small or non-existent, and even CCPs would disappear for many crops. The mean results from the 500 stochastic outcomes suggest similar levels of crop prices. Only in the case of rice is the mean of stochastic prices noticeably lower than the deterministic estimate.

Given the asymmetric nature of U.S. farm programs, the estimated variation in stochastic results takes on special significance. For example, even though mean corn prices from the stochastic analysis are well above the $1.95 loan rate, the $0.33-$0.38 per bushel standard deviation in corn prices is large enough that some of the 500 outcomes for corn prices are low enough to generate considerable marketing loan benefits. It is precisely this asymmetry that accounts for some of the differences between deterministic baseline prices and the mean prices of the stochastic analysis. In the case of rice, large average stochastic loan program benefits increase average coupled producer returns relative to the deterministic estimates, and result in a higher mean level of rice production. The higher mean level of rice production, in turn, contributes to a lower mean level of rice prices than in the deterministic baseline.

Table 1. Deterministic and stochastic baseline crop price projections

	2006	2007	2008	2009	2010	2011	2012	2013	2014
Corn	(dollars per bushel)								
Deterministic	2.19	2.22	2.23	2.26	2.28	2.30	2.32	2.32	2.33
Stochastic mean	2.18	2.21	2.22	2.25	2.27	2.29	2.31	2.32	2.32
Stochastic standard deviation	0.33	0.36	0.36	0.36	0.37	0.37	0.38	0.38	0.38
Soybeans	(dollars per bushel)								
Deterministic	4.99	5.27	5.41	5.42	5.43	5.44	5.44	5.44	5.43
Stochastic mean	5.01	5.24	5.37	5.41	5.42	5.42	5.41	5.41	5.43
Stochastic standard deviation	0.89	0.92	0.96	0.88	0.89	0.91	0.91	0.85	0.88
Wheat	(dollars per bushel)								
Deterministic	3.24	3.31	3.36	3.42	3.47	3.51	3.56	3.60	3.63
Stochastic mean	3.24	3.30	3.35	3.41	3.46	3.50	3.55	3.60	3.63
Stochastic standard deviation	0.38	0.37	0.41	0.42	0.43	0.41	0.42	0.42	0.42
Upland cotton	(dollars per pound)								
Deterministic	0.45	0.46	0.46	0.48	0.50	0.51	0.52	0.53	0.55
Stochastic mean	0.46	0.46	0.46	0.48	0.50	0.51	0.51	0.53	0.54
Stochastic standard deviation	0.06	0.06	0.06	0.07	0.07	0.07	0.07	0.07	0.07
Rice	(dollars per hundredweight)								
Deterministic	6.98	7.26	7.42	7.58	7.73	7.89	8.09	8.27	8.41
Stochastic mean	6.98	7.25	7.34	7.46	7.58	7.69	7.84	7.95	8.06
Stochastic standard deviation	1.36	1.42	1.50	1.51	1.46	1.62	1.64	1.72	1.77

Note: Projections were prepared in January-February 2005 based on available market information and an assumed continuation of existing agricultural policies.

For the major field crops, the bulk of the estimated product-specific AMS can be attributed to marketing loan program benefits. The means reported in Table 2 mask a wide range of stochastic outcomes. In most of the 500 stochastic outcomes, for example, corn marketing loan benefits are zero in every year after 2006. In some of the outcomes, however, prices are low enough to generate very large marketing loan benefits. For example, in 2010, corn LDPs exceed $3.6 billion in 10 percent of the outcomes.

At the mean of the stochastic outcomes, dairy and sugar account for more than half of the total product-specific AMS. Once the dairy MILC program expires in 2005, the AMS for those two commodities is simply equal to production multiplied by the gap between a legislatively-fixed support price and a WTO-fixed world reference price (based on 1986-1988 world market prices). Thus, for dairy and sugar under current U.S. policies, the only source of variation in the AMS is production uncertainty.

Table 2. AMS calculations, mean of 500 stochastic outcomes

	2006	2007	2008	2009	2010	2011	2012	2013	2014
	(million dollars)								
Product-specific calc. AMS	11,228	10,863	10,705	10,200	9,979	9,949	9,925	9,790	9,790
Product-specific current AMS	11,018	10,660	10,483	9,983	9,746	9,724	9,703	9,555	9,581
Barley	42	41	46	43	44	41	40	37	34
Corn	1,340	1,351	1,361	1,190	1,067	993	936	915	951
Upland cotton	1,452	1,474	1,409	1,253	1,162	1,167	1,151	1,086	1,014
Dairy	4,740	4,788	4,832	4,870	4,909	4,947	4,986	5,030	5,074
Minor oilseeds	14	12	13	11	9	11	14	12	14
Oats	13	11	12	9	8	8	7	7	7
Peanuts	21	23	24	25	22	25	25	26	23
Rice	341	295	288	271	248	257	239	230	209
Sorghum	104	97	94	83	72	60	50	44	41
Soybeans	1,407	1,037	910	740	739	775	825	739	770
Sugar	1,285	1,311	1,275	1,290	1,285	1,288	1,291	1,298	1,307
Wheat	158	120	117	99	82	53	40	32	37
All other	100	100	100	100	100	100	100	100	100
Nonproduct-specific calc. AMS	7,436	7,275	7,299	7,049	6,992	6,812	6,720	6,561	6,474
Countercyclical payments	4,254	4,019	3,905	3,639	3,481	3,282	3,147	2,942	2,822
Crop insurance	2,764	2,839	2,977	2,993	3,093	3,112	3,155	3,201	3,234
All other	418	418	418	418	418	418	418	418	418
Value of agricultural production	210,633	214,229	218,115	222,249	225,124	227,876	231,139	235,995	240,833
5% de minimis trigger	10,532	10,711	10,906	11,112	11,256	11,394	11,557	11,800	12,042
Nonproduct-specific in current AMS	1,056	958	696	594	487	432	272	282	221
Total current AMS	12,073	11,618	11,179	10,578	10,234	10,156	9,975	9,838	9,802
URAA current AMS limit	19,103	19,103	19,103	19,103	19,103	19,103	19,103	19,103	19,103
Proportion of outcomes where:									
Product-spec. current AMS exceeds AMS limit	6.0%	4.0%	4.2%	3.8%	2.2%	1.8%	3.4%	2.8%	2.8%
Nonproduct-specific calc. AMS exceeds de minimis 5%	9.6%	8.4%	6.2%	5.2%	4.0%	3.6%	2.4%	2.4%	1.8%
Total current AMS exceeds AMS limit	12.6%	12.0%	10.0%	8.4%	6.0%	5.4%	5.6%	5.0%	4.6%

In the case of product-specific support, the difference between the calculated AMS and the current AMS used to determine compliance with the WTO agreement is modest, generally a little over $200 million per year. The difference is due to the effect of the product-specific *de minimis* rule that excludes from the current AMS product-specific support that is less than 5 percent of the value of production of the commodity in question.

In contrast, there is a very large difference between the mean calculated nonproduct-specific support (primarily CCPs and crop insurance benefits) and the proportion included in the mean estimate of the current AMS. In the vast majority of outcomes (over 90 percent of outcomes in 2006 and over 98 percent of outcomes in 2014), total nonproduct-specific support is less than the *de minimis* level of 5 percent of the value of total agricultural production. As a result, none of the nonproduct-specific support counts toward the current AMS in the majority of possible outcomes. However, in the few cases when nonproduct-specific support exceeds the *de minimis* level, it is a major component of the estimate of total current AMS. The mean contribution of less than $1 billion in every year after 2006 reflects a very low probability of a very large contribution.

At the mean of the 500 outcomes, the total current AMS declines from about $12 billion in 2006 to less than $10 billion by 2014. This estimate is far below the URAA limit of $19.1 billion, and would seem to suggest that the United States would face little difficulty complying with its URAA commitments, or even with a hypothetical DDA agreement that would require significant reductions in the permitted current AMS.

The means, however, do not tell the whole story. In 6.0 percent of the outcomes for 2006, for example, the product-specific current AMS exceeds the WTO limit, even before considering nonproduct-specific support measures. That share declines to 2.8 percent by 2014, primarily because projected increases in mean commodity prices reduce the likelihood of large marketing loan expenditures.

In addition to the effects of product-specific support, in 9.6 percent of the 2006 outcomes, nonproduct-specific support exceeds the *de minimis* level, and in 12.6 percent, the 2006 total current AMS (including both product-specific and nonproduct-specific support) exceeds the WTO limit. The proportion of cases of product-specific and nonproduct-specific support exceeding respective triggers cannot always be simply added to estimate the proportion of cases where the total current AMS will exceed the WTO limit, because some of the outcomes with high levels of product-specific AMS also have high levels of nonproduct-specific support. The share of outcomes where the total current AMS exceeds the WTO limit declines from 12.6 percent in 2006 to 4.6 percent by 2014, under current U.S. policies and URAA commitments.

The framework also makes it possible to estimate the proportion of outcomes where the total current AMS exceeds the URAA commitment levels at least once over the nine-year period. In 41.8 percent of the 500 outcomes, the URAA commitments are exceeded at least once between 2006 and 2014. If the results for individual years were independent of one another, the probability of at least one violation of the AMS commitments would be 51.8 percent. The difference suggests that AMS estimates are correlated positively across time. For example, suppose a high stochastic yield draw results in low market prices and a large AMS in year t. High yields in year t are also likely to result in large carry-out stocks that increase the likelihood of lower prices and a large AMS in year t+1.

These stochastic results tell a very different story than suggested by deterministic analysis (Table 3). Product-specific current AMS is more than $2 billion per year lower in the deterministic analysis than the mean of the 500 stochastic outcomes. Two crops account for most of the difference. For both corn and soybeans, deterministic baseline prices are high enough that marketing loan benefits are small or non-existent, and what little support is provided by loan interest rate subsidies is less than the crop-specific *de minimis* level. In contrast, many of the stochastic outcomes yield sizable marketing loan benefits and, consequently, sizable current AMS.

Table 3. Deterministic and stochastic AMS calculations

	2006	2007	2008	2009	2010	2011	2012	2013	2014
	(million dollars)								
Product-specific calculated AMS									
Deterministic	8,626	8,094	7,979	7,796	7,682	7,673	7,645	7,563	7,414
Stochastic mean	11,228	10,863	10,705	10,200	9,979	9,949	9,925	9,790	9,790
Difference	2,602	2,769	2,726	2,403	2,298	2,276	2,279	2,227	2,375
Product-specific current AMS									
Deterministic	7,937	7,950	7,798	7,628	7,522	7,523	7,500	7,354	7,268
Stochastic mean	11,018	10,660	10,483	9,983	9,746	9,724	9,703	9,555	9,581
Difference	3,081	2,710	2,686	2,356	2,225	2,201	2,202	2,201	2,314
Corn contribution to product-specific current AMS									
Deterministic	0	0	0	0	0	0	0	0	0
Stochastic mean	1,340	1,351	1,361	1,190	1,067	993	936	915	951
Difference	1,340	1,351	1,361	1,190	1,067	993	936	915	951
Soybean contribution to product-specific current AMS									
Deterministic	0	0	0	0	0	0	0	0	0
Stochastic mean	1,407	1,037	910	740	739	775	825	739	770
Difference	1,407	1,037	910	740	739	775	825	739	770
Other product contribution to product-specific current AMS									
Deterministic	7,937	7,950	7,798	7,628	7,522	7,523	7,500	7,354	7,268
Stochastic mean	8,270	8,272	8,211	8,054	7,941	7,956	7,942	7,902	7,860
Difference	334	322	414	426	419	433	442	547	592
Nonproduct-specific calculated AMS									
Deterministic	6,732	5,920	5,605	5,264	5,106	4,872	4,719	4,574	4,406
Stochastic mean	7,436	7,275	7,299	7,049	6,992	6,812	6,720	6,561	6,474
Difference	704	1,355	1,694	1,785	1,885	1,940	2,001	1,987	2,067
Countercyclical payments contribution to nonproduct-specific calculated AMS									
Deterministic	4,104	3,222	2,856	2,463	2,267	1,993	1,794	1,613	1,414
Stochastic mean	4,254	4,019	3,905	3,639	3,481	3,282	3,147	2,942	2,822
Difference	151	797	1,049	1,175	1,214	1,289	1,353	1,329	1,408
Nonproduct-specific support included in current AMS									
Deterministic	0	0	0	0	0	0	0	0	0
Stochastic mean	1,056	958	696	594	487	432	272	282	221
Difference	1,056	958	696	594	487	432	272	282	221
Total current AMS									
Deterministic	7,937	7,950	7,798	7,628	7,522	7,523	7,500	7,354	7,268
Stochastic mean	12,073	11,618	11,179	10,578	10,234	10,156	9,975	9,838	9,802
Difference	4,137	3,668	3,382	2,950	2,712	2,633	2,474	2,483	2,534

Nonproduct-specific support is also significantly smaller in the deterministic analysis than the mean of the stochastic analysis. CCPs account for most of the difference, but crop insurance benefits also contribute. The relationship between deterministic and stochastic estimates of CCPs depends on baseline prices, and there are cases where deterministic estimates of CCPs can be greater than the mean of stochastic outcomes, specifically, where deterministic baseline CCPs are near their maximum levels, there will be some stochastic outcomes where CCPs are at less than maximum levels. However, on balance, CCPs are smaller in the deterministic baseline than the mean of the stochastic outcomes.

The deterministic estimate of the total current AMS is actually closer to the 10th percentile of the stochastic outcomes than to the mean (Figure 1). In the deterministic analysis, the current AMS for several crops is zero in most or all years, so the total current AMS is only slightly larger than the AMS for dairy and sugar. The same occurs in most of the stochastic outcomes as well. In a substantial minority of the stochastic outcomes, however, marketing loan benefits, CCPs, and/or crop insurance benefits are large, contributing to a skewed distribution of total current AMS.

Sorting the stochastic results for 2006 illustrates the factors that contribute to the cases where WTO triggers are exceeded (Table 4). In the 6.0 percent of outcomes where product-specific support exceeds the AMS limit, the average corn and cotton prices are far lower than in the other 94.0 percent of outcomes, and these low prices can largely be attributed to above-average yields. In one-third of the cases where product-specific support exceeds the AMS limit, nonproduct-specific support also exceeds the *de minimis* level, as above-average CCPs and below-average value of production more than offset the impact of below average crop insurance benefits.

The 9.6 percent of 2006 outcomes where nonproduct-specific support exceeds the *de minimis* level suggests a very different pattern. In particular, crop insurance benefits far exceed their average levels, as corn and cotton yields and corn and cotton prices are all below their mean values. Normally, one would expect prices and yields to be inversely related, and that is indeed the more common relationship in the stochastic outcomes. However, there can be cases where large carry-in stocks and/or weak demand can result in below-average prices in spite of below-average yields. Such cases are relatively rare, but they do occur often enough to play a major factor in determining the share of outcomes that exceed AMS commitments.

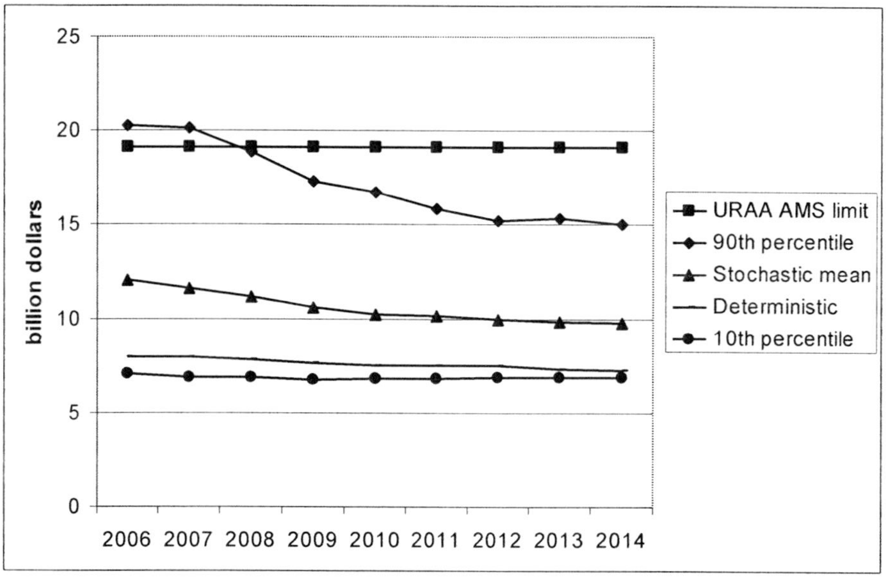

Figure 1. Deterministic and stochastic estimates of total current AMS

Table 4. Sorted stochastic results for 2006

	Mean of 500 outcomes	Product-specific current AMS > AMS limit		Non-product-specific support > de minimis		Total current AMS > AMS limit	
		No	Yes	No	Yes	No	Yes
	(million dollars)						
Product-spec. current AMS	11,018	10,338	21,589	10,670	14,238	10,140	17,069
Calc. nonproduct-specific	7,436	7,343	8,879	7,057	10,997	7,053	10,085
Total current AMS	12,073	11,234	25,121	10,670	25,235	10,261	24,608
Counter-cyclical payments	4,254	4,073	7,103	4,041	6,262	3,909	6,656
Crop insurance contribution	2,764	2,852	1,358	2,598	4,318	2,727	3,011
Value of agricultural production	210,633	211,267	200,684	211,514	202,322	211,929	201,629
	(bushels per acre)						
Corn yield	148.0	147.3	159.1	148.7	142.0	147.8	149.4
	(pounds per acre)						
Upland cotton yield	714	711	754	716	697	713	722
	(dollars per bushel)						
Corn price	2.18	2.22	1.65	2.21	1.90	2.24	1.80
	(dollars per pound)						
Upland cotton price	0.456	0.461	0.378	0.461	0.406	0.464	0.395
Proportion where product-specific support exceeds AMS limit	6.0%	0.0%	100.0%	4.4%	20.8%	0.0%	47.6%
Proportion where nonproduct-specific support exceeds de minimis	9.6%	8.1%	33.3%	0.0%	100.0%	1.1%	68.3%
Proportion where total current AMS exceeds AMS limit	12.6%	7.0%	100.0%	4.4%	89.6%	0.0%	100.0%

To the extent these results are plausible, it illustrates the importance of drawing on both supply and demand side exogenous variables in doing stochastic analysis. If only supply side variables were drawn, downward-sloping demand curves would ensure a negative relationship between price and yields would hold in almost all cases (carry-in stocks could cause a few exceptions). Many of the cases where the nonproduct-specific support level exceeds the *de minimis* level could never have occurred if only supply side variables were considered, as there would be very few outcomes where production and prices would simultaneously be below mean levels.

When aggregating across all the outcomes where AMS commitments are exceeded, corn and cotton yields are near mean levels. The outcomes where high yields result in low prices, large marketing loan benefits, and a large product-specific AMS are offset by the cases where below-average yields and low prices result in high crop insurance expenditures and a large level of non-commodity specific support.

The value of agricultural production is systematically lower in the outcomes where the various WTO triggers are exceeded than in other outcomes. This suggests that in estimating the critical level of nonproduct-specific support it is not adequate to take 5 percent of the deterministic value of production or even 5 percent of the stochastic mean of the value of production.

As this is written, the shape of any eventual DDA agreement remains unclear. For purposes of illustration, consider a hypothetical agreement that would reduce the AMS limit in 10 percent increments until the 2011 limit equals 50 percent of the limit in 2006 but keep all other accounting rules the same as assumed in generating the other estimates (Table 5). Under current U.S. farm policies, the proportion of outcomes exceeding the hypothetical AMS limit would increase quickly, reaching almost 38 percent in 2011 before declining slightly in later years. The relationship between these estimates and U.S. policy changes remains uncertain, but the probability of policy change seems much higher at the lower AMS limit.

Results from assuming alternative levels of hypothetical reductions in AMS limits demonstrate the nonlinearity of the estimates. For example, 23 percent of outcomes exceed a 2011 AMS limit set 40 percent lower than the current limit, but 100 percent exceed a 2011 limit that is set 70 percent lower than the current limit. This occurs primarily because the AMS for dairy and sugar are largely predetermined under current policy. Dairy and sugar account for more than $6 billion in AMS at the mean, and only production variability can change the estimate unless policies are altered.

If CCPs are included in measures of nonproduct-specific support, the likelihood of exceeding the *de minimis* trigger increases dramatically when the trigger is reduced below the current 5 percent. If, on the other hand, CCPs are excluded from the nonproduct-specific category, the share of outcomes where crop insurance and the other minor components of nonproduct-specific support exceed the *de minimis* level is low unless the trigger is lowered below 3 percent of the value of production.

Under one interpretation of the 2004 WTO framework agreement (WTO 2004), CCPs would be shifted out of the amber box to a redefined blue box that would be limited to 5 percent of the value of production. Given current program provisions, it is mathematically impossible for CCPs to exceed $8 billion, and in none of the stochastic results does the value of agricultural production fall below $160 billion. Only if the proposed blue box limit were reduced to less than 4 percent of the value of production does the stochastic model estimate any probability of exceeding the limit under current U.S. policies. Note that these estimates are contingent on the value of production being based on current market outcomes; if the value of production is based on some historical level, the results could be significantly different (in general, the value of production has increased over time, so using an historical value of production would tend to increase the proportion of outcomes exceeding hypothetical limits, all else equal).

Finally, the framework agreement and recent negotiations suggest the possibility of limits on AMS for particular products. How any such limits would be set is uncertain at this writing, but suppose the limits were set at some percentage of 1999-2001 average levels of reported current AMS for each commodity. Stochastic model results suggest that almost any plausible limit would have a significant chance of being exceeded under current U.S. policies (Table 6). For example, even if a commodity-specific limit were set at 150 percent of the 1999-2001 current AMS level, in 20.4 percent of outcomes the limit would be exceeded for corn in 2006 and in 13.0 percent in 2014. At lower commodity-specific limits, the proportion of outcomes exceeding the limit increases, but perhaps less than might have been anticipated. This occurs because in any given year, the most likely outcome is that prices will be high enough that marketing loan benefits and thus the product-specific AMS will be near zero.

Table 5. Proportion of outcomes exceeding alternative AMS limits

	2006	2007	2008	2009	2010	2011	2012	2013	2014
	(million dollars)								
URAA current AMS limit	19,103	19,103	19,103	19,103	19,103	19,103	19,103	19,103	19,103
Proportion where:									
Product-specific > AMS limit	6.0%	4.0%	4.2%	3.8%	2.2%	1.8%	3.4%	2.8%	2.8%
Nonproduct-spec. > de minimis	9.6%	8.4%	6.2%	5.2%	4.0%	3.6%	2.4%	2.4%	1.8%
Total current AMS > AMS limit	12.6%	12.0%	10.0%	8.4%	6.0%	5.4%	5.6%	5.0%	4.6%
	(million dollars)								
Hypothetical AMS limit: 50% lower by 2011	19,103	17,193	15,283	13,372	11,462	9,552	9,552	9,552	9,552
Proportion where:									
Product-specific > AMS limit	6.0%	8.2%	14.6%	17.0%	23.0%	37.6%	33.8%	31.2%	31.6%
Nonproduct-spec. > de minimis	9.6%	8.4%	6.2%	5.2%	4.0%	3.6%	2.4%	2.4%	1.8%
Total current AMS > AMS limit	12.6%	15.4%	18.4%	20.0%	24.0%	37.8%	33.8%	31.8%	31.6%
Proportion where product-specific current AMS > AMS limit if:									
Limit unchanged ($19.103 bil.)	6.0%	4.0%	4.2%	3.8%	2.2%	1.8%	3.4%	2.8%	2.8%
Limit reduced 10%	10.6%	8.2%	7.8%	6.2%	5.8%	4.2%	5.2%	5.4%	5.2%
Limit reduced 20%	18.2%	13.4%	14.6%	8.8%	9.2%	8.0%	7.6%	8.8%	8.0%
Limit reduced 30%	24.8%	22.6%	21.4%	17.0%	14.8%	14.2%	13.4%	13.0%	13.4%
Limit reduced 40%	33.2%	35.2%	29.4%	26.6%	23.0%	23.0%	22.4%	21.0%	20.0%
Limit reduced 50%	49.0%	45.8%	43.8%	39.4%	36.2%	37.6%	33.8%	31.2%	31.6%
Limit reduced 60%	77.6%	74.2%	72.2%	67.2%	63.0%	67.0%	66.4%	60.8%	61.8%
Limit reduced 70%	100.0%	100.0%	100.0%	100.0%	100.0%	100.0%	100.0%	100.0%	100.0%
Proportion where nonproduct-specific support > de minimis if:									
CCPs included; de minimis = 5%	9.6%	8.4%	6.2%	5.2%	4.0%	3.6%	2.4%	2.4%	1.8%
CCPs inc.; 4%	33.2%	30.6%	27.6%	23.4%	20.8%	18.6%	13.8%	12.2%	11.4%
CCPs inc.; 3%	70.8%	64.0%	63.4%	58.0%	54.4%	48.6%	49.4%	43.0%	38.4%
CCPs inc.; 2%	92.6%	89.4%	90.4%	83.6%	85.8%	81.0%	81.6%	77.2%	72.4%
CCPs excluded ; de minimis = 5%	0.0%	0.0%	0.0%	0.0%	0.0%	0.0%	0.0%	0.0%	0.0%
CCPs exc.; 4%	0.2%	0.4%	0.0%	0.2%	0.4%	0.2%	0.0%	0.2%	0.0%
CCPs exc.; 3%	9.0%	8.0%	8.6%	8.0%	8.4%	9.4%	8.2%	8.6%	6.6%
CCPs exc.; 2%	28.0%	29.0%	29.2%	28.8%	30.2%	28.4%	30.0%	29.0%	28.0%
Proportion where CCPs exceed hypothetical blue box limit if limit is:									
5% of value of production	0.0%	0.0%	0.0%	0.0%	0.0%	0.0%	0.0%	0.0%	0.0%
4%	0.0%	0.0%	0.0%	0.0%	0.0%	0.0%	0.0%	0.0%	0.0%
3%	25.4%	20.8%	18.2%	13.6%	11.2%	8.4%	6.0%	4.0%	3.8%
2%	50.6%	45.6%	42.0%	37.2%	35.6%	32.6%	28.0%	23.8%	22.6%

The consequences of the hypothetical product-specific limits are very different for different commodities. For example, the hypothetical limits are especially large for soybeans, in part because special oilseed payments made in the 1999-2001 period were classified as product-specific support, while market loss assistance payments made to grain and cotton producers were classified as nonproduct-specific. With a higher base, the proportion of outcomes where the soybean AMS would exceed the hypothetical limit is much smaller than the corresponding proportions for corn.

Given the nature of the AMS calculations for dairy, in almost all outcomes even a modest reduction in a product-specific limit would be exceeded without a change in policy. With rising milk production over time, even setting the limit at 100 percent of the 1999-2001 current AMS would be almost certain to require a policy change.

Table 6. Proportion of outcomes exceeding hypothetical product-specific AMS limits (limits expressed as percentage of 1999-2001 average current AMS)

Limit	2006	2007	2008	2009	2010	2011	2012	2013	2014
Corn									
150%	20.4%	18.4%	18.4%	16.0%	14.0%	13.2%	12.2%	13.4%	13.0%
100%	28.2%	28.6%	27.4%	24.0%	21.2%	20.6%	19.0%	17.0%	18.6%
75%	31.4%	34.0%	31.6%	27.8%	26.6%	25.2%	22.8%	20.4%	22.2%
50%	36.4%	39.0%	36.4%	32.4%	31.2%	29.2%	26.6%	23.0%	24.4%
25%	42.8%	43.0%	42.8%	37.2%	37.6%	32.0%	30.6%	29.4%	28.8%
Soybeans									
150%	4.0%	1.8%	2.2%	1.0%	0.6%	1.2%	1.4%	0.8%	2.4%
100%	15.4%	11.4%	8.4%	7.0%	6.6%	5.2%	7.4%	5.8%	6.2%
75%	22.6%	19.0%	14.6%	12.2%	11.8%	11.4%	15.0%	13.2%	12.2%
50%	38.0%	26.8%	25.0%	19.0%	20.6%	21.6%	23.0%	20.2%	20.6%
25%	50.8%	38.0%	33.4%	29.6%	28.8%	32.0%	31.4%	29.8%	31.2%
Wheat									
150%	7.0%	6.0%	5.6%	3.8%	3.8%	1.2%	0.8%	1.0%	1.8%
100%	12.2%	9.2%	9.0%	7.0%	6.4%	3.6%	3.4%	2.2%	2.4%
75%	15.2%	11.6%	11.8%	9.6%	8.2%	5.2%	5.0%	3.4%	3.8%
50%	18.6%	14.4%	13.8%	12.8%	9.4%	7.8%	6.0%	4.4%	4.4%
25%	24.2%	19.6%	18.6%	16.0%	13.6%	11.2%	8.6%	6.8%	6.8%
Cotton									
150%	1.0%	0.6%	0.8%	0.4%	0.4%	0.4%	0.4%	0.6%	0.6%
100%	18.8%	20.4%	20.0%	14.6%	12.4%	12.4%	11.6%	9.8%	10.2%
75%	41.4%	45.0%	41.8%	34.2%	28.4%	29.2%	26.6%	24.4%	22.2%
50%	68.0%	68.8%	65.4%	54.8%	49.6%	49.0%	48.8%	44.0%	39.2%
25%	94.2%	91.8%	88.0%	81.4%	73.8%	74.8%	77.2%	72.2%	63.4%
Rice									
150%	6.2%	5.0%	5.4%	4.6%	3.2%	5.2%	4.4%	4.2%	2.6%
100%	27.4%	23.4%	23.6%	21.8%	21.0%	20.6%	20.0%	19.2%	18.4%
75%	34.6%	30.0%	29.4%	27.6%	26.4%	26.6%	25.0%	23.4%	24.0%
50%	43.6%	39.4%	36.6%	33.6%	31.0%	32.2%	29.4%	29.4%	26.6%
25%	57.4%	51.0%	51.2%	49.0%	44.6%	45.0%	41.8%	39.6%	35.2%
Dairy									
150%	0.0%	0.0%	0.0%	0.0%	0.0%	0.0%	0.0%	0.0%	0.0%
100%	54.4%	69.8%	82.6%	90.2%	95.4%	97.8%	99.4%	99.6%	100.0%
75%	100.0%	100.0%	100.0%	100.0%	100.0%	100.0%	100.0%	100.0%	100.0%
50%	100.0%	100.0%	100.0%	100.0%	100.0%	100.0%	100.0%	100.0%	100.0%
25%	100.0%	100.0%	100.0%	100.0%	100.0%	100.0%	100.0%	100.0%	100.0%

Note: Figures assume the commodity-specific de minimis rule is eliminated. With the existing de minimis rule, the current AMS would be zero whenever the calculated AMS is less than 5% of the value of production.

Concluding Remarks

For many policy questions, traditional point estimates often miss the point. Many government policies have asymmetric features, so a deterministic point estimate may differ systematically from the mean of possible outcomes. Furthermore, there are many times where there is interest in the tails of distributions, such as policies that provide support only when abnormal events occur. Both of these concerns are important in examining the potential impacts of any agreement to establish new WTO disciplines on internal support measures.

The stochastic results detailed here illustrate the value of a model that can generate a range of possible outcomes rather than a single set of point estimates. Deterministic analysis suggests that projected U.S. support to producers as measured by the current AMS is well below the levels permitted under the URAA. Stochastic analysis reveals that the mean of possible AMS outcomes exceeds the deterministic level by several billion dollars per year, and that in 41.8 percent of the outcomes, the URAA limits would be exceeded at least once over the period between 2006 and 2014 if current rules and policies remained in place. While deterministic analysis would suggest that even a large reduction in AMS limits need have no effect on U.S. farm policy, stochastic analysis suggests that even a modest reduction in AMS limits could significantly increase the probability that limits will be exceeded in any given year. Commodity-specific limits are particularly likely to prove an issue for current U.S. farm policy.

The estimates reported here should be treated with caution. Stochastic analysis remains as much an art as a science, and future model developments will yield different results. Furthermore, stochastic analysis does not eliminate the problem of baseline dependence of scenario results. If deterministic baseline prices were higher (lower) than reported here, the proportion of outcomes that exceed various WTO limits would be lower (higher) than indicated in the tables. The results should be used to identify potential issues, but should not be considered definitive to the third (or even first) decimal place.

References

Abler, D, and D. Blandford. "A Review of Empirical Studies on the Production Impacts of PFC and MLA Payments under the U.S. FAIR Act." Presentation at the USDA Economic Research Service workshop, "Modeling U.S. and EU Agricultural Policy: Focus on Decoupled Payments," Washington, D.C. October 4, 2004

Anderson, K., W. Martin, and D. van der Mensbrugghe. "Doha Agricultural and Other Merchandise Trade Reform: What's at Stake." AAEA organized session paper, Providence, Rhode Island, July 2005.

Economic Research Service, USDA. 2005. "United States Support and Support Reduction Commitments by Policy Category." Table on ERS WTO briefing room website, http://www.ers.usda.gov/briefing/farmpolicy/data/totalusa.xls.

Fabiosa, J., J. Beghin, S. de Cara, A. Elobeid, C. Fang, M. Isik, H. Matthey, A. Saak, P. Westhoff, D.S. Brown, B. Willott, D. Madison, S. Meyer, and J. Kruse. 2005. "The Doha Round of the World Trade Organization and Agricultural Markets Liberalization: Impacts on Developing Economies." *Review of Agricultural Economics* 27(3):317-335.

Food and Agricultural Policy Research Institute (FAPRI). 2003. "FAPRI Analysis of Stricter Payment Limitations." *FAPRI-UMC Staff Report* #05-03. Columbia, Missouri: FAPRI, June.

—. 2005a. "FAPRI 2005 U.S. and World Agricultural Outlook." *FAPRI Staff Report* 1-05. Ames, Iowa: FAPRI, January.

—. 2005b. "FAPRI 2005 U.S. Briefing Book." *FAPRI-UMC Report* #02-05. Columbia, Missouri: FAPRI, March.

—. 2005c. "The President's Budget: Implications of Selected Proposals for U.S. Agriculture." *FAPRI-UMC Staff Report* #03-05. Columbia, Missouri: FAPRI, March.

—. 2005d. "Implications of Increased Ethanol Production for U.S. Agriculture." *FAPRI-UMC Staff Report* #10-05. Columbia, Missouri: FAPRI, August.

—. 2005e. "FAPRI Stochastic Model Documentation." FAPRI-UMC Staff Report. Columbia, Missouri: *FAPRI*, forthcoming.

Just, R. 2001. "Addressing the Changing Nature of Uncertainty in Agriculture." *American Journal of Agricultural Economics* 83(5):1131-1153.

World Trade Organization (WTO). 1994. "Agreement on Agriculture." *http://www.wto.org/english/docs_e/legal_e/14-ag.pdf.*

—. 2004. "Text of the 'July Package'—the General Council's post-Cancun Decision." *http://www.wto.org/english/tratop_e/dda_e/draft_text_gc_dg_31july04_e.htm.*

WTO Appellate Body. 2005. "United States—Subsidies on Upland Cotton." Report of the Appellate Body. Document #05-0884. *http://docsonline.wto.org.*

In: International Agricultural Trade and Development
Editor: Dragan Miljkovic, pp. 111-128
ISBN: 978-1-60021-965-8

Chapter 7

MODELING PRODUCTION RESPONSE TO "MORE DECOUPLED" PAYMENTS*

Jesús Antón[1]

ABSTRACT

Several significant changes in agricultural policy in OECD countries over the last two decades have been driven by the concept of "decoupling". In practice, these "more decoupled" payments have changed from linking support to the output to linking the payments to land, and they have been implemented with increasing freedom to produce. This paper explores the economics that explains why these movements are likely to reduce production effects. However, a broad perspective of all the economic mechanisms that affect farmers′ decision making does not allow for the conclusion that there are no impacts. The magnitude of the impacts of "more decoupled" payments is an empirical question that needs to be investigated using econometric estimation methods. Although the small amount of empirical literature available in this area shows, in general, some impacts, is not conclusive as to their magnitude. This reduces the confidence in simulation results that involve this type of payments. Relevant technical difficulties may explain, but not justify, this lag on the empirical work dealing with the main policy change that has recently occurred in OECD countries. Recent studies using micro data are promising and should be enhanced, while further work is needed to improve the comparability and applicability of estimation results in simulation models.
JEL classification: Q18

Key words: Decoupling, agricultural policy, simulation models.

---

* Paper prepared for presentation at the Annual Meeting of The International Agricultural Trade Consortium (IATRC), San Diego, California, 4-6 December 2005.

1. Jesús Antón is Economist in the Spanish Ministry of Agriculture and in the Organization for Economic Co-operation and Development, OECD. The views expressed in this paper are those of the author and not necessarily those of the Spanish Ministry of Agriculture, the OECD Secretariat or its member countries. This paper has benefited from the input of many. Among others, I am grateful to Catherine Benjamin, Carmel Cahill, Frank Fuller, Hsin Huang, Pierre Luigi Londero, Roger Martini, Richard Stillman, Wyatt Thompson, Martin von Lampe, and Patrick Westhoff. All remaining errors are my own.

Over the last two decades there has been a number of reforms in agricultural policies in certain OECD countries and sectors. The US 1996 FAIR Act created the Production Flexibility Contract (PFC) payments that were followed by the 2002 Direct Payments under the 2002 Farm Bill. In the European Union, the 1992 reform was a first step followed by the 2003 Common Agricultural Policy (CAP) reform that created the Single Farm Payment (SFP). These reforms have been guided by the concept of decoupling domestic support measures from production decisions. Governments and trade negotiators demand estimates and quantifications of the impacts of these reforms and measures. The estimated impacts using different models depend on the features and assumptions of the modeling tool and the policy representation in this modeling framework. It is clear that the representation and assumptions attached to both the original policies and the new policies after reform substantially affect the quantitative results (Gohin).

This paper investigates the modeling challenges posed by some of the policy measures implemented under these reform processes. The focus is on modeling the payments with the purpose of estimating their impact on production decisions and trade. It is not obvious which instruments should be considered under the heading of "more decoupled" payments. Much of the confusion in the debate on modeling and quantifying "decoupling" is due to the fact that the set of payments that are called "decoupled" or "more decoupled" is not well defined. We apply a pragmatic approach by considering under "more decoupled" payments the main instruments that have been used in this process of reform, out from price / output support and border measures. The discussion of the 2003 CAP Reform has created additional confusion in the terminology and in the technical debate: in this European context, the term "degree of decoupling" is applied to the % of eligible CAP payments that are moved to the new single farm payment. This definition can only be applied to the specific EU policy reform framework and it differs from the empirical definition of the degree of decoupling as the relative production and trade impacts of a given payment as compared to price support (Cahill, OECD). This latter empirical approach is followed in this paper, which implies that the SFP, just as any other program, has a degree of decoupling that needs empirical investigation.

The discussion is organized in three sections. The first section analyses the economics behind the production response to "more decoupled" payments and identifies the mechanisms of response through which this support measures can affect production decisions. The second section identifies the main modeling challenges associated with the main policy developments towards decoupling; that is, linking payments to land (instead of output), and broadening the commodities and activities that can benefit from the payments. The third section briefly assesses how some relevant models represent these policies. The conclusions identify areas where more empirical research is needed.

The Economics of Production Response to "More Decoupled" Payments

The different production response to payments can be due to two interrelated causes. First, different programs can generate a different set of incentives to producers. These incentives are determined by the characteristics and implementation criteria that define a specific program. Second, the structural features of the farming sector in a given country or region where the instrument is applied affect the capacity and willingness to adjust for a given set of new incentives.

The Characteristics of the Payments

Table 1 summarizes some basic implementation criteria that are relevant in determining the type of incentives created by a payment scheme. They have been arbitrarily classified under four criteria: a) the nature of the "variable" that determines the amount of the payment received; b) the mathematical relationship between variable a) and the amount of the payment; c) the limits or conditions imposed that constrain the direct application of a) and b); and, finally, d) the commodities and activities that are covered by variable a).

Payments provided proportionally to the output quantities are normally considered as fully coupled payments. But payments can be provided on the basis of the area used for a given activity on the basis of other non land inputs, or even on the basis of the use of risk reducing strategies such as insurance or price hedging. The incentive created in each case can differ significantly. Payments based on output (and also market price support) create incentives to use all the production inputs in order to maximize profits from higher producer net output prices. Payments based on area create incentives to use more land on production instead of other inputs and, therefore, to reduce yields. The same type of reasoning can be applied to any possible variable determining the amount of the payment.

Table 1. Some relevant implementation criteria

Implementation criteria	Some possible options
(a) The amount of and the right for the payment depends on:	1. Output quantity 2. Output price 3. Area 4. Non-land inputs 5. Risk-reducing input (insurance, hedging...)
(b) The payments are provided:	1. Proportional to a) 2. Positively related to A but not proportional 3. Negatively related to a)
(c) There are limits or conditions attached To the payments:	1. Quantitative limits on a) and / or b) 2. Cross compliance conditions on technologies and practices
(d) Commodity coverage of the payments	1. Single commodity 2. Several commodities with • Same rate • Different rate 3. Allowing idling (no production required) 4. Excluding some commodities 5. Maintaining land in agricultural use

Once the variable defining the amount of the payment is found, the relationship between the amount of the payment and variable a) needs to be identified. This relationship is often proportional: the payment is defined as a given amount of dollars per ton or per hectare, but it is sometimes the case that this relationship is not proportional. It could be digressive or progressive and create in both cases different types of incentives. It could also be negative or countercyclical. For instance, US countercyclical payments depend negatively on prices. There is also emergency aid in many countries that is provided as a compensation for a production loss: the lower the production, the higher the payment. This type of countercyclical payment typically generates risk related incentives on production that are called insurance effects (Hennessy).

Payments are often subject to different types of constraints that can affect the type and magnitude of the incentives they create whenever the constraints are binding for some farmers. These constraints could limit the eligible quantity of variable a); for instance, the set aside conditions and the maximum eligible area in the area payments in the European Union. They can also truncate, displace or curve the set of incentives created by the payments (OECD, 2002). It is often the case that the effects of those limits are asymmetric: the magnitude of the impacts of the constraint is different for increasing payments as compared to decreasing payments. Additionally, many payments have different types of conditions attached to them, sometimes called cross compliance conditions which are related to agricultural practices and technologies. These conditions impose technological constraints that influence the type and magnitude of farmers' response.

The set of commodities that are supported by a given program or set of programs determines the relative incentives among different activities that typically compete for the use of some scarce resources. A support program that covers a single agricultural production will generate a reallocation of resources that otherwise would be used in other activities in the agricultural sector or in other sectors. On the contrary, a program that covers all agricultural activities will allocate to the agricultural sector resources that otherwise would be used in other sectors. It has been argued that not requiring production, that is that the payment covers the possibility of idling, eliminates the production effects of payments. This is obviously erroneous since idling is an additional activity that is allowed, but there may be other activities that are not eligible for the payment (OECD, 2005). Several "more decoupled" programs cover the possibility of not producing, but requiring maintaining land in agricultural use defined as doing some minimum maintenance agricultural activities. This can be a different activity with different cost incentives than just "idling".

Structural Response from Producers

Given the set of incentives created by the implementation criteria in Table 1, the response of farmers to these incentives can vary for very different reasons. I will mention some of these without any ambition of being exhaustive:

I. The technology available and the possibilities of adjusting this technology. The use of capital and labor and, particularly, the possibilities of technological substitution between these, other inputs and land are crucial determinants of production response.

II. The relative availability of different resources or inputs. This includes the prices and the mobility of resources, particularly land, but also of other inputs. Legal, physical and other constraints can affect the adjustability of these resources.
III. Whenever some of the input markets are not perfectly competitive or they are incomplete, be it the land market, the labor market, the capital markets or the risk related markets, the preferences of the farmer can influence his business decisions. These preferences include, for instance, labor / leisure and risk preferences. This is likely to be the case for non-commercial farmers.
IV. The expectations created by the implementation criteria of the payment, the government decision making process, or any other source of information. Farmers′ expectations, that are not necessarily an immediate consequence of any objective information, can influence the incentives to adjust or respond to the economic incentives.

The combination of these elements is often correlated with the structural characteristics of the farms in a given country or region, the degree of economic development, the development of markets and legal frameworks, the availability of infrastructures and services, the geography, the climate and the agronomic conditions. All these circumstances are often summarized empirically into a matrix of elasticities of output supply. This matrix is a very useful tool to determine response to support that is provided to the outputs through payments or prices, but it provides insufficient information to determine response to the "more decoupled" payments.

What is Decoupling and How Can "More Decoupled" Payments be Modeled?

A pragmatic and applied use of the concept of "decoupling" identifies this process with the type of agricultural policy reform that has been experienced in some OECD countries and sectors over the last two decades. For example, the main policy changes occurred in the arable crops sector in the United States and the European Union. The main characteristic of these "decoupling" reforms is the movement away from output related payments or support, mainly market price support. The "decoupling" reforms have substituted this support by "more decoupled" payments. Where are the "decoupling" reforms moving the support to? The principal idea is to provide support to farmers while reducing its incidence on farmers' resource allocation decisions and, therefore, on production and trade. Historically, two main axes have been used for decoupling:

1. From support that depends on the quantity produced to payments based on land.
2. From support defined for individual commodities to payments with more freedom on what to produce.

All current payments that are normally called "more decoupled" are paid on a per hectare basis and, therefore, are based on area. Eligibility for some of these payments is based on historical parameters, but all available examples impose some current conditions on some current land. Why should the movement from output support to land support reduce the production response? Let us assume first that land is a perfect complementary input with respect to the rest of the inputs. This is a Leontief technology between area and the other inputs. If this was the case, it is not important whether a subsidy is given to land or to other inputs: in both cases production will increase in the same way because inputs have to be used in fixed proportions. If there are no economies of scale[2], output support will also have the same impact on production as support to any input.

We need to assume some degree of substitution between area and other inputs (that for simplification we will call "yields") in order to obtain a differentiated output response when supporting each type of input. In this case, there is an incentive to use more of the subsidized input as compared to the unsubsidized one. For an area payment, more land is brought into production at the expense of other inputs (yields). When moving from price support to area payments one could expect an increase in the use of land and a reduction in yields. A reduction in production will be observed whenever the reduction in yields is larger than the increase in area. This should be the case if the supply of land is inelastic relative to the supply of other inputs. The larger the substitution possibilities and the larger the differences in the elasticity of supply of land as compared to other inputs, the larger the potential for a lower supply response to area payments. But theory does not solve the question of the relative magnitude of production response to payments based on output, area or other inputs.

This is very much related to the degree of capitalization of the area payments on land values and rents. If land supply was fully inelastic, the payment would be fully capitalized on the price of land, and the owner of the land would fully benefit from the payment with no consequence on production. But normally land supply would respond to land payments, and the additional land brought into production would displace the use of other inputs, generating a fall in yields. In this more general case, farmers who do not own the land would also benefit from the area payment and there would be some production response. The magnitude of this response is an empirical question. There are some empirical studies trying to estimate the impact of "more decoupled" payments on land prices in the United States (for instance Roberts, Kirwan and Hopkins), even if there are important technical difficulties in this estimation (Goodwin, Mishra and Ortalo-Magné). This evidence shows partial capitalization of payments such as PFC payments.

The second axis for decoupling has been to broaden the area based payments to a larger set of agricultural activities that are allowed in the benefiting area. In the European context, these two axes have been applied in successive steps: the 1992 CAP reform created commodity specific area payments; the 2003 reform have broadened the eligible activities under the new SFP. What are the economic reasons that underpin the idea that broadening the activities would reduce the production response? The explanation is straight forward: if the farmer has the freedom to decide what to produce (or not to produce) on the land benefiting from the payments, the probability of the payment affecting land allocation decisions is reduced. In other words, the total supply of land for a large set of agricultural activities is expected to be less elastic to payments and rent prices because there are fewer alternative activities to which land could be devoted. However, it is always the case in all known "more

[2]. This is a common assumption when considering response for a whole country or region where the production technology can be replicated when output expands.

decoupled" payments that some agricultural activities are excluded from the land benefiting from the payment[3].

In the context of these two axes, if a "more decoupled" payment is in fact more decoupled, this must be due to one or both of these reasons. The first reason is that the "more decoupled" payments are based on area and producers substitute land for other inputs in production, which generates an important reduction in yields. The second reason is that "more decoupled" payments are provided for a larger set of agricultural activities and, therefore, there is less scope for bringing land from other uses into production.

The main modeling challenges created by the "more decoupled" payments are precisely related to the capacity of models to represent the nuances of these two axes. The first axis demands for a good representation of the technical substitution between land and other inputs. A theoretically consistent model requires both land and yields response to the payments and, very likely, in opposing directions. A proper production function with some degree of technical substitution would capture these effects through a demand for land that can be differentiated from land supply. Several technical possibilities are easily available for this construction. The second axis requires an exhaustive representation of different land uses or, at least, a good estimate of the land supply for the set of activities allowed under the payment. Again there are several technical possibilities to represent this type of land supply system, such as a Constant Elasticity of Transformation (CET) functional form.

There are other relevant modeling issues raised in the literature. For instance, the risk effects of some payments and the income effects of payments in the farm household decision making. Both fall under bullet III on the structural response analyzed in the previous section and they are not specific to "more decoupled" measures. Risk effects can be significant when payments are provided counter-cyclically. Despite the fact that both US Direct Payments and Countercyclical Payments are provided on the same basis (per hectare of historical land with some current conditions), counter-cyclical payments generate additional commodity specific risk-related incentives to produce. The magnitude of these incentives is normally smaller than those created by deficiency payments and its modeling poses challenging questions (Antón and LeMouel). Modelers should not underestimate possible risk-related effects of programs that are not designed as counter-cyclical, but whose provision of resources (the level of the payment) is determined on an *ad hoc* counter-cyclical basis. There is evidence of *ad hoc* counter-cyclicality in aggregate support measures of several OECD countries (OECD, 2004). In this area, the empirical evidence on the degree of farmers′ risk aversion is scarce and not unanimous.

Farm households make decisions — such as on work and leisure, and on savings, investment and consumption — that are conditioned by their levels of income, and all types of payments will have an effect on these decisions. To the extent that "more decoupled" payments are more efficient in transferring income to the farm household (Dewbre, Antón and Thompson), they have the potential for a larger response. The impact on agricultural production is likely to be small in magnitude and unclear in terms of its direction (USDA, OECD 2005b)). The investigation of these effects would better be undertaken using individual data on farm households. This line of research could clarify issues on farm

[3]. In the case of US Direct payments, fruits and vegetables are excluded. In the EU, Single Farm Payment, fruits and vegetables and potatoes are excluded in most of the countries. In both cases, land must be maintained in good agricultural use, even if practical terms this later condition is more demanding in the European Union than in the United States.

structures and adjustment that have great policy relevance; they are not, however, the focus of this paper.

Finally, there are some modeling questions that are particularly difficult to analyse (OECD, 2005). First, the existence of complex sets of cross compliance conditions covering issues such as animal welfare and environmental standards. Second, the existence of expectations about future policies in a context of reforms that do not change dramatically the level of support but which may cover for cyclical decreases in revenues and may allow for the updating of historical variables that determine the amount of the payment. Third, in many OECD countries the level of support is already very high and this can potentially affect (likely reduce) the responsiveness to payments.

The main challenges for modeling the production response of "more decoupled" payments are not due to the technical structure of the model, but to the difficulty of finding robust and consistent empirical estimations of the response parameters that can feed simulation models. The need for this empirical work is accentuated by the complexity and the number of response mechanisms that can be identified. The technical difficulties for undertaking such sophisticated estimations have contributed to the scarcity of the empirical literature in this area, particularly for structural models. The lack of variability of total support levels and the use of quantitative restrictions that may prevent farmers' response are also part of these difficulties. The absence of a control group of farmers not receiving the support is also signalled as a difficulty in Key et al. The explicit consideration of variables capturing the policy instruments and changes in policy regimes is a prerequisite for obtaining useful estimations of response parameters. The scarce empirical literature that has been published often deals with area response, leaving open the very relevant issue of yield response A review of the empirical literature in the US (Abler) reports only one published study on land response to US payments (Adams et al.). Most studies are focused on only part of the effects that are discussed in this article (Moro and Sckokai). Furthermore, some studies underline the uncertainties associated with the quantification of the yield response to area payments (Benjamin and Houée). There are also difficulties in building the bridge between the empirical results and the parameter needs of specific models. The production ratios and the corresponding degree of coupling / decoupling in Cahill and OECD (2001a) are attempts to overcome this difficulty.

How Do Models Deal with "More Decoupled" Payments?

Driven by the demand from policy makers and negotiators, several models have tried to simulate the impact of agricultural policy reform in production and trade. The original focus of most of these models was trade and trade policy measures. However, the policy changes that have occurred in the last two decades have increased the relative importance of domestic measures of the "more decoupled" nature in the agricultural policy mix and models have often adapted their structure to capture some of these measures. There is scarce econometric evidence of the nature and scope of farmers´ response to these payments. Under this circumstance we must accept that simulation models cannot perform as well as we would like, and their stories are very much influenced by a set of assumptions about the impact of the new payments. These assumptions are often based on valuable "expert assessment", but rarely on true empirical evidence.

This section briefly discusses the representation of main domestic programs in a selection of simulation models: FAPSIM (Economic Research Service of USDA), FAPRI (Universities of Missouri and Iowa State), AGLINK and PEM (both from OECD), ESIM (EU Commission) and WEMAC (INRA). The sample of models does not pretend to be exhaustive (Table 2). They are all partial equilibrium models[4]. The information is based on the responses to a questionnaire sent to the modelers[5].

Table 2. Payments represented in selected models

	FAPSIM Linker (ERS)	FAPRI	AGLINK (OECD)	PEM (OECD)	ESIM (EC)	WEMAC (INRA)
EU 1992 Area Payments[1]	Yes	Yes	Yes	Yes	Yes	Yes
EU 2003 Single Farm Payment	No	Yes	Yes	Yes	No	No
US 1996 AMTA / 2002 Direct Payment	No	Yes	Yes	Yes	No	Yes
US 2002 Counter-cyclical Payments	No	Yes	Yes	Yes	No	Yes
Other Programmes	Indian wheat	EU new members		Mexican Procampo		

1. This heading refers to both the original 1992 payments and the 1999 reform.

What payments are included in these models? We focus our discussion on four "more decoupled" programs implemented by the main players in agricultural trade, avoiding the discussion about inclusion or exclusion from this list. The objective is to be illustrative, with no intended empirical or legal implication. The four programmes are the 1992 area payments and the 2003 single farm payment in the European Union, and the 1996 AMTA payments (called direct payments in the 2002 farm bill) and the countercyclical payments in the United States. All six models include a representation of the 1992 EU area payments (Table 2). The other three programs are just assumed to be fully decoupled (with no effect on production decisions) in FAPSIM and ESIM. The SFP is also considered as fully decoupled in WEMAC. FAPRI, AGLINK and PEM have a representation of some response to all these payments.

Land Allocation and Non Price Effects

The land allocation system is a main modeling element and it is briefly described in Table 3. Most of the partial equilibrium models represent production of agricultural commodities by a combination of land and yield equations. The yield variable is assumed to

[4] The OECD's GTAP-PEM based on one of the most popular general equilibrium models (GTAP) follows a representation of land markets and "more decoupled" payments that is similar to the standard representation in PEM.

summarize all the information about non-land inputs. Most of these models exclude the substitution between land and other inputs: a payment to land does not reduce the relative use of non-land inputs as we have theoretically argued. This is not the case of ESIM and PEM where input substitution occurs. Excluding area / yield substitution implies that a commodity specific area payment will be partially decoupled only if land response to area payments is weaker than land response to price support, which seems unlikely to occur. Land response is most often represented with a single system of land equations that summarize the interaction between supply and demand in the land market. The exception is the PEM model that has an explicit production function with a representation that is similar to some general equilibrium models like GTAP-PEM, with a CES production function that allows the substitution of land for other inputs. All models assume the heterogeneity of land with a system that accounts for the imperfect substitution of land for different uses. However, the empirical evidence on the degree of substitution in production between land and other inputs, and the degree of differentiation between different types of land is scarce[6]. Several models include in their standard work a systematic use of sensitivity analysis. This is a welcome improvement that helps understand the results, but which cannot substitute for an empirical estimation of the magnitude of these parameters, and their confidence intervals.

Table 3. Elements in the land allocation structure of each model

	FAPSIM Linker (ERS)	FAPRI	AGLINK (OECD)	PEM (OECD)	ESIM (EC)	WEMAC (INRA)
Inputs represented in the model	Land and yields	Land and yields	Land and yields	Land + set of other inputs	Land + set of other inputs	Land and yields
Input substitution in production	No	No	No	CES	Yes	No
Market of land: demand and supply	Yes	1 land equation[1]	1 land equation[1]	Yes	1 land equation[1]	1 land equation[1]
Land heterogeneity for different uses	Yes	Yes	Yes	Yes	Yes	Yes
Idling	Yes	Compulsory exogenously	Endogenous voluntary set aside equ.	Compulsory exogenously	Compulsory exogenously	Exogenous

[1] One system of equations for land response, as reduced form of supply / demand interactions.

[5]. These questionnaires were sent to the economists in charge of the models on the occasion of an *ad hoc* World Outlook Conference held in Rome, May 2005.

[6] See, for example, OECD (2001b) for a revision of the empirical literature that is used for determining the parameter values in the PEM.

An important challenge raised by payments that allow voluntary idling or set aside is the representation of the land that is "idle" but receiving the payment in the land allocation system. All models include an exogenous representation of idling (compulsory set aside) or an implicit effect on land. The need for a good representation of the endogenous response of idling is exacerbated by the existence of some conditions attached to the land that is idled, but receives the payment. This land should be differentiated from land just leaving the sector. For instance, AGLINK has an endogenous voluntary set aside equation for the EU. The statistical identification of these two types of lands is not always well defined and the challenge of estimating "idling" supply and demand seems to be open.

Table 4. Representation of non-price effects

	FAPSIM Linker (ERS)	FAPRI	AGLINK (OECD)	PEM (OECD)	ESIM (EC)	WEMAC (INRA)
Cross Compliance	No	No	No	No	No[1]	No
Risk effects	No	No[2]	Yes[3]	Yes[4]	No	No
Wealth / Income effects	No	No[2]	Only risk related	Only risk related	No	No
Other effects	No	No	No	No	No	No

1. Maintaining land in agricultural use is included.
2. FAPRI uses a reduced form that it is assumed to capture risk and wealth effects. Lagged prices may capture some risk effects for counter-cyclical payments.
3. Risk premiums are calculated for countercyclical payments from truncation if price distributions.
4. There is a risk version of PEM that calculates risk premiums for main PSE categories having a significant effect in reducing farming revenue.

Cross compliance conditions that are attached to some of these payments, particularly the SFP, are excluded from the analysis despite their potential to affect relative incentives (Table 4). Their influence needs to be analyzed at the individual level before aggregating at the national level that is the geographical framework of analysis of these models. Risk effects are included in some applications of AGLINK and PEM, though the weakness of the empirical evidence about the coefficient of risk aversion to include in the equations is recognized. Risk effects are of relevance only for US counter-cyclical payments. Wealth / income effects (other than risk related that are typically estimated to be very small) and any other effects are absent in all models. Some models, like the FAPRI, have a reduced form approach that is difficult to interpret in terms of the precise type of economic effects it is designed to capture.

"More Decoupled" Programs in the European Union

The original EU 1992 area payments for crops are payments per hectare of land used for specific activities. The Agenda 2000 reform that aligned most of the rates of support and allowed some voluntary set aside introduced changes in the initial 1992 policy.

Table 5. Representation of the 1992 EU Area Payments

	FAPSIM Linker (ERS)	FAPRI	AGLINK (OECD)	PEM (OECD)	ESIM (EC)	WEMAC (INRA)
Commodities whose equations are affected	Cereals, oilseeds (beef)	Cereals and oilseeds (beef)	Cereals, oilseeds (beef)	Cereals, oilseeds (beef)	Cereals, oilseeds (beef)	Cereals, oilseeds
First incidence of the payment[1]	Additional returns per ton	GrainArea= f(AP),ε=0.02 Commodity area shares depend on AP	Cereals Area = f (returns + 0.267*AP) Beef Inv = =f(ret.+HP...)	Commodity area supply = f (Pa+AP) (substitution with other inputs)	Commodity area supply = f (returns + a* P…)	Impact on area equation ε = 0.06
Incidence on other land uses	Set aside	Set aside	Set aside	Set aside	Idling is an alternative	Set aside
Payment rates	Same per hectare	AP / ton * *Hist.Yield	Same per hectare (after 2000)	Commodity Specific rates (observed)	Same AP/ hectare	Specific historical rates
Eligible base limit	Yes	Not out of range	No	Yes in specific applications	No, but legal limits	No

1. When a functional formula is written, ε denotes the corresponding elasticity of area with respect to the payment “AP”.

All models consider EU 1992 area payments as having an impact on production (Table 5). FAPSIM considers the payments as additional returns per ton (they are fully coupled), meanwhile the rest of models introduce area payments in the grain or cereals area equations with different elasticities. PEM adds the payments per hectare to the rental price of land received by land owners. The ratio of PEM production response to area payments as compared to price support is used to weigh the incidence of area payment on land returns in the AGLINK equations. Other land uses is only implicit in all models, except for compulsory set aside that is explicitly included as an exogenous shock (except in ESIM). The payment rate for different commodities can differ in most of the models, which is relevant for the cross effects among eligible commodities. The eligible area base limits are not represented in most of the models. FAPSIM is an exception and ESIM includes the legal limits for transferring land from one use to another, such as from pasture to crops.

The 2003 Single Farm Payment substitutes a large portion of the 1992 CAP payments (including livestock payments per head or per ton) by a new single farm payment largely independent of the agricultural activity conducted on the land. In general, the design of the SFP as farm level average of payments per hectare generates different rates per hectare for different pieces of land. However, the rate of payment for a given entitlement does not change for different land uses, including idling with an extensive list of cross compliance conditions. This hybrid between a flat rate payment and a payment rate differentiated by commodity introduces additional uncertainty about the magnitude of the cross effects of the SFP.

The SFP is assumed to be fully decoupled in half of the models (Table 6). The share of old CAP payments included in the SFP is used in all models to determine the amount of remaining old "partially decoupled" payments. FAPRI[1] applies a 0.75 coefficient to the payments in the land share equations. PEM expands the types of land uses that are eligible for the payment, including other arable land, and, therefore, reduces the possibility of substitution with alternative uses. AGLINK uses the smaller PEM production ratio of SFP to weigh their impact on cereal area equation. Compulsory set aside is explicit in all three models, but voluntary set aside can only be interpreted as implicit, except in AGLINK. The chosen options on the rate of support are also different across models.

"More Decoupled" Programs in the United States

In the United States the PFC payments of the 1996 FAIR Act, were substituted by the Direct Payments program in the 2002 Farm Bill. The program maintains its basic structure, even if a voluntary partial updating of base acres has been adopted with potential expectation effects about future updates (OECD, 2005). It is considered as fully decoupled by FAPSIM and ESIM, but incidence on land returns are modeled in the other four models (Table 7). FAPRI identifies this response with a wealth effect. In most cases a uniform rate per hectare is applied using historical basis and no limit is imposed to eligible land. The amount of the PFC payments was topped up since 1998 to cover for smaller market prices. This top-up payment was institutionalized in the counter-cyclical payments program in the 2002 Farm Bill.

[1] FAPRI has two different models for the EU. The model described in this paper is the FAPRI-ISU model.

Table 6. Representation of the 2003 EU Single Farm Payment

	FAPSIM Linker (ERS)	FAPRI	AGLINK (OECD)	PEM (OECD)	ESIM (EC)	WEMAC (INRA)
Commodities whose equations are affected	None	Cereals and oilseeds (dairy)	Crops and Beef, Sheep and dairy	Land for crops, pasture and other	None	None
First incidence of the payment[1]		Grain Area= F(.75*SFP…) ε = 0.02 Commodity areas shares = f (.75*SFP..) ε = 0.038	Cereals Area = f (returns +0.11*SFP..) Beef Inv = = f (ret. + 0.06*SFP..)	Commodity area supply= f (Pa+SFP) (substitution with other inputs)		
Incidence on other land uses		Compulsory set aside	Implicit in non-homogeneity	Compulsory set aside and other arable		
Payment rates		Same SFP per hectare *0.75 * Decoupling ratio	Same SFP per hectare	Specific rates (observed)		
Eligible base limit		Not, but low supply elasticity	No	No		

1. When a functional formula is signaled, ε denotes the corresponding elasticity of area with respect to the payment "SFP".

Table 7. Representation of the US 1996 PFC and 2002 Direct Payments

	FAPSIM Linker (ERS)	FAPRI	AGLINK (OECD)	PEM (OECD)	ESIM (EC)	WEMAC (INRA)
Commodities whose equations are affected	None	Cereals and oilseeds	All grains and oilseeds	All crops and oilseeds and other ara.	None	Cereals and oilseeds
First incidence of the payment[1]		All land= f (.25* net coeff. on returns*DP..) ε ≈ 0.01	Commodity area supply = f (returns +0.09*DP)	Commodity area supply= f (Pa+DP) (substitution with other inputs)		Impact on area equation
Incidence on other land uses		Only implicit	Not explicitly	Idling is under other arable land		Not explicitly
Payment rates		Same rate per hectare	Same rate per hectare	Historical average rates		Historical rates
Eligible base limit		No, but low supply elasticity	No	No		No

1. When a functional formula is signaled, ε denotes the corresponding elasticity of area with respect to the payment "SFP".

FAPSIM and ESIM consider these counter-cyclical payments as fully decoupled. WEMAC considers the same impact as direct payments (Table 8). FAPRI models an additional response as compared to the "decoupled" component already considered for the direct payments. This "coupled" component is attributed to insurance and policy expectation effects, and it almost doubles the response to these payments as compared to direct payments. AGLINK also adds to the "price" component of direct payments a risk component that is estimated from the truncation of price distributions. Similarly, the PEM model considers a risk reducing effect on price premiums additional to the effect on land prices.

Table 8. Representation of the US 2002 Counter-cyclical Payments

	FAPSIM Linker (ERS)	FAPRI	AGLINK (OECD)	PEM (OECD)	ESIM (EC)	WEMAC (INRA)
Commodities whose equations are affected	None	Cereals, Oilseeds and Cotton	All grains and oilseeds	All crops and oilseeds and other arable	None	Cereals and oilseeds
First incidence of the payment[1]		"decoupled" component = (.25* net coeff.on returns*CCP..) "coupled" component= 0.25*CCP(EP) (by commodity)	"Risk" component= Risk price premium "Price" component= f (returns +0.09*DP)	Variance Land price		Same as in direct payments
Incidence on other land uses		Only implicit	Not explicitly	Idling is under other arable		Not explicitly
Payment rates		Commodity specific rates (E(CCP))	Same CCP/h Different risk premium	Historical rates		Historical rates
Eligible base limit		Not, but low supply elasticity	No	No		No

1. When a functional formula is signaled, ε denotes the corresponding elasticity of area with respect to the payment "CCP".

The Degree of Decoupling of Different Programs

This is a complex panorama of imperfect *ad hoc* second best solutions to modeling payments whose incidence on farmers' response remains an open empirical question. The assumptions in each model have implications about the response to additional support through each program, and the relative impact as compared to price support (the production ratio as defined in Cahill and OECD, 2001). The numerical value of these production ratios is very sensitive to the details of calculation and, therefore, the ratios in Table 9 are merely illustrative of the large different implications and assumptions across models. Assumptions, policy representation and response can also change for different applications of the same model. For instance, the response to Counter Cyclical Payments is typically contingent on expected prices and variability. The response to prices in each model also affects the value of the denominator in the ratio. Therefore, this information should not be used as an assessment of the degree of decoupling of each program.

There are good economic and empirical reasons to argue that these payments are "more decoupled" than price or output support. There are also good reasons to argue that the SFP is more decoupled than the 1992 EU area payments program, and the US Direct Payment is more decoupled than the Counter-cyclical Payments. Any further step on quantifying the degree of decoupling and the expected response to these payments would need further empirical evidence and work on comparability.

Table 9. Implied approximate estimated degree of coupling / decoupling[1]

	FAPSIM Linker (ERS)	FAPRI	AGLINK (OECD)	PEM (OECD)	ESIM (EC)	WEMAC (INRA)
EU 1992 Area Payments	1	≈ 1.00	< 0.27	0.27	(0 , 1)	(0 , 1)
EU 2003 Single Farm Payment		≈ 0.60	< 0.11	0.11	0	0
US 1996 AMTA / 2002 Direct Payment		≈ 0.34	< 0.09	0.09		(0 , 1)
US 2002 Counter-cyclical Payments		≈ 0.59	< (0.09+Risk)	?		(0 , 1)

1. These numbers are calculated as production ratios: increase in production per dollar of additional payments as compared to the increase in production per dollar of additional price support (OECD, 2001). Calculations in this table are sensitive to the details of the experiment design and are approximate with the purpose of illustrating the range of potential available assumptions only. When no calculation was available but the magnitude could be inferred as the interval (0 , 1), this interval is shown in the table and represents partial decoupling. When the modeler makes no claim of representing a given program, the cell is left empty.

Conclusions and Further Needs

Economists have to be aware of the limitations of their analysis. There are many things we do not know about the quantitative response to "more decoupled" payments. Unfortunately, the simulation work to date is weakened by the scarcity of the econometric evidence in this area. But simulation exercises with these models are and have been useful. If they are done and interpreted with the maximum rigor, these exercises help to understand the implications of reforms and develop the empirical agenda required to quantify their impact.

They are also second best approaches to quantifying these impacts, under the constraints imposed by the current state of knowledge and art.

The lack of a body of empirical literature on farmers' response to "more decoupled" payments implemented in several countries is surprising and regrettable, because it imposes limitations on the analysis of the consequences of what is probably the most important agricultural policy change that has occurred in decades. But there is room for being optimistic. There are some very recent studies that are improving our empirical knowledge of the response to these payments in the European Union and the United States (Sckokai and Antón, Goodwin and Mishra 2005a and 2005b, and Key, Lubowski and Roberts). They use mostly micro data with different approaches. Agricultural economists and research institutions should learn from this experience. There are important potential gains from devoting more resources to generate the appropriate data (often micro data) and facilitate and promote the econometric analysis of response to "more decoupled" payments using these data. Some effort is also needed to facilitate the comparability of empirical results and to build the bridges between these results and the parameters needed in simulation models. If these payments continue to be provided per hectare, special efforts should be dedicated to the empirical knowledge of land markets, their interaction with yields and their representation in simulation models.

REFERENCES

Abler, D. "*A Review of Empirical Studies of the Acreage and Production Response to US Production Flexibility Contract Payments under the FAIR Act and related Payments under Supplementary Legislation*". Paris: Organization for Economic Co-operation and Development, 2004

Adams, G., P. Westhoff, B. Willott, and R.E. Young II (2001), "Direct Payments, Safety Nets and Supply Response: Do "decoupled" Payments Affect US Crop Area? Preliminary Evidence from 1997-2000", *American Journal Of Agricultural Economics* 83, pp. 1190-1195.

Antón, J. and C. LeMouel. "Do counter-cyclical payments in the 2002 US Farm Act create incentives to produce?" *Agricultural Economics* 31(2004): 277-284

Benjamin, C., and M. Houée. " *The impact on yields of moving from price support to area payments – a study of the 1992 Cap Reform*". Paris: Organization for Economic Co-operation and Development, 2005.

Cahill, S. "Calculating the Rate of Decoupling for Crops under CAP/Oilseeds Reform." *Journal of Agricultural Economics* 48 (1997): 349-378.

Dewbre, J., J. Antón and W. Thompson. "The Transfer Efficiency and Trade effects of Direct Payments". *American Journal of Agricultural Economics* 83(2001): 1204-1214.

Gohin, A. "Assessing the Impacts of the 2003 CAP Mid Term Review: How Sensitive are they to the assumed Production Responsiveness to Agenda 2000 Direct Payments?" *Contributed Paper to the 8th Conference of Global Economic Analysis*. Lübeck, June 2005.

Goodwin, B.K. and A. Mishra. "Are Decoupled Payments really Decoupled?" *American Journal of Agricultural Economics*. In press, 2005a

Goodwin, B.K. and A, Mishra. " Another Look at Decoupling: Additional Evidence on the Production Effects of Direct Payments." *American Journal of Agricultural Economics*, 87(2005): 1200-1210.

Goodwin, B.K., A. Mishra and F. Ortalo-Magné. "What´s Wrong with Our Models of Agricultural Land Values?" *American Journal of Agricultural Economics* 85(2003): 744-752.

Hennessy, D. "The Production Effects of Agricultural Income Support Policies under Uncertainty." *American Journal of Agricultural Economics* 80(1998): 46-57.

Key, N., R.N. Lubowsky and M.J. Roberts. "Farm-Level Production Effects from Participation in Government Comodity Programs: Did the 1996 Fedaral Agricultural Improvement and Reform Act Make a Difference?" *American Journal of Agricultural Economics,* 87(2005): 1211-1219.

Moro, D. and P. Sckokai. "Modelling the CAP Arable Crop Regime in Italy: Degree of Decoupling and Impact of Agenda 2000." *Cahiers d´Economie et Sociologie Rurales,* 53(1999): 49-73.

OECD. "*Decoupling: A Conceptual Overview.*" Paris: Organization for Economic Co-operation and Development, 2001.

________. "*Market Effects of Crop Support Measures.*" Paris: Organization for Economic Co-operation and Development, 2001b.

________. "*Effects of quantitative constraints on the degree of decoupling of crop support measures.*" Paris: Organization for Economic Co-operation and Development, 2002.

________. "*Risk Effects of Crop Support Measures." Paris: Organization for Economic Co-operation and Development*, 2004.

________."*Decoupling –Illustrating some open questions on the production impacts of different agricultural policy instruments.*" Paris: Organization for Economic Co-operation and Development, 2005a.

________."*The Challenge of Decoupling Agricultural Support*". Website. Paris: OECD, 2005b. *http://www.oecd.org/document/47/0,2340,en_2649_33777_25110575_1_1_1_1,00.html*

Roberts, M.J., B. Kirwan and J. Hopkins. "The Incidence of Government Program Payments on Agricultural Land Rents: The Challenges of Identification." *American Journal of Agricultural Economics* 85(2003): 762-769.

Sckokai, P. and J. Antón. "The Degree of Decoupling of Area Payments for Arable Crops in the European Union". *American Journal of Agricultural Economics* 87(2005): 1220-1228.

United States Department of Agriculture: "Decoupled Payments in a Changing Policy Setting." Economic Research Service. *Agricultural Economic Report* 838.

In: International Agricultural Trade and Development
Editor: Dragan Miljkovic, pp. 129-160
ISBN: 978-1-60021-965-8

Chapter 8

THE EXTENT AND IMPACT OF FOOD NON-TARIFF BARRIERS IN RICH COUNTRIES

Scott Bradford
Brigham Young University
Provo, UT

ABSTRACT

International trade negotiations have significantly reduced food tariffs in rich countries, increasing the relative importance of non-tariff barriers (NTBs). Since reducing them often requires deeper integration, the resulting negotiations have been more fractious and difficult than earlier efforts. The Uruguay Round took almost eight years, by far the longest round on record. The Doha Round has faced trouble in Seattle, Cancun, and Hong Kong. Given these considerations, we need to weigh the benefits of reducing NTBs. If these benefits are small, then perhaps the time has come to place a lower priority on achieving deeper economic integration. On the other hand, if the barriers remain substantial, it could be worthwhile to invest considerable political capital in their elimination.

This paper presents a new method for estimating tariff equivalents of NTBs for final food goods in OECD countries. The analysis exploits detailed, comprehensive, and careful price comparisons: matched retail prices that the OECD collects on a regular basis in order to calculate purchasing power parity (PPP) estimates. Since this method does not identify policies, I strive to supplement the numbers by presenting preliminary information on possible sources of the barriers. I then use an applied general equilibrium model to provide a broad-brushed assessment of the impact of these NTBs. The results imply that NTBs significantly restrict trade in OECD nations and that removing them would bring large gains to them and to developing countries. Thus, this research implies that continued efforts to negotiate the reduction of NTBs will indeed exceed the costs.

1. INTRODUCTION

International trade negotiations over the past few decades have greatly reduced food[1] tariffs in rich nations, leading to a commensurate increase in the relative importance of food non-tariff barriers (NTBs). This has presented two challenges for trade analysts and negotiators alike. First, since NTBs cannot be measured as easily as tariffs, we have become less sure about how much food protection rich nations have. Second, since NTBs lack tariffs' transparency and are often embedded within complex domestic regulatory regimes, reducing these NTBs generally requires more work than reducing tariffs does.

This extra work stems not just from more difficult and technical subject matter but also from more intense political opposition to deeper integration. The Uruguay Round took almost eight years, the longest round on record, in part because it reduced NTBs more than any other previous round. The Doha Round, which seeks major opening in food sectors, suffered setbacks in Seattle and Cancun and had to settle for disappointing results in Hong Kong mainly because of a stalemate on agriculture. Food producer interests remain politically strong in rich nations, even to the point of possibly preventing a global trade deal that would bring great benefits to the world.

Despite this opposition, the desire for more integration still drives policy, and support for significant liberalization in agriculture and food products is widespread. Many nations continue to negotiate bilateral and regional agreements, which almost always call for substantial barrier reductions in food. The United States has moved beyond free trade agreements (FTAs) with Canada (CUSFTA) and Mexico (NAFTA) and concluded FTAs with at least 10 other nations. Several other deals are in the works. Even Japan has gotten into the FTA act lately, and there are signs there that it may soon begin to open agriculture as part of multilateral and bilateral deals.

Given strong support for, and opposition to, reducing food NTBs, we need to weigh the benefits of doing so. If they are small, then perhaps we should place a lower priority on achieving deeper economic integration. On the other hand, large potential gains could make it worthwhile to invest considerable political capital in the reduction of food NTBs.

Assessing the worth of food NTB reduction involves two tasks: 1) Reliably measuring the height of the NTBs, and 2) Using an economic model to infer the potential economic gains from their removal. Accordingly, I first present a new method for estimating tariff equivalents of NTBs for food final goods in OECD economies. The analysis exploits detailed, comprehensive, and careful price comparisons. I also present some preliminary information on the policies behind the estimates. Then, I use an applied general equilibrium (AGE) model to provide a broad-brushed assessment of the impact of these NTBs.[2] The results imply that food final goods NTBs greatly restrict trade in many OECD nations, especially in Japan, and that removing them would bring large gains to the world economy, for rich and poor countries alike. Thus, this research implies that continued efforts to negotiate the reduction of food NTBs will indeed exceed the costs.

---

[1] By "food" I mean agricultural products; fishery products; and processed food, drink, and tobacco products.

[2] This analysis gives an overview of the size and shape of the protection "forest", without detailed descriptions of individual "trees". Assessing the effects of particular policies, however, is important future work since it would probably facilitate the negotiations that this paper implies are worthwhile.

2. MEASURING NTBS

Nations can protect their markets in many different ways, making it hard to determine just how much protection different industries enjoy. As trade agreements have brought tariff reductions, governments have relied on a variety of more opaque but effective tools for insulating domestic food markets from foreign competition. For the purposes of this paper, I will define NTBs as follows: "A government policy or practice, other than a tariff, that raises the domestic price of a good above its import price". Note that this definition does not include subsidies, since they do not drive wedges between domestic and import prices, even though such subsidies could restrict imports. This definition encompasses barriers that drive wedges between prices. Such NTBs include quotas and the procedures used to administer them; regulations that limit or completely exclude imports, such as sanitary and phytosanitary restrictions, testing and certification standards, labeling and packaging requirements, and food additive rules; inadequate protection for trademarks and geographical indications; restrictive distribution systems; burdensome customs procedures; safeguards, including anti-dumping duties; biased government procurement; rules of origin; sanctions; and threats of protection. Even when not created with protectionist intent, these policies can inhibit international arbitrage, shield producers, and shrink the world economy.

2.1. Other Approaches to Measuring NTBs

This section discusses three prominent NTB measurement approaches that have been applied to food: 1) Counting NTBs and computing coverage ratios, 2) Inferring protection from trade flows, and 3) Inferring protection from price gaps. Then, this paper's method is discussed.

2.1.1. Compute NTB "Coverage Ratios"

The United Nations has developed "NTB coverage ratios" by computing what percentage of products within a sector has an NTB. Unfortunately, this measure does not take account of how restrictive each barrier is. One sector may have many products that are subject to minor NTBs. Another sector may have just a few products with very restrictive NTBs. The first sector would have a much higher NTB coverage ratio, while we would expect the second sector to actually have more restrictive trade barriers. Also, the UN's accounting probably does not cover all NTBs. For instance, these coverage ratios do not include inefficient customs procedures, even though they probably significantly restrict a wide variety of imports.

2.1.2. Infer Protection from Trade Flows

This approach seeks to measure the effects of NTBs by estimating their impact on the volume of trade in different industries. Researchers use models to predict trade patterns absent any barriers (on the basis of factors such as country size, distance from other economies, and factor endowments) and then use the gap between actual and predicted trade flows to infer protection. This method has the advantage of being able to capture the aggregate impact of all barriers combined, even ones not considered by NTB list-makers.[3] This approach, however, depends on having a trade model that can accurately account for all determinants of trade, besides barriers, which is an ambitious requirement. One wonders how much of the gap between predicted and actual flows results from barriers and how much results from model misspecification or data mismeasurement or both. The fact that one has to specify demand elasticities in order to convert the quantity shortfalls into tariff-equivalents introduces another source of uncertainty.

2.1.3. Price Gaps

Like the second approach, this method has the virtue of capturing the full impact of all NTBs. It has the additional virtues of not relying on any single model and providing tariff-equivalent measures directly. Although it has pitfalls, I believe that the price gap approach has the most promise for measuring NTBs. With many possible barriers to trade, I believe that one can best account for all of them by using the information that prices concisely convey.

The basic philosophy behind this approach is that barriers to arbitrage across national borders should be considered barriers to trade.[4] If international markets are integrated, sellers cannot raise domestic prices above prices that would attract arbitrage from abroad. One needs to carefully account for unavoidable costs associated with shipping goods between economies. Once one has done this, however, if a price gap exists for equivalent goods in two different nations, then one can conclude that the higher-priced market is protected. Moreover, one can use the price gap as a measure of the extent of protection. Thus, a single number can give the total effect of all trade barriers. These gaps may be caused in part by policies that are not explicitly designed to impede trade, such as overly harsh sanitary standards. No matter what the intent, however, which can be difficult to judge anyway, I presume that policies that segment national markets are trade barriers.[5]

The key to using this approach is obtaining appropriate price measures. Such efforts confront three challenges. The first is comparing prices of equivalent goods. Even if they have the same name, goods may have very different levels of quality. Thus, surveyors need to work hard to ensure comparability. Many researchers have used unit values as price proxies because they are widely available. These can provide reasonable estimates of price gaps at very detailed classification levels (eg, Harmonized System 10-digit), but, at higher levels of aggregation, unit values tend to be notoriously inexact measures of prices because of large quality differences in products.

A second challenge is using producer, rather than consumer, prices. Most price surveys are undertaken with a view to comparing costs to the consumer. In order to accurately gauge protection for producers, though, one should compare producer prices. Data gathered at the retail level include non-traded value added, such as distribution margins and transportation costs. These prices may therefore provide an inaccurate picture of protection since they

---

[3] One popular version of this approach is to use so-called gravity equations. For an excellent review of this methodology, see Frankel 1997.

[4] This does not depend on individual consumers engaging in arbitrage. Organized and well-informed trading companies and other international wholesalers can easily seize arbitrage opportunities.

[5] This notion corresponds to that of Knetter and Goldberg 1996, which argues that "A market is segmented if the location [sic] of the buyers and the sellers influences the terms of the transaction in a substantial way (i.e. by more than the marginal cost of physically moving the good from one location to another)." (pp 3-4.)

include elements that cannot be eliminated through arbitrage. The price of a pound of coffee purchased in a supermarket in Tokyo may be higher than a pound of the same brand of coffee purchased in New York, either because trade barriers raise the wholesale price of coffee or because the costs of distributing coffee in Tokyo are higher, or both. One who seeks to isolate the role of trade barriers needs to compare producer, rather than consumer, prices.

A third challenge relates to the comprehensiveness of coverage. Samples of a few products gathered at selective retail outlets may not be representative of the full array of goods sold. Also, many international surveys are undertaken to establish differences in the cost of living experienced by business executives and their families. These naturally focus on a set of products that are not representative of all purchases.

2.2. This Paper's Method[6]

Other studies have used price differentials as evidence of protection and to estimate the benefits of integration.[7] This section discusses how I have tried to overcome the challenges mentioned above, in order to produce improved estimates of NTB food final goods protection and its effects. I use data in which every effort has been made to ensure comprehensive coverage and comparability. In addition, I have endeavored to compare producer prices by eliminating the effects of distribution margins. The data is also analyzed at a fairly disaggregated level, to mitigate weighting problems.

I start with carefully matched retail prices that the OECD collects on a regular basis in order to calculate purchasing power parity (PPP) estimates. With the cooperation of member governments, OECD researchers build on the resources, expertise, and data possessed by various national consumer price index (CPI) agencies and sample prices of over 3000 final goods, about half of which are in food. They make every effort to compare equivalent products across countries. For the most part, they rely on identical brand names or exact descriptions of the items to be priced. When they cannot find appropriate matches based on descriptions, researchers from the nations involved travel abroad to determine which items would be most appropriate matches for the items in their country. This has occurred with grain, some vegetables, and tobacco. The researchers also call upon the expertise of producers, trade associations, and buyers for large stores in order to determine matches.

Prices are collected from many markets and outlets at different times during the year in order to obtain a single annual, national average (World Bank 1993, p10). Also, prices of the average-sized purchase for that country are compared. After collecting the data, apparent mismatches in quality are dealt with either by refining the specifications or discarding the data (OECD 1995, p5). This method does not produce perfect data, but the scale of resources expended on accurate matching indicates that these are excellent measures of price differences for equivalent products.

The researchers aggregate the most detailed price data into categories called "basic headings". These are defined as "groups of similar well-defined commodities for which a sample of products can be selected that are both representative of their type and of the

[6] See Bradford and Lawrence 2004 and Bradford 2003 for more discussion of the methodology and data presented in this paper and for welfare analyses of total protection.

[7] See in particular Hufbauer et al 2002.

purchases made in participating countries" (OECD 1995, p5). Thus, a basic heading should not be too broad or too narrow. It should not be so broad that very different products are compared; it should not be so narrow that few economies in the sample sell it. For instance, seaweed is too narrow, and food is too broad.

In multilateral comparisons, one usually cannot find products that are representative of the category and typical of what is bought in every country, since consumers in different nations buy different mixes of products. Thus, while most items are priced in most or all of the nations, not every product in the sample is priced in each country. To be included in the sample, a product needs to be a "representative product" in at least one country and it must be sold in large enough quantities in at least one other country so as to be price-able. A "representative product" is one that accounts for a large share of that country's expenditure on that basic heading. For instance, cheddar is a representative product for the cheese basic heading in France but not for Italy. Cheddar cheese, however, is price-able in Italy. As long as nations price their own major products and a share of all other products, relative prices for each product and country can be calculated indirectly as well as directly. For details on how the prices are combined into one average price for each country see Eurostat-OECD PPP Programme 1996. There are about 200 basic headings in the whole sample. I obtained unpublished basic heading price data for 1999 and trimmed the sample to about 50 traded food goods. All prices were converted to US dollars using the 1999 exchange rates. See Table 1 for the list of categories.

The consumer price measures were converted to producer prices using data on margins—wholesale trade, retail trade, transportation, and taxes—which come from national input-output tables.[8] I did so for nine countries: Australia, Belgium, Canada, Germany, Italy, Japan, the Netherlands, the United Kingdom (UK), and the United States (US). Although I wanted to include more nations, such as France, the availability of detailed margins data determined which ones became part of the sample. I matched these margins with the OECD retail price data and derived estimates of producer prices by peeling off the relevant margins. Thus,

$$[1]\quad p_{ij}^{p} = \frac{p_{ij}^{c}}{1+m_{ij}},$$

p_{ij}^{p}: the producer price of good *i* in country *j*,
p_{ij}^{c}: the consumer price of good *i* in country *j*, as taken from the OECD data,
m_{ij}: the margin for good *i* in country *j*, as taken from the national IO table.

Unfortunately, margins data only become available with a considerable time lag.[9] The producer price estimates were therefore obtained by assuming that distribution margins were the same percentage of overall value-added as they were in the most recent year for which data were available.

[8] Roningen and Yeats 1976 also use retail prices and adjust for taxes and transport costs, but they do not adjust for wholesale and retail trade margins, which significantly outweigh taxes and transportation.

[9] The margins data come from the following years: Australia, 1995; Belgium, 1990; Canada, 1990; Germany, 1993; Italy, 1992; Japan, 1995; Netherlands, 1990; UK, 1990; and US,1992.

Table 1.

Rice	Fresh fruit
Flour and other cereals	Dried fruit and nuts
Bread	Frozen and preserved fruit and juices
Other bakery products	Fresh vegetables
Pasta products	Dried vegetables
Other cereal products	Frozen vegetables
Fresh, frozen and chilled beef	Preserved vegetables, juices, soups
Fresh, frozen and chilled veal	Potatoes and other tuber vegetables
Fresh, frozen and chilled pork	Potato products
Fresh, etc. lamb, mutton and goat	Raw and refined sugar
Fresh, frozen and chilled poultry	Coffee and instant coffee
Delicatessen	Tea and other infusions
Other meat preparations, extracts	Cocoa excluding cocoa preparations
Other fresh, frozen, chilled meat	Jams, jellies, honey and syrups
Fresh, frozen or deep-frozen fish	Chocolate and cocoa preparations
Dried, smoked or salted fish	Confectionery
Fresh, frozen, deep-frozen seafood	Edible ice and ice-cream
Preserved or processed fish & seafood	Salt, spices, sauces, condiments
Fresh, pasteurised, sterilised milk	Mineral water
Condensed, powdered milk	Other soft drinks nec
Other milk products excluding cheese	Spirits and liqueurs
Processed and unprocessed cheese	Wine (not fortified or sparkling)
Eggs and egg products	Beer
Butter	Other wines and alcoholic beverages
Margarine	Cigarettes
Edible oils	Other tobacco products
Other animal and vegetable fats	

Producer prices allow us to get a sense of which industries in which nations have the lowest prices, but inferring the extent of insulation from foreign competition requires one more step: taking account of transport costs from one nation's market to another. A foreign good must travel from the foreign factory to the foreign border and then to the domestic border in order to compete with a domestic good.[10] Thus, one cannot infer protection simply by comparing producer prices. The domestic producer price must be compared to the import price of the foreign good. Such import price data that matches the producer prices in this data does not exist independently and needs to be inferred. This is done by combining data on export margins, also available from national input-output tables, with international transport costs.[11]

I could only get detailed data on international transport costs for Australia and the US. Each reports import values for detailed commodities on both a basis that includes insurance and freight (cif) and one that does not—so-called free on board (fob). The cif/fob ratio is a good measure of all the costs of shipping goods from abroad to these economies. The ratios

[10] For a discussion of the importance of export margins, see Rousslang and To 1993.

[11] I have export margins for all countries except the UK, for which I used the Netherlands export margins. Export margins tend not to vary much by country, so I feel confident that using the Netherlands margins does not compromise the results.

for both nations are small, so that the gap between the two is also small: the average for all products for the US is 1.05, while the overall average for Australia it is 1.09. Thus, for each detailed sector, the average of the two cif/fob ratios is used as an estimate for the international transport cost for that product for all the countries.

These data on export margins and international transport costs are used to compute import prices for each product and country, as follows. Adding the export margins to the producer prices enables one to calculate the export price for each product in each country. The lowest export price plus the common international transport cost is the import price. Thus, the export price is given by:

$$[2]\quad p_{ij}^{e} = p_{ij}^{p}(1 + em_{ij}),$$

p_{ij}^{e}: the export price of good i for country j,
em_{ij}: the export margin of good i for country j.

The import price is then given by:

$$[3]\quad p_{i}^{I} = p_{iM}^{e}(1 + tr_{i}),$$

p_{i}^{I} : the import price of good i (the same for each nation),
tr_{i}: the international transport margin for good i,
$p_{iM}^{e} = \min(p_{i1}^{e}, p_{i2}^{e}, \ldots, p_{i9}^{e})$: the minimum of the 9 export prices.

The ratio of each country's producer price to the import price gives us an initial measure of protection, pr_{ij}^{IN} :

$$[4]\qquad pr_{ij}^{IN} = \frac{p_{ij}^{p}}{p_{i}^{I}}.$$

For a given good, these measures will differ from true protection if all of the countries in the sample have barriers to imports for that good. For such goods, the calculated import price will exceed the true import price to the extent that the low cost producer has barriers against imports. This will bias the protection estimates downward. By the same token, if just one of the nine has no barriers to imports in that good, then pr_{ij}^{IN} will approximate true protection, because, in this case, the price in the free trading country will approximate the import price. Since the sample includes Australia, Canada, and the US, which are fairly free traders, the low price in the sample approximates the import price the great majority of the time.

Nevertheless, data on trade taxes are used to correct, at least partially, for the possible downward bias. These tariff data come from the OECD tariff database, which gives most favored nation tariff rates for member countries at the Harmonized 6-digit level. The final measure of total protection, pr_{ij}^{TOT}, is given by:

[5] $pr_{ij}^{TOT} = max(pr_{ij}^{IN}, 1 + tar_{ij})$,

tar$_{ij}$: the tariff rate for good *i* in country *j*.

I simply use the fact that tariffs provide a lower bound on protection. If the initial measures do not exceed the overall tariff rate, then that tariff rate is used as the measure of protection. This happened about one-third of the time. After this correction, the only time that these protection measures will be biased downward is when all nations in the sample have NTBs against the rest of the world.

These measures provide estimates of the protective effect of all kinds of barriers—tariffs and NTBs alike. For our purposes, we want to focus on the impact of NTBs alone, so I perform one final, simple modification. Tariffs are subtracted from these total protection numbers. Mathematically, NTB protection is given by

[6] $pr_{ij}^{NTB} = pr_{ij}^{TOT} - tar_{ij} = \max(pr_{ij}^{IN} - tar_{ij}, 1)$.

Note that, since we measure protection as a ratio of the world price, a value of 1 indicates no protection. Thus, I conclude that there is no NTB protection whenever $pr_{ij}^{IN} - tar_{ij} < 1 \Rightarrow pr_{ij}^{IN} < 1 + tar_{ij}$, that is, whenever the percentage by which the producer price exceeds the import price does not exceed the tariff rate.

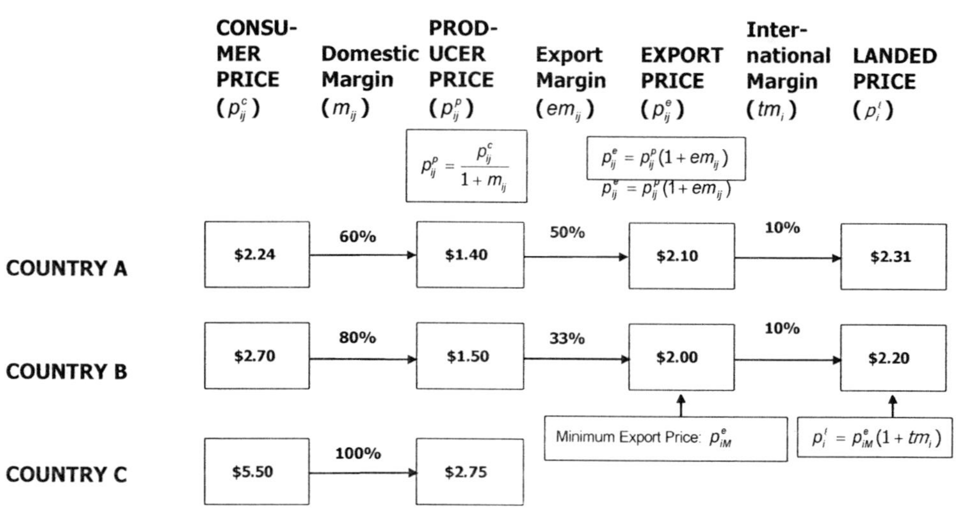

➔ NTB Protection in C = $\frac{p_{iC}^p}{p_i^l} - tar_{ij} = \frac{2.75}{2.20} - tar_{ij} = 1.25 - tar_{ij}$, ie, (25% - tariff rate), if the tariff rate is 25% or less. Otherwise, NTB protection is inferred to be zero.

Note: *i* indexes products, and *j* indexes countries.

Figure 1. NTB Protection Calculation: Schematic Example

Figure 1 shows a schematic example that illustrates this methodology. Suppose that there are three countries, with consumer prices as shown: Country A with the lowest and Country C with the highest. C's consumer price is nearly 2.5 times that of A, but such a facile comparison can mislead. After peeling off domestic distribution costs for this good, the ratio of C's producer price to A's is lower, though still large. As is often the case in reality, in this example, the country with the high consumer price also has the highest percentage domestic distribution margin. Converting to producer prices gets us closer to our goal, since these provide a clearer indication of how efficient producers in different nations are. Still, as discussed above, a straight comparison of producer prices would overstate protection, since doing so would not take account of the costs required to sell in foreign markets. So, to each of the producer prices, we add the unavoidable export margins and the international transport costs. Note that, because of its relatively small export margin, Country B ends up with the lower border price, even though its consumer and producer prices are higher than A's. In the end, the NTB protection level for C that we calculate is (25% - the tariff rate) (if the tariff rate is lower than that), a much smaller gap than that between the underlying consumer and producer prices.

3. Mary and Assessment

3.1. Key Characteristics

I believe that measures using this method, while not perfect, will shed useful new light on NTB protection because they possess, to a large degree, four key characteristics: completeness, comprehensiveness, accuracy, and international comparability.

3.1.1. Completeness

Using price gaps enables one, in principle, to capture the combined effects of **all** NTBs, which can include any number of regulations and bureaucratic procedures. For example, a UN study analyzed how excess paperwork and cumbersome customs procedures impede the international flow of goods. The study points out that, in addition to direct costs, these regulations impose indirect costs, such as losses due to "deterioration or pilferage" while cargo is waiting to be cleared, or the "strong disincentive for potential exporters" imposed by complicated procedures. (See United Nations Conference on Trade and Development (1992).) The study estimated that these barriers imposed costs that averaged 10 to 15%, on top of any other trade barriers. Protection measures that rely on lists of individual barriers, such as the UN's own NTB measures, will tend to overlook subtle but real barriers such as these. This paper's method, however, will capture the protective impact of such barriers if they raise domestic prices above the import price implied by the sample.

3.1.2. Comprehensiveness

These measures cover all traded final goods, instead of a small subset thereof. Some other studies (such as Hufbauer and Elliott 1994) have limited their coverage to sectors in which protection had been previously thought to exist, without testing whether other sectors might enjoy well-disguised insulation from foreign competition. The approach in this paper allows one to construct a more comprehensive picture of final goods NTB protection in these nations. By the same token, this method does exclude non-final goods, which account for most output and trade.

3.1.3. Accuracy

Accuracy stems from comparing actual prices of identical or equivalent goods. Differences in quality have bedeviled attempts to use prices, except for certain homogeneous goods. The data here, on the other hand, have resulted from intensive multilateral efforts to correct for quality differences.

3.1.4. International Comparability

Many other estimates have only been derived for a single country at a time, making it difficult to rank economies in terms of openness. These measures use the same data and apply the same method to each country in the sample, thus allowing one to make such rankings, for individual products, for aggregated categories, and for each country as a whole.

3.2. Possible Concerns

3.2.1. Imperfect Competition

Is it possible that market power could lead to estimates that do not really reflect NTBs? I argue that this is not so. If the domestic producer price exceeds the prevailing import price by more than the tariff rate, an NTB must support that gap, no matter how those prices came to be. Market power does not change this fact. With market power, a trade barrier may endogenously change prices, but the fact remains: an un-arbitraged gap between the domestic price and the tariff-inclusive import price cannot persist without NTBs that segment the domestic and world markets, and the gap measures the amount of NTB protection.

3.2.2. Terms of Trade Effects

A related concern is the impact of terms of trade effects, for which this method makes no adjustment. If an NTB drives down the import price, should one measure NTB protection with respect to the NTB-ridden import price or the free trade import price? For instance, suppose that the latter is 1.00 and that a country imposes an NTB of 0.2 that drives the domestic price to 1.10 and the import price to 0.90. Is the amount of NTB protection 22% $(\frac{1.1}{0.9}-1)$ or 10% $(\frac{1.1}{1}-1)$? One could make an argument for either, but this paper's method presumes that the amount of NTB protection is 22%, because that is the size of the wedge. With the barrier in place, domestic consumers have to pay 22% more than people who can buy the good at world prices. Consider a more extreme case. Suppose in the above example that the domestic price remains at 1.00, while the import price gets driven to 0.80. It seems that one should not conclude that NTB protection is zero simply because the domestic price did not move; after all, the domestic price is 25% higher than the world price. In practice, the terms of trade rarely, if ever, move as much as in the above examples and will usually not matter. Even if one does want to correct for terms of trade effects, one does not observe the free trade import price, so speculation would drive the correction, and it would introduce a fair amount of uncertainty into the measures. Thus, for theoretical and practical reasons, there is no correction for terms of trade effects.

3.2.3. Dumping

Dumping can possibly bias the inferred import price downward, which would bias the protection measures upward. While protectionists make much of dumping, true cases of dumping in which firms sell goods overseas below cost are rare to non-existent. Most economists would agree that, the vast majority of the time, policymakers use anti-dumping duties as alternative ways to protect inefficient industries, not as justified defenses against artificially low prices and the predatory threats they pose. Even if such dumping occurs, and the resulting import price is lower than otherwise, that does not invalidate it as a proper benchmark. Again, gaps between domestic and import prices only result from barriers, even if the import prices are artificially low.

3.2.4. Demand Differences

One may wonder whether these measures are valid if consumers in different economies have different demands. The question arises: If Country A's citizens have a higher demand for good *X* than do Country B's citizens, won't that drive up the price of good *X* in Country A in the absence of trade barriers? Answer: Only if there is a barrier in Country A that allows such a gap to emerge. If Country A and Country B are truly integrated, then good *X* will have one single demand curve, and the price will be the same everywhere. Demand differences without barriers cannot sustain price gaps.

3.2.5. Price vs. Quantity Effects

Finally, in deriving these estimates, I realize that there is no clear connection between tariff equivalents and the amount by which imports are reduced. Quantity changes depend on market structure and such key parameters as the elasticities of supply and of demand. Thus, a high NTB on a good with a low elasticity of demand may reduce imports by less than a small NTB on a good with a high elasticity of demand. I do not purport, however, to analyze prices and quantities at the same time. In order to assess the impact of the barriers on quantities, and thus on welfare, one would need a model of the particular sector in question. I claim that the cleanest, most effective way to measure NTB protection is to derive tariff equivalents and leave quantity and welfare analysis for the next step.

4. The Extent of NTB Protection

Table 2 presents the NTB data for the nine nations. Again, these are reported as the ratio of the domestic producer price to the world price. Thus, a reading of 2.00 would be a protection rate of 100%. As mentioned above, the measures were constructed using 50 categories, but, to facilitate the presentation, I have aggregated up to 13 sectors, which correspond to the GTAP sectors that will be used in the AGE analysis below. The table also reports weighted geometric means for each country. I used the value of consumption as weights in constructing these means. Two factors motivated this choice: 1) Protection skews the value of consumption less than protection skews the value of production or of imports, and 2) The OECD reports the value of consumption along with its price data, so consumption data that exactly matches the protection aggregation was available. While these expenditure shares vary by country, the first column of the table presents median expenditure shares to indicate the importance of each sector.

Table 2.

Fresh Vegetables, Fruit, Nuts	8.2	1.055	1.031	1.046	1.257	1.036	2.048	1.000	1.317	1.203
Other Crops: Garden Products	2.6	1.000	2.231	3.227	1.956	1.326	2.478	1.197	2.529	1.524
Live Animals: Pets	1.9	1.000	1.081	1.000	1.321	1.113	2.305	1.000	1.473	1.000
Other Ag Products: Eggs	0.7	1.429	1.098	1.000	1.020	1.000	1.000	1.072	1.657	1.000
Fresh Fish	1.9	1.137	1.181	1.114	1.206	1.000	1.398	1.000	1.056	1.301
Beef, Sheep, Goat, Horse Meat Products	4.1	1.000	1.563	1.021	2.140	1.259	5.332	1.773	2.026	1.001
Other Meat Products: Poultry, Pork	8.7	1.010	1.165	1.003	1.346	1.085	2.600	1.157	1.256	1.004
Vegetable Oils and Fats	1.0	1.313	1.472	1.204	1.249	1.087	2.348	1.000	1.000	1.447
Dairy Products	9.5	1.274	1.164	1.237	1.022	1.065	1.759	1.056	1.081	1.145
Processed Rice	0.3	1.000	1.067	1.000	1.028	1.023	2.773	1.000	1.000	1.119
Sugar	0.4	1.000	1.157	1.052	1.000	1.000	1.216	1.199	1.000	1.000
Other Food Products	27.7	1.083	1.194	1.042	1.053	1.044	2.048	1.013	1.117	1.071
Beverages and Tobacco Products	28.5	1.488	1.012	1.166	1.004	1.009	1.519	1.047	1.234	1.063
WEIGHTED GEOMETRIC MEANS		1.202	1.131	1.098	1.116	1.062	1.908	1.069	1.219	1.073
Fresh Vegetables, Fruit, Nuts		0.101	0.097	0.068	0.074	0.126	0.082	0.111	0.076	0.059
Other Crops: Garden Products		0.014	0.035	0.025	0.037	0.026	0.029	0.046	0.023	0.004
Live Animals: Pets		0.037	0.023	0.021	0.014	0.006	0.000	0.019	0.018	0.036
Other Ag Products: Eggs		0.007	0.005	0.008	0.016	0.009	0.006	0.005	0.004	0.007
Fresh Fish		0.016	0.032	0.021	0.019	0.048	0.085	0.012	0.012	0.009
Beef, Sheep, Goat, Horse Meat Products		0.041	0.036	0.049	0.028	0.098	0.020	0.041	0.029	0.092
Other Meat Products: Poultry, Pork		0.086	0.148	0.082	0.146	0.101	0.044	0.116	0.087	0.067
Vegetable Oils and Fats		0.010	0.011	0.013	0.006	0.037	0.004	0.011	0.005	0.008
Dairy Products		0.097	0.095	0.095	0.089	0.126	0.045	0.121	0.065	0.069
Processed Rice		0.003	0.002	0.001	0.001	0.008	0.048	0.003	0.003	0.002
Sugar		0.003	0.004	0.003	0.004	0.007	0.002	0.006	0.002	0.006
Other Food Products		0.299	0.259	0.311	0.277	0.233	0.406	0.274	0.210	0.342
Beverages and Tobacco Products		0.285	0.253	0.304	0.288	0.174	0.229	0.236	0.466	0.299

These results imply that Canada, Italy, the Netherlands, and the US have the lowest food NTB barriers, averaging less than 10%. Australia, Belgium, Germany, and the UK rank in the middle, ranging from 11% to 22%. Japan is a huge outlier: its food NTBs average more than 90%, and Japan's NTBs are the highest in each category listed except garden products (mostly houseplants and planting products) and eggs. Overall, this analysis suggests that there is nontrivial NTB food protection in industrial nations, but Japan's barriers loom very large. Much work needs to be done to bring greater transparency and openness to Japan's food markets.

Looking at individual sectors, these results imply that, in addition to Japan, Germany, the UK, and the US have significant NTBs in fresh fruits and vegetables. As one would expect, the data show Australia, Canada, and the US with low barriers in the two meat sectors, while the Europeans and Japanese have extensive NTBs. In dairy products, in addition to Japan, Australia, Belgium, Canada, and the US seem to have nontrivial NTBs. Belgium and the UK have higher barriers than average in the large processed food sector, but, once again, Japan's barriers loom much larger than anyone else's. The beverages and tobacco sector probably has the most measurement error because of the difficulties involved in correcting for large taxes. With this caveat in mind, we have some evidence that Australia, Canada, and the UK join Japan with significant barriers.

One may wonder about the sugar estimate for the US: 0% NTB protection. Three factors contribute to this result. First, Australia is the low-price producer sample, but its import price is probably higher than the true world price, biasing sugar protection estimates downward. Second, to make its sugar restrictions more WTO-compatible, the US has converted its quotas to tariff-rate quotas, which means that its official tariff rate is high (about 75%; see Table 3 below). The tariff rate ends up exceeding the inferred NTB price gap, resulting in a finding of no NTB protection. Finally, the underlying price data only includes sugar sold to final demand, not sugar sold to food processing firms; the price gaps for final demand sugar are probably lower than the gaps for sugar sold to produers.

Table 3.

	AUS	BEL	CAN	GER	ITA	JAP	NET	UK	US
Vegetables, fruit, nuts	1.009	1.119	1.053	1.119	1.119	1.098	1.119	1.119	1.064
Crops n.e.c.	1.000	1.092	1.054	1.092	1.092	1.003	1.092	1.092	1.020
Live Animals	1.106	1.058	1.097	1.058	1.058	1.074	1.058	1.058	1.043
Other Ag Products	1.000	1.060	1.044	1.060	1.060	1.220	1.060	1.060	1.092
Fishing	1.000	1.122	1.003	1.122	1.122	1.055	1.122	1.122	1.005
Bovine cattle, sheep and goat, horse meat products	1.000	1.000	1.192	1.000	1.000	1.497	1.000	1.000	1.108
Meat products n.e.c.	1.015	1.158	1.079	1.136	1.125	1.128	1.122	1.139	1.060
Vegetable oils and fats	1.052	1.136	1.105	1.127	1.091	1.100	1.174	1.146	1.065
Dairy products	1.006	1.086	1.099	1.088	1.110	1.250	1.086	1.083	1.082
Processed rice	1.000	1.120	1.006	1.120	1.120	1.000	1.120	1.120	1.054
Sugar	1.048	1.150	1.095	1.150	1.150	1.553	1.150	1.150	1.745
Food products n.e.c.	1.038	1.145	1.059	1.132	1.142	1.167	1.136	1.137	1.040
Beverages and tobacco products	1.070	1.384	1.141	1.403	1.507	1.163	1.430	1.317	1.126
WEIGHTED GEOMETRIC MEANS	1.036	1.190	1.096	1.198	1.171	1.149	1.186	1.210	1.082
TRANSPARENCY: Average Tariff/Total Protection	0.153	0.593	0.495	0.630	0.735	0.141	0.729	0.490	0.529

For comparison purposes, Table 3 provides tariff data. Not surprisingly, tariffs are generally lower and more tightly distributed. The Europeans have the highest average tariffs in food. One can use the tariff and NTB numbers to calculate a measure of "protection transparency", which is defined as the ratio of tariff protection to total protection (which is simply the sum of NTB and tariff protection). These data imply that Japan and Australia have the most opaque food protection regimes, while Italy and the Netherlands have the most transparent.

Obstfeld and Rogoff 2000 concludes that "a recurring theme here is that the markets for most 'traded' goods are not fully integrated, and segmentation due to various trade costs can be quite pervasive. In fact, the spectrum of goods subject to low trade costs may be very narrow." Our data provide support for this view in the realm of food.

5. Policies Behind the Price Gaps

These NTB estimates may help policy makers in one of two ways. First, for known NTBs, these measures provide estimates of the extent to which those NTBs actually restrict trade. Thus, these results may provide useful information to trade negotiators as they decide how to efficiently focus their efforts on freeing up trade. Second, some sectors that have not reached the trade negotiation agenda may, in fact, enjoy significant disguised NTB protection that is worth negotiating down. This research can help to flag such sectors.

To illustrate how these results can help in the first way mentioned, Table 4 shows possible barriers for some of the NTB gaps, though much more work along these lines needs to be done. I have drawn on the *EU Market Access Database*, the USTR's 2000 *Report on Foreign Trade Barriers*, and 2000 WTO *Trade Policy Review* for the European Union, the US, and Japan. A more detailed analysis would reveal more policies behind the NTBs. Also, for any given price gap, the policies listed may not be major causes, but they are initial candidates.

Looking back at Table 2, there are a number of NTBs for which there are no listed possible policies. In these cases, more detailed research may reveal particular sources of the gaps, which might then become subject to negotiation. Also, any of these gaps, as well the ones which have listed policies, could result from burdensome customs procedures and other administrative friction, as discussed above. Thus, efforts by trade negotiators to remove such widespread sand from the wheels of trade could potentially have large benefits across many sectors and economies.

6. The Welfare Effects of Integration

To provide insights into the importance of NTBs, this section simulates their removal. For eight of the nine nations, the simulations compare real incomes in the world as it is with one in which the NTBs are eliminated. (Unfortunately, data problems prevent Belgium from being included.) I use an AGE model based on one developed by Harrison, Rutherford, and Tarr (HRT).[12] The model has considerable country and sectoral detail: 16 regions and 33 sectors (See Table 5).[13] The model also allows for both increasing returns to scale and

[12] The model is based on the computer code provided by Glenn Harrison, Thomas F. Rutherford, and David Tarr. Their code is available for public access at http://theweb.badm.sc.edu/glenn/ur_pub.htm and was used in their 1995, 1996, and 1997 articles.

[13] The underlying data come from Version 5 (1997) of the Global Trade Analysis Project (GTAP) database.

dynamic adjustment of the capital stock. The next two subsections describe the model and then report the simulation results.

Table 4.

	PANEL A	
EU		**SOURCE**
Fresh Vegetables, Fruit, Nuts	Restrictive banana trade regime	USTR
Other Crops: Garden Products	Unreasonable water solubility standards for fertilizers	USTR
Live Animals: Pets	Animal products have to be sourced from EU-approved 3rd country establishments	USTR
Other Ag Products: Eggs	Animal products have to be sourced from EU-approved 3rd country establishments	USTR
Fresh Fish	Animal products have to be sourced from EU-approved 3rd country establishments	USTR
	Italy has overly strict interpretation of sanitary requirements	USTR
Beef, Sheep, Goat, Horse Meat Products	Animal products have to be sourced from EU-approved 3rd country establishments	USTR
	Ban on hormone beef	USTR
	Italy has overly strict interpretation of sanitary requirements	USTR
	Beef labeling requirementsw	WTO
Other Meat Products: Poultry, Pork	Animal products have to be sourced from EU-approved 3rd country establishments	USTR
	Ban on anti-microbial treatments for poultry	USTR
Dairy Products	Animal products have to be sourced from EU-approved 3rd country establishments	USTR
Other Food Products	Modern biotech products face lengthy and unpredictable approval process	USTR
	Standards for flour	WTO
Beverages and Tobacco Products	Strict standards on wine-making practices for imported wine	USTR
	Alcohol and tobacco labeling requirements	USTR
US		
Fresh Fish	Certification requirements for yellowfin tuna	EU
Beverages and Tobacco Products	Burdensome wine labelling requirements that vary by state	EU

Table 4. (Continued)

	PANEL B	
JAPAN		**SOURCE**
Fresh Vegetables, Fruit, Nuts	Overly restrictive sanitary standards	EU
	Complex regulations	EU
	Excessive fumigation	USTR
	Potato ban	USTR
Other Crops: Garden Products	Overly restrictive sanitary standards	EU
Fresh Fish	Quotas	EU
Beef, Sheep, Goat, Horse Meat Products	Restrictive Safeguards; Overreaction to Mad Cow	USTR
Other Meat Products: Poultry, Pork	Excessive bird flu quarantines for poultry	USTR
Processed Rice	Import ban	
Other Food Products	Licensing and distribution barriers for imports	USTR
	Food additive restrictions	USTR
	Quota for chocolate	WTO
Beverages and Tobacco Products	Burdensome wine testing	EU
	Term "mineral water" not backed by legal obligations in Japan	EU
	High taxes on beer and spirits	USTR
CANADA		
Fresh Vegetables, Fruit, Nuts	Overly restrictive sanitary standards	EU
	Packaging requirements	EU
Vegetable oils and fats	Rules on coloring of margarine	EU
Dairy Products	Inspection requirements	EU
Other Food Products	Different labeling requirements across provinces	EU
Beverages and Tobacco Products	Discriminatory price controls, taxes, listing procedures, delivery regulations	EU
AUSTRALIA		
Fresh Vegetables, Fruit, Nuts	Overly strict quarantine laws	EU
Other Ag Products: Eggs	Overly strict quarantine laws	EU
Fresh Fish	Overly strict quarantine laws	EU
Vegetable oils and fats	Overly strict quarantine laws	EU
Dairy Products	Overly strict quarantine laws	EU
Other Food Products	Overly strict quarantine laws	EU

6.1. Description of the Model

Some sectors are assumed to have constant returns to scale. Other sectors, though, are modeled with increasing returns to scale and imperfect competition.[14] In these sectors, there is firm-level product differentiation, with output being a composite of varieties. Firms have fixed costs and constant marginal costs, meaning that reducing the number of firms leads to

[14] See Table 6 for the sectors and the mark-ups used. This table also presents alternative mark-ups from the GTAP model. The results are robust to the set of mark-ups used.

rationalization gains. These firms compete using quantity conjectures, with entry and exit that drive profits to zero.

Table 5.

33 SECTORS	**16 REGIONS**
Fruits, Nuts, Vegetables	Australia
Other Crops	Japan
Other Agriculture	Korea
Live Animals	China
Other Animal Products	Rest of Asia
Fish	Canada
Coal, Gas, Oil	United States
Other Minerals	Brazil
Bovine Cattle, Sheep, Goat, and Horse Products	Rest of Latin America
Other Meat Products	Germany
Vegetable Oils and Fats	Italy
Dairy Products	Netherlands
Processed Rice	United Kingdom
Sugar	Rest of Europe
Other Food Products	Middle East
Beverages and Tobacco Products	Rest of World
Textiles	
Wearing Apparel	
Leather Goods	
Lumber and Wood Products	
Pulp, Paper Products, Publishing	
Coal and Petroleum Products	
Chemicals, Plastics,and Rubber	
Non-metallic Mineral Products	
Primary Ferrous Metals	
Non-ferrous Metals	
Fabricated Metal Products	
Motor Vehicles and Parts	
Electronic Equipment	
Machinery and Equipment	
Other Manufacturing Products	
Trade and Transport Services	
Other Services	
Investment Good	

Sectors in bold are the food sectors for which we inserted our protection measures.
Underlined sectors are the ones which are assumed to have increasing returns to scale.

Dynamics are incorporated by allowing the capital stock to vary in response to changes in the rate of return caused by liberalization. If the rate of return increases, investment increases the capital stock until its return is driven back down to the long-run equilibrium. The results, therefore, reflect the model's predictions for what happens after the capital stock has changed enough to return the price of capital to its original level. The capital adjustment process is not modeled, and the time horizon implied by these results depends on how long one thinks it takes capital to respond to interest rate differentials. The model ignores the consumption foregone by the increased investment, which may overstate the estimated benefits. On the other hand, the model ignores any impact of growth on productivity and innovation, which leads to an underestimate of the gains.

6.1.1. Production Structure

Production involves the use of intermediate goods and five factors—capital, skilled labor, unskilled labor, land, and natural resources. Only capital can move across national boundaries; all factors can move freely across sectors. Value added in each sector has a CES (constant elasticity of substitution) production function. This formulation means that, within each sector, the elasticity of substitution between any two of the factors is the same. I use HRT's values for these elasticities, which they estimated econometrically using US time series data from 1947 to 1982 and using the same functional form as is used in this AGE model. In their estimates, however, they used only three factors—capital, labor, and land—instead of five. See Table 6 for these estimates and their standard errors. The production function for intermediates and the value-added composite is Leontief.[15]

6.1.2. Demand Structure

On the demand side, each region has a representative consumer and a single government agent, each of whom has a nested CES utility function and practices multi-stage budgeting. At the top level, demand across the 33 sectors is Cobb-Douglas. Consumers first decide how much to spend on each of the 33 aggregate goods, given total income and aggregate prices. Each of these goods is a CES composite of domestic output and an import composite, which are imperfect substitutes. In this second level, consumers divide spending between the domestic and import good by maximizing a CES utility function subject to the total spending they have allocated to that sector and given the aggregate prices in that sector. At the third level, the model invokes the Armington assumption in that imports of the same good from different economies are assumed to be imperfect substitutes. Preferences across these different goods from different economies are given by a CES utility function. At this third level, consumers choose quantities of each import subject to the amount they have budgeted for aggregate imports at the second level and subject to the various prices. I follow HRT and set the elasticity of substitution across import varieties, σ_{MM}, equal to eight and the elasticity of substitution between the import composite and the domestic good, σ_{DM}, equal to four. These elasticities affect the magnitude of the results. Higher values of these parameters lead to greater substitution in response to price reductions and, in general, higher welfare gains from liberalization. Roughly speaking, cutting these elasticities in half reduces the gains by 10% to 50%, depending on the region and the simulation. Similarly, doubling these elasticities increases the estimated gains by about 20% to 100%. Even such wide changes in the calibration, however, do not change any of the main conclusions.

[15] Relaxing this assumption does not significantly change the results.

Table 6.

SECTOR	Factor Substitution Elasticities	Lerner Indices* HRT	GATT
Fruits, Nuts, Vegetables	0.945 (0.041)	0	0
Other Agriculture	0.945 (0.041)	0	0
Other Crops	0.945 (0.041)	0	0
Live Animals	0.945 (0.041)	0	0
Other Animal Products	0.945 (0.041)	0	0
Fish	0.945 (0.041)	0,05	0
Coal, Gas, Oil	0.293 (0.102)	0,03	0,05
Other Minerals	0.426 (0.105)	0,08	0,05
Bovine Cattle, Sheep, Goat, and Horse Products	0.945 (0.041)	0,10	0
Other Meat Products	0.945 (0.041)	0,10	0
Vegetable Oils and Fats	0.945 (0.041)	0,03	0
Dairy Products	0.945 (0.041)	0	0
Processed Rice	0.945 (0.041)	0,13	0
Sugar	0.945 (0.041)	0,03	0
Other Food Products	0.945 (0.041)	0,03	0
Beverages and Tobacco Products	0.945 (0.041)	0,03	0
Textiles	0.927 (0.077)	0,06	0,14
Wearing Apparel	0.927 (0.077)	0,13	0,13
Leather Goods	0.927 (0.077)	0,13	0,13
Lumber and Wood Products	0.945 (0.041)	0,05	0
Pulp, Paper Products, Publishing	1.202 (0.090)	0,05	0,15
Coal and Petroleum Products	0.293 (0.102)	0,03	0,05
Chemicals, Plastics,and Rubber	1.009 (0.027)	0,04	0,15
Non-metallic Mineral Products	0.426 (0.105)	0,08	0,05
Primary Ferrous Metals	0.911 (0.241)	0,05	0,13
Non-ferrous Metals	0.958 (0.132)	0,05	0,13
Fabricated Metal Products	1.189 (0.055)	0,05	0,12
Motor Vehicles and Parts	1.202 (0.090)	0,11	0,12
Electronic Equipment	1.202 (0.090)	0,06	0,15
Machinery and Equipment	1.202 (0.090)	0,06	0,15
Other Manufacturing Products	1.202 (0.090)	0,06	0,15
Trade and Transport Services	1.283 (0.525)	0	0
Other Services	3.125 (0.817)	0	0
Investment Good	1.988 (0.477)	0	0
	Standard Errors in Parentheses	*(P-MC)/P	

In the sectors with increasing returns, yet another level of constrained choice is introduced. In this set-up, the domestic good and each import good produced in each region, instead of being homogeneous goods, are themselves composites of different varieties produced by the different firms. Consumers have CES preferences over these varieties and allocate spending across them subject to the amount they budgeted for each good at the third level. The elasticity of substitution across these varieties is set at 15. All results are robust to wide changes in this parameter.

6.1.3. Incorporating the New Data

6.1.3.1. Protection Data

To simulate the impact of NTBs, the model was benchmarked with the total protection measures—NTBs plus tariffs—instead of the GTAP protection data, which consists almost entirely of tariffs. In the model, all policy distortions enter as ad valorem price wedges[16], which, conveniently, is the form that this paper's new protection data take. So, replacing the GTAP tariff equivalents with these data is fairly straightforward. I did not, however, simply use the new measures as is, since they apply only to final goods, while all of the sectors of the model contain a combination of final and intermediate goods. Instead, I used a weighted average of the new data and the original GTAP data. The weight on the former was the fraction of output in that sector sold to final demand; the GTAP measure got the complementary weight. Thus, letting B and GTAP be the two protection measures and α, the final demand fraction, the protection estimate used was $\alpha B + (1 - \alpha)GTAP$. Using this method ensures that model sectors with a high proportion of final goods use a protection estimate close to mine, while sectors with a low fraction of final goods use a protection estimate close to the GTAP measure. Put another way, the lower the final demand fraction, the less the data deviated from the standard GTAP data. See Table 7 for a comparison of these weighted data and the original GTAP data. This table shows the food estimates in bold; it also includes total protection estimates for non-food sectors in the model. Replacing the GTAP data with these does not significantly affect the food results.

6.1.3.2. Distribution Margins Data

The margins data used to derive the protection measures allow one to model distribution more accurately within the AGE framework. Most AGE trade models do not account for margins explicitly. All distribution services are lumped into the trade and transport sector and consumed as a separate good, instead of being linked to the goods that use those distribution services. Since margins vary across sectors, this obscures the role of distribution in the economy and can skew the results of AGE analyses. For instance, simulations of price reductions in other sectors may imply a large substitution out of trade and transport services, even though actual consumption of these will probably increase in order to facilitate commodity flows. Also, not accounting for margins implies that consumers base choices on producer prices instead of the higher consumer prices that include margins.

---

[16] Government revenue is held constant throughout all simulations by assuming that lump-sum taxes are used to replace any lost tax revenue.

Table 7.

				NEW DATA*									GTAP DATA				
SECTOR	AUS	CAN	GER	ITA	JAP	NET	UK	US		AUS	CAN	GER	ITA	JAP	NET	UK	US
Fruits, Nuts, Vegetables	**4.6**	**6.0**	**35.1**	**15.3**	**94.1**	**13.9**	**34.0**	**17.4**		2.0	1.9	14.5	14.5	44.9	14.5	14.5	4.7
Other Agriculture										1.0	2.0	3.0	18.0	30.0	4.5	23.0	3.0
Other Crops	**2.1**	**66.8**	**83.0**	**6.9**	**52.5**	**9.7**	**89.1**	**32.2**		2.7	2.4	3.1	3.1	22.1	3.1	3.1	21.5
Live Animals	**1.0**	**0.3**	**36.6**	**31.4**	**149.1**	**34.9**	**38.2**	**1.1**		0.8	0.2	36.6	36.6	149.1	36.6	36.6	1.1
Other Animal Products	**7.2**	**19.3**	**6.7**	**6.4**	**7.8**	**7.2**	**25.6**	**2.3**		0.5	19.8	6.7	6.7	5.0	6.7	6.7	0.6
Fish	**8.6**	**1.2**	**11.4**	**11.4**	**16.2**	**8.7**	**7.7**	**5.1**		0.3	0.4	6.8	9.6	4.9	7.5	6.9	0.6
Coal, Gas, Oil										0.0	0.0	0.0	0.0	-0.8	0.0	0.0	0.2
Other Minerals										0.1	0.0	0.0	0.0	0.0	0.0	0.0	0.4
Bovine Cattle, Sheep, Goat, Horse Products	**0.0**	**18.1**	**109.7**	**39.0**	**265.4**	**80.6**	**99.6**	**8.3**		0.1	16.3	88.9	88.9	36.4	88.9	88.9	5.3
Other Meat Products	**3.0**	**29.3**	**41.8**	**23.3**	**119.8**	**29.6**	**37.6**	**5.5**		4.1	72.4	30.9	30.9	58.2	30.9	30.9	3.6
Vegetable Oils and Fats	**20.2**	**13.1**	**27.3**	**15.4**	**46.0**	**13.8**	**12.2**	**6.0**		2.8	8.6	11.4	11.4	6.6	11.4	11.4	4.3
Dairy Products	**19.1**	**77.8**	**30.8**	**33.8**	**173.7**	**53.0**	**43.4**	**32.0**		7.3	214.8	87.7	87.7	287.0	87.7	87.7	42.5
Processed Rice	**0.4**	**0.6**	**47.9**	**28.9**	**224.3**	**25.4**	**23.7**	**13.1**		1.0	0.7	87.4	87.4	409.0	87.4	87.4	5.3
Sugar	**11.7**	**8.3**	**66.3**	**37.2**	**111.0**	**72.4**	**69.2**	**46.9**		13.9	4.9	76.4	76.4	116.1	76.4	76.4	53.4
Other Food Products	**10.9**	**11.4**	**21.5**	**24.8**	**98.3**	**23.8**	**27.1**	**11.3**		5.6	14.1	28.8	28.8	38.3	28.8	28.8	11.4
Beverages and Tobacco Products	**54.1**	**35.6**	**33.9**	**37.8**	**59.6**	**35.2**	**45.2**	**15.4**		9.2	62.5	8.3	8.3	16.2	8.3	8.3	3.0

These problems are addressed by incorporating distribution explicitly into each final demand sector for which there is margins data. This is done by treating margins like taxes, since margins create a wedge between consumer and producer prices. For the eight nations involved, therefore, margin wedges were insertedinto each of the relevant sectors.[1] The value of the trade and transport sector was reduced by the total value of these margins. Finally, inputs into the trade and transport sector were reduced and re-distributed across the final goods sectors in accordance with the amount of distribution used in those sectors.[2]

6.2. Welfare Analysis

This section presents estimates of the potential gains from including food NTBs on the trade negotiation agenda. Since tariffs presumably require much less work to remove, it is not likely that negotiators will remove NTBs and not tariffs. So two sets of scenarios are simulated: one in which nations remove all food protection—NTBs and tariffs alike—and one in which nations only remove tariffs. For each of these two situations, I conduct two types of simulations: unilateral barrier removal in each of the eight nations and multilateral worldwide opening by all eight at once. I focus on changes in equivalent variation (which, given the model structure, is the same as changes in real consumption) as a percentage of GDP.

Tables 8 and 9 show the main results for total protection and just tariffs. These tables report the permanent, annual effect of trade opening on consumption, as a percentage of GDP, once the capital stock has changed to its new equilibrium. Alternatively, they report the welfare costs, born at home and abroad, of tariff and total protection in the eight nations separately and as a group. Table 10 shows the difference between the two scenarios and thus the predicted extra gains from removing food NTBs. (Alternatively, the results in Tables 8A and 8B are simply the sum of the results from Tables 9 and 10.) For each table, Panel A reports these gains as a percentage of GDP, while Panel B shows them in billions of 1997 US dollars.

Tables 8A and 8B imply that, overall, food protection in these eight nations imposes significant costs on the world. If all food barriers in all eight were removed, world welfare would increase by 0.73% of GDP, or about $185 billion (in 1997 dollars). About $135 billion of that would accrue to rich countries, with less developed countries (LDCs) getting permanent annual gains of about $50 billion. All but Canada, Germany, and the US would reap significant gains from unilateral opening, and all but Germany would benefit greatly from opening in all eight. Germany suffers from adverse terms of trade effects when all eight open: the reallocation of resources causes demand for the goods that Germany tends to export to decline, relative to demand for the goods that Germany tends to import. Japan's food barriers impose large costs on poor countries. Every poor region would benefit most from Japanese opening. ("Rest of Europe" is mostly rich countries.) Interestingly, the US would get significant gains from Japanese food barrier removal but not from its own.

---

[1] See Gohin 1998 and Komen and Peerlings 1996 for other examples of modeling margins in this way within AGE models. Bradford and Gohin 2006 explicitly model the distribution sector for the US within an AGE model.

[2] These modifications only apply to final goods. Due to lack of data, I do not modify the model to account for intermediate distribution. It turns out that these intermediate margins are quite a bit smaller than the margins for final goods.

Tables 9A and 9B reveal that poor countries would reap most of their gains from the removal of tariffs, not NTBs: about $33 billion from tariff removal, compared to $50 billion for all protection removal. Food tariffs in Japan, Germany, the UK, and the US impose the largest burdens on poor countries. Since tariffs are much easier to reduce than NTBs, it appears that poor countries will get more bang from their negotiating buck by focusing on food tariff removal in rich countries, rather than food NTBs.

Table 8 A.

	REGION IN WHICH PROTECTION IS REMOVED:									8 COUNTRY
IMPACT ON:	AUS	CAN	GER	ITA	JAP	NET	UK	US	ALL 8	PTA
Australia	0.03	0.01	0.05	0.00	1.54	0.02	0.16	0.07	1.90	4.35
Canada	0.02	0.35	0.02	0.09	0.34	0.01	0.06	0.23	1.18	3.66
Germany	0.02	0.00	-0.01	-0.02	-0.07	-0.04	-0.02	0.00	-0.14	1.96
Italy	0.02	0.01	0.09	0.23	-0.14	-0.01	0.02	0.01	0.28	4.61
Japan	0.02	0.00	-0.02	-0.01	2.16	0.00	-0.02	0.00	2.14	2.18
Netherlands	0.04	0.01	0.27	0.19	-0.01	0.47	0.02	0.12	1.16	9.38
United Kingdom	0.00	0.01	0.02	0.01	0.16	0.01	0.36	0.03	0.60	2.79
United States	-0.01	0.04	0.01	0.00	0.31	0.01	0.02	-0.05	0.31	1.35
China	0.01	0.00	0.00	-0.01	0.27	0.00	-0.01	0.00	0.31	-0.57
South Korea	-0.01	0.00	-0.01	-0.01	0.38	0.00	-0.01	0.02	0.40	-0.51
Rest of Asia	0.01	0.00	0.04	0.02	0.62	0.02	0.03	0.05	0.78	-0.81
Brazil	-0.02	0.01	0.12	0.10	0.34	0.07	0.10	0.12	0.81	0.00
Rest of Latin America	0.00	0.00	0.12	0.08	0.41	0.03	0.08	0.24	0.98	-0.53
Rest of Europe	0.01	0.01	0.08	0.00	0.04	-0.01	0.03	0.02	0.17	-0.88
Middle East	-0.01	0.00	0.14	0.07	0.39	0.05	0.11	0.07	0.77	-0.05
Rest of the World	-0.01	0.02	0.19	0.09	0.39	0.06	0.17	0.04	0.91	0.03
LDC's	0.00	0.01	0.10	0.06	0.42	0.04	0.08	0.08	0.76	-0.36
DEVELOPED NATIONS	0.00	0.02	0.02	0.01	0.62	0.00	0.03	-0.01	0.72	1.76
WORLD	0.00	0.02	0.04	0.03	0.57	0.01	0.04	0.02	0.73	1.25

Focusing on Table 10, most of these nations do not get significant extra annual boosts to GDP from unilateral food NTB opening. Multilateral opening from all eight, however, would bring nontrivial annual gains of at least 0.1% of GDP for all except Canada and Germany. Global GDP would rise an additional 0.4%, or $90 billion, with NTB removal in just the food sectors. It appears that poor countries have little to gain from NTB reductions in Europe or the US. Japan, however, remains a large burden, and their food NTBs warrant close attention from poor and rich countries alike. In fact, Japanese opening of food NTBs accounts for almost as many gains as having all eight open.

Table 8 B.

TOTAL PROTECTION
NET WELFARE CHANGE (EQUIVALENT VARIATION)

IN BILLIONS OF 1997 DOLLARS.

	REGION IN WHICH PROTECTION IS REMOVED:										8 COUNTRY	
IMPACT ON:	AUS	CAN	GER	ITA	JAP	NET	UK	US	ALL 8		PTA	GDP
Australia	0.10	0.03	0.17	0.00	5.22	0.07	0.54	0.24	6.44	15.338		339.12
Canada	0.10	1.76	0.10	0.45	1.71	0.05	0.30	1.15	5.92	18.991		501.69
Germany	0.34	0.00	-0.17	-0.34	-1.19	-0.68	-0.34	0.00	-2.38	35.497		1701.3
Italy	0.19	0.10	0.86	2.21	-1.35	-0.10	0.19	0.10	2.69	46.984		960.91
Japan	0.81	0.00	-0.81	-0.41	87.71	0.00	-0.81	0.00	86.89	95.985		4060.4
Netherlands	0.12	0.03	0.79	0.56	-0.03	1.38	0.06	0.35	3.40	28.643		293.47
United Kingdom	0.00	0.11	0.23	0.11	1.80	0.11	4.05	0.34	6.76	33.707		1125.9
United States	-0.72	2.87	0.72	0.00	22.26	0.72	1.44	-3.59	22.26	101.507		7179.7
China	0.09	0.00	0.00	-0.09	2.39	0.00	-0.09	0.00	2.75	-5.047		885.51
South Korea	-0.04	0.00	-0.04	-0.04	1.49	0.00	-0.04	0.08	1.57	-1.996		391.37
Rest of Asia	0.13	0.00	0.52	0.26	8.09	0.26	0.39	0.65	10.17	-10.566		1304.5
Brazil	-0.13	0.07	0.80	0.66	2.26	0.46	0.66	0.80	5.38	0.000		664.19
Rest of Latin America	0.00	0.00	1.32	0.88	4.50	0.33	0.88	2.63	10.75	-5.815		1097.1
Rest of Europe	0.28	0.28	2.24	0.00	1.12	-0.28	0.84	0.56	4.75	-24.604		2796
Middle East	-0.06	0.00	0.79	0.40	2.21	0.28	0.62	0.40	4.36	-0.283		565.88
Rest of the World	-0.15	0.31	2.94	1.39	6.04	0.93	2.63	0.62	14.08	0.464		1547.7
LDC's	0.00	0.65	6.46	3.87	27.12	2.58	5.16	5.16	49.07	-23.242		6456.2
DEVELOPED NATIONS	0.00	3.79	3.79	1.90	117.54	0.00	5.69	-1.90	136.50	350.824		18958
WORLD	0.00	5.08	10.17	7.62	144.86	2.54	10.17	5.08	185.53	329.867		25415

Table 9 A.

TARIFFS
NET WELFARE CHANGE (EQUIVALENT VARIATION)

AS FRACTION OF GDP

	REGION IN WHICH PROTECTION IS REMOVED:									8 COUNTRY
IMPACT ON:	AUS	CAN	GER	ITA	JAP	NET	UK	US	ALL 8	PTA
Australia	-0.03	0.01	0.05	0.01	1.06	0.02	0.13	0.06	1.28	2.79
Canada	0.00	0.33	0.02	0.09	0.48	0.00	0.05	0.08	1.20	1.41
Germany	0.00	0.00	0.03	-0.04	-0.07	-0.05	-0.04	-0.01	-0.14	0.12
Italy	0.00	0.01	-0.03	0.36	-0.12	-0.01	-0.03	-0.01	0.18	0.69
Japan	0.00	0.00	-0.02	-0.01	0.96	-0.01	-0.02	-0.01	0.94	0.91
Netherlands	0.00	0.00	-0.28	-0.11	-0.07	0.59	-0.14	0.03	0.02	0.18
United Kingdom	-0.01	0.00	0.00	-0.01	0.09	-0.01	0.33	0.00	0.42	0.57
United States	0.00	0.04	0.01	0.00	0.14	0.01	0.02	-0.02	0.16	0.48
China	0.01	0.01	0.01	0.00	0.10	0.01	0.00	0.01	0.13	-0.23
South Korea	0.00	0.00	-0.01	-0.01	0.16	0.00	-0.01	0.02	0.17	-0.17
Rest of Asia	0.01	0.00	0.04	0.02	0.21	0.02	0.04	0.05	0.36	-0.37
Brazil	-0.01	0.00	0.06	0.09	0.22	0.07	0.07	0.10	0.62	0.10
Rest of Latin America	0.00	0.00	0.14	0.09	0.21	0.03	0.08	0.19	0.72	-0.22
Rest of Europe	0.00	0.00	-0.04	-0.02	-0.02	-0.03	-0.05	0.00	-0.13	-0.26
Middle East	0.00	0.00	0.15	0.07	0.17	0.04	0.10	0.05	0.58	0.12
Rest of the World	0.00	0.02	0.19	0.09	0.22	0.06	0.16	0.04	0.73	0.13
LDC's	0.00	0.00	0.09	0.05	0.19	0.03	0.07	0.07	0.51	-0.10
DEVELOPED NATIONS	0.00	0.02	-0.01	0.01	0.28	0.00	0.01	-0.01	0.32	0.51
WORLD	0.00	0.02	0.02	0.03	0.26	0.01	0.03	0.02	0.37	0.36

Table 9 B.

TARIFFS
NET WELFARE CHANGE (EQUIVALENT VARIATION)

IN BILLIONS OF 1997 DOLLARS.

	REGION IN WHICH PROTECTION IS REMOVED:									8 COUNTRY
IMPACT ON:	AUS	CAN	GER	ITA	JAP	NET	UK	US	ALL 8	PTA
Australia	-0.10	0.03	0.17	0.03	3.59	0.07	0.44	0.20	4.34	
Canada	0.00	1.66	0.10	0.45	2.41	0.00	0.25	0.40	6.02	
Germany	0.00	0.00	0.51	-0.68	-1.19	-0.85	-0.68	-0.17	-2.38	
Italy	0.00	0.10	-0.29	3.46	-1.15	-0.10	-0.29	-0.10	1.73	
Japan	0.00	0.00	-0.81	-0.41	38.98	-0.41	-0.81	-0.41	38.17	
Netherlands	0.00	0.00	-0.82	-0.32	-0.21	1.73	-0.41	0.09	0.06	
United Kingdom	-0.11	0.00	0.00	-0.11	1.01	-0.11	3.72	0.00	4.73	
United States	0.00	2.87	0.72	0.00	10.05	0.72	1.44	-1.44	11.49	
China	0.09	0.09	0.09	0.00	0.89	0.09	0.00	0.09	1.15	
South Korea	0.00	0.00	-0.04	-0.04	0.63	0.00	-0.04	0.08	0.67	
Rest of Asia	0.13	0.00	0.52	0.26	2.74	0.26	0.52	0.65	4.70	
Brazil	-0.07	0.00	0.40	0.60	1.46	0.46	0.46	0.66	4.12	
Rest of Latin America	0.00	0.00	1.54	0.99	2.30	0.33	0.88	2.08	7.90	
Rest of Europe	0.00	0.00	-1.12	-0.56	-0.56	-0.84	-1.40	0.00	-3.63	
Middle East	0.00	0.00	0.85	0.40	0.96	0.23	0.57	0.28	3.28	
Rest of the World	0.00	0.31	2.94	1.39	3.40	0.93	2.48	0.62	11.30	
LDC's	0.00	0.00	5.81	3.23	12.27	1.94	4.52	4.52	32.93	
DEVELOPED NATIONS	0.00	3.79	-1.90	1.90	53.08	0.00	1.90	-1.90	60.67	
WORLD	0.00	5.08	5.08	7.62	66.08	2.54	7.62	5.08	94.03	

Table 10 A.

NTBS NET WELFARE CHANGE (EQUIVALENT VARIATION) AS FRACTION OF GDP										
	REGION IN WHICH PROTECTION IS REMOVED:									8 COUNTRY
IMPACT ON:	AUS	CAN	GER	ITA	JAP	NET	UK	US	ALL 8	PTA
Australia	0.06	0.00	0.00	-0.01	0.48	0.00	0.03	0.01	0.62	1.56
Canada	0.02	0.02	0.00	0.00	-0.14	0.01	0.01	0.15	-0.02	2.25
Germany	0.02	0.00	-0.04	0.02	0.00	0.01	0.02	0.01	0.00	1.84
Italy	0.02	0.00	0.12	-0.13	-0.02	0.00	0.05	0.02	0.10	3.92
Japan	0.02	0.00	0.00	0.00	1.20	0.01	0.00	0.01	1.20	1.27
Netherlands	0.04	0.01	0.55	0.30	0.06	-0.12	0.16	0.09	1.14	9.20
United Kingdom	0.01	0.01	0.02	0.02	0.07	0.02	0.03	0.03	0.18	2.22
United States	-0.01	0.00	0.00	0.00	0.17	0.00	0.00	-0.03	0.15	0.87
China	0.00	-0.01	-0.01	-0.01	0.17	-0.01	-0.01	-0.01	0.18	-0.34
South Korea	-0.01	0.00	0.00	0.00	0.22	0.00	0.00	0.00	0.23	-0.34
Rest of Asia	0.00	0.00	0.00	0.00	0.41	0.00	-0.01	0.00	0.42	-0.44
Brazil	-0.01	0.01	0.06	0.01	0.12	0.00	0.03	0.02	0.19	-0.10
Rest of Latin America	0.00	0.00	-0.02	-0.01	0.20	0.00	0.00	0.05	0.26	-0.31
Rest of Europe	0.01	0.01	0.12	0.02	0.06	0.02	0.08	0.02	0.30	-0.62
Middle East	-0.01	0.00	-0.01	0.00	0.22	0.01	0.01	0.02	0.19	-0.17
Rest of the World	-0.01	0.00	0.00	0.00	0.17	0.00	0.01	0.00	0.18	-0.10
LDC's	0.00	0.01	0.01	0.01	0.23	0.01	0.01	0.01	0.25	-0.26
DEVELOPED NATIONS	0.00	0.00	0.03	0.00	0.34	0.00	0.02	0.00	0.40	1.25
WORLD	0.00	0.00	0.02	0.00	0.31	0.00	0.01	0.00	0.36	0.89

Table 10 B.

NTBS NET WELFARE CHANGE (EQUIVALENT VARIATION) IN BILLIONS OF 1997 DOLLARS.											
	REGION IN WHICH PROTECTION IS REMOVED:									8 COUNTRY	
IMPACT ON:	AUS	CAN	GER	ITA	JAP	NET	UK	US	ALL 8	PTA	GDP
Australia	0.2	0.0	0.0	0.0	1.6	0.0	0.1	0.0	2.1	5.876	339.123
Canada	0.1	0.1	0.0	0.0	-0.7	0.1	0.1	0.8	-0.1	11.917	501.691
Germany	0.3	0.0	-0.7	0.3	0.0	0.2	0.3	0.2	0.0	33.455	1701.311
Italy	0.2	0.0	1.2	-1.2	-0.2	0.0	0.5	0.2	1.0	40.354	960.906
Japan	0.8	0.0	0.0	0.0	48.7	0.4	0.0	0.4	48.7	59.036	4060.425
Netherlands	0.1	0.0	1.6	0.9	0.2	-0.4	0.5	0.3	3.3	28.115	293.466
United Kingdom	0.1	0.1	0.2	0.2	0.8	0.2	0.3	0.3	2.0	27.289	1125.922
United States	-0.7	0.0	0.0	0.0	12.2	0.0	0.0	-2.2	10.8	67.044	7179.693
China	0.0	-0.1	-0.1	-0.1	1.5	-0.1	-0.1	-0.1	1.6	-3.011	885.506
South Korea	0.0	0.0	0.0	0.0	0.9	0.0	0.0	0.0	0.9	-1.331	391.37
Rest of Asia	0.0	0.0	0.0	0.0	5.3	0.0	-0.1	0.0	5.5	-5.740	1304.452
Brazil	-0.1	0.1	0.4	0.1	0.8	0.0	0.2	0.1	1.3	-0.664	664.185
Rest of Latin America	0.0	0.0	-0.2	-0.1	2.2	0.0	0.0	0.5	2.9	-3.401	1097.129
Rest of Europe	0.3	0.3	3.4	0.6	1.7	0.6	2.2	0.6	8.4	-17.335	2795.951
Middle East	-0.1	0.0	-0.1	0.0	1.2	0.1	0.1	0.1	1.1	-0.962	565.879
Rest of the World	-0.2	0.0	0.0	0.0	2.6	0.0	0.2	0.0	2.8	-1.548	1547.675
LDC's	0.0	0.6	0.6	0.6	14.8	0.6	0.6	0.6	16.1	-16.786	6456.195
DEVELOPED NATIONS	0.0	0.0	5.7	0.0	64.5	0.0	3.8	0.0	75.8	254.136	18958.49
WORLD	0.0	0.0	5.1	0.0	78.8	0.0	2.5	0.0	91.5	238.374	25414.68

Three main forces drive the gains for any given country: the amount of protection removed, the share of trade in GDP for that country, and terms of trade effects. The US's relatively low barriers and its low trade/GDP share lead to relatively low predicted gains for the US. Similarly, the Netherlands' high trade share amplifies its percentage gains. On the other hand, Japan's NTBs are so high that it reaps substantial extra gains from NTB liberalization despite the fact that Japan has the lowest trade share in the sample: only about 10%. Terms of trade changes mute gains for Canada, Germany, and Italy.

For all economies except Canada and Japan, the extra gains from multilateral food NTB opening are significantly more than the gains from unilateral opening. These six economies have incentives to engage in multilateral NTB reform, as opposed to going it alone.

Overall, these results imply that the potential gains to be reaped from food protection are not trivial, whether one considers tariffs or NTBs. Of course, such extensive liberalization in these nations is not on the table right now. Complete opening may not be an option because of short run political stresses caused by contraction in protected sectors. Our analysis does not provide a recipe for reform, but it does show that the potential gains from future attempts to integrate markets remain quite large.

These estimates of the benefits of integration do not take account of certain costs. In particular, differences in national languages, policies, and institutions may well create barriers to price arbitrage, but they may also provide benefits that would be lost if the world economy was to be deeply integrated in the sense we are exploring in this study. Also, I have not considered adjustments costs as workers and other factors move out of shrinking sectors into expanding sectors.

On the other hand, these results may understate the costs of the barriers by treating them as if they were tariffs. There are at least two ways in which the costs of NTBs may be higher. First, they do not generate revenue for the government as tariffs do, so this benefit is foregone. An NTB such as excessive fumigation raises costs to the foreign exporter without necessarily generating income for the importing country. The fumigators in that country may get paid more than otherwise, but this is a transfer from within the economy, not an extra source of revenues as with tariffs. Second, removing barriers may actually save resources and therefore yield even larger benefits than estimated here. As Anderson and van Wincoop 2002 emphasizes, tariffs generate deadweight losses, but NTBs may consume resources directly. Suppose, for example, that two nations each require meat to be certified as safe even though their criteria are very similar. Firms that wish to sell in both markets must expend real resources to meet foreign requirements. Meat approved in one economy cannot simply be sold abroad. Under these circumstances, in addition to the gains from removing the barriers, freeing the resources that are consumed by the (unnecessary) duplicative regulatory processes could produce additional gains.

The estimates are also conservative because they ignore the potential benefits from opening nations outside the sample of eight used in the study.

7. Conclusion

This paper has presented a method for estimating food NTB protection in rich countries. The estimates imply that rich nations harbor significant food NTB protection, in addition to food tariffs. Japan has unusually high food NTBs. AGE simulations imply that negotiating the removal of food NTBs, especially in Japan, would bring large benefits to rich and poor nations alike, implying that the extra work required to open these markets would probably pay off.

Of course, the trade opening devil lurks in the details, so trade analysts need to determine the actual policies that underlie the protection we have quantified in this paper. It is easy for governments to claim that certain policies in other economies act as trade barriers; the more difficult task is to provide evidence for these claims. We have taken an initial step toward this goal by matching up suspected policies with sectors for which we have evidence of NTB protection. As shown in Table 4, we find that, for agriculture and food products, overly restrictive phytosanitary and sanitary requirements, apparently unfounded import bans of certain products, and onerous labeling rules emerge as potentially damaging trade barriers and worthwhile targets of negotiations. Various experts for individual sectors are probably well aware of such barriers; this paper has provided potentially valuable information by putting numbers on the extent and effects of a wide range of barriers.

This initial analysis could be improved in a number of ways. More recent price data are available, making it possible to derive updated protection data. Including more countries in the price comparisons would improve the accuracy of the barrier estimates and would provide a more complete picture of the potential gains from trade opening. The AGE analysis could be improved by accounting for technological change. Also, it would probably be worthwhile to add confidence intervals to the AGE estimates, something which is quite feasible.

I hope that this paper has provided useful initial insights on the extent of, the effects of, and the policies underlying food NTB protection in rich countries. I also hope that this paper will stimulate much-needed future research in this area.

ACKNOWLEDGEMENTS

This work draws on joint work with Robert Lawrence, to whom I am greatly indebted. I thank David Blandford, Michael Ferrantino, Tim Josling, Suchada Langley, Christine McDaniel, William Meyers, Pat Westhoff, and Linda Young for their help. I also thank participants in the BYU Economics Department Raw Research Seminar, the APEC Non-tariff Measure Workshop (Bangkok, October 2003), the Empirical Trade Analysis Conference (Washington, DC, January 2004), the 2004 AAEA annual meeting in Denver, and the 2005 IATRC annual meeting in San Diego. I take full responsibility for any errors in this paper.

REFERENCES

J.E. Anderson and E. van Wincoop. 2002. "Borders, Trade and Welfare" in S.M. Collins and D. Rodrik, eds. *Brookings Trade Forum 2001*. Washington DC: Brookings Institution.

S.C. Bradford. February 2003. "Paying the Price: Final Good Protection in OECD Countries." *Review of Economics and Statistics*. 85(1):24-37.

S.C. Bradford and A. Gohin. 2006. "Modeling Distribution Services and Assessing Their Welfare Effects in a General Equilibrium Framework." *Review of Development Economics*. 10(1):87-102.

S.C. Bradford and R.Z. Lawrence. February 2004. *Has Globalization Gone Far Enough?* Washington, DC: Institute for International Economics.

Eurostat-OECD PPP Programme. 1996. "The Calculation and Aggregation of Parities." Unpublished.

J.A. Frankel. 1997. *Regional Trading Blocs in the World Economic System*. Washington DC, Institute for International Economics.

A. Gohin. 1998. *Modelisation du Complexe Agro-alimentaire Francais dans un Cadre D'equilibre General.* PhD Dissertation, Universite de Paris I, Panthéon-Sorbonne.

G.W. Harrison, T.F. Rutherford, and D. Tarr. December 1995. "Quantifying the Outcome of the Uruguay Round." *Finance and Development*. 32(4):38-41.

G.W. Harrison, T.F. Rutherford, and D. Tarr. 1996. "Quantifying the Uruguay Round" in W. Martin and L.A. Winters, eds. The Uruguay Round and the Developing Countries. New York: Cambridge University Press.

G.W. Harrison, T.F. Rutherford, and D. Tarr. September 1997. "Quantifying the Uruguay Round." *Economic Journal*. 107:1405-1430.

G.C. Hufbauer et al. 2002. *The Benefits of Price Convergence: Speculative Calculations*. Washington, DC: Institute for International Economics.

G.C. Hufbauer and K.A. Elliot. 1994. *Measuring the Costs of Protection in the United States*. Washington, DC: Institute for International Economics.

M.M. Knetter and P.K. Goldberg. 1995. "Measuring the Intensity of Competition in Export Markets." Cambridge, MA: National Bureau of Economic Research Working Paper.

M.H.C. Komen and J.H.M. Peerlings. 1996. "WAGEM: an Applied General Equilibrium Model for Agricultural and Environmental Policy Analysis." Wageningen Economic Papers: 1996-4, The Netherlands

M. Obstfeld and K. Rogoff. 2000. "The Six Major Puzzles in International Macroeconomics: Is There A Common Cause?" *NBER Macroeconomics Annual 2000*. Cambridge, MA: NBER.

Organization for Economic Cooperation and Development (OECD). 1995. *Purchasing Power Parities and Real Expenditure*. Paris: OECD.

V. Roningen and A. Yeats. 1976. "Nontariff Distortions of International Trade: Some Preliminary Empirical Evidence." *Weltwirtschaftliches Archiv*. 112(4):613-625.

D.J. Rousslang and T. To. 1993. "Domestic Trade and Transportation Costs as Barriers to International Trade." *Canadian Journal of Economics*. 26(1):208-221.

United Nations Conference on Trade and Development (UNCTAD). 1992. *Analytical Report by the UNCTAD Secretariat to the Conference*. New York: United Nations.

World Bank. 1993. *Purchasing Power of Currencies: Comparing National Incomes Using ICP Data*. Washington, DC: World Bank.

In: International Agricultural Trade and Development ISBN: 978-1-60021-965-8
Editor: Dragan Miljkovic, pp. 161-164

Chapter 9

ELIMINATING NON-TARIFF BARRIERS TO TRADE: FEASIBLE? DESIRABLE?

Linda M. Young

Bradford's (2005) paper is part of a growing literature that addresses the extent, nature and impact of non tariff barriers to trade. Some these catalog non-tariff barriers with the purpose of developing systematic datasets (USITC 2001; UN 2005); others provide background and present the conceptual issues presented by NTBs with a liberal use of case studies due to the complexity and uniqueness of the issues presented by regulations (Josling, Orden and Roberts 2004; Bredahl and Hollerin 1997; ERS 2003). The general question of the legitimacy of sanitary and phytosanitary (SPS) and technical barriers to trade (TBT) standards, or at least their conformity to World Trade Organization (WTO) standards, has a high profile due to the intersection of increasing consumer demand for quality and food safety at the same time that many countries are frustrated over the difficulty of improving market access. Developing countries in particular have cited high SPS and TBT barriers as an obstacle in developing new agricultural exports (Wilson 2001; Otsuki, Wilson, and Sewadeh 2000; Oyejide, Ogundkola and Bankole 2000) and in realizing the benefits from WTO membership.

Bradford estimates that the removal of all non tariff barriers to trade would result in the possible realization of US$91.5 billion dollars of efficiency gains. Bradford first estimates the gaps between domestic and international prices, and then uses a computable general equilibrium model to estimate the gains from removing the wedges between domestic and international prices. While Bradford explains the estimation procedures with care, relatively little discussion is focused on the nature of the possible gains and how those gains might be realized. Their realization first requires an assessment of what portion of the 91.5 billion represents opaque protectionism and a violation of member's WTO commitments. The balance then, includes the legitimate outcomes of national preferences and regulatory outcomes for SPS regulations and quality standards. The second question is how likely is the removal of protectionism hidden by excessive SPS and TBT standards?

Economists are acutely aware of the argument, advanced many years ago by Stigler (1971) that regulations may result from industry capture of regulatory agencies. Producers lobby for, and at times achieve, a higher level of import regulations than is warranted by a dispassionate calculation of costs and benefits (Josling, Orden and Roberts). Effective action by industry groups may result in SPS barriers that meet the WTO criteria while still being higher than warranted by national preferences, or at times may result in regulations that violate the SPS or TBT agreements of the WTO.

However, under the SPS agreement of the WTO, countries are allowed to apply high standards to achieve low levels of risk as long as appropriate risk assessment procedures have been used, and the standards do not distort trade more than is necessary. This is the situation described by Otsuki, Wilson and Sewadeh, who evaluate the impact of European Union standards for aflatoxin on the quantity of cereals, dried fruits and nuts imported from African nations. They estimate the loss of African exports due to EU standards that are higher than international standards, but that are still permitted under the SPS agreement. It is estimated that application of the new standards will result in a reduction of 1.4 deaths per billion a year while African nations lose US$670 million in exports.

Standards set by private retail chains are increasing important. Reardon and Berdequé (2002) examine the rise of powerful grocery chains which frequently maintain standards for food safety and quality that exceed those set by governments. This is an indication of the increasing importance of quality and safety to consumers. If trade policy were to dictate the harmonization of standards at a lower level than that demanded by consumers, it is possible that consumer demand would be reduced and the anticipated efficiency gains would not materialize (Thilmany and Barrett 1996).

Incidence of pest and disease may also create the price gaps for agricultural goods and food. For example, beef products are differentiated by origin, and whether or not they originate from a country with hoof and mouth disease free status will affect their price. The outbreak of disease, such as BSE, and the temporary imposition of import restrictions will also cause divergence in prices of traded goods.

The difficulty in interpreting Bradford's results lies in differentiating between price differences from TBT and SPS regulations that meet current WTO standards and those that don't. However, even if this were possible, it remains unclear that it would be easy to remove them.

Regulations that don't meet WTO standards can be contested under the WTO dispute settlement understanding. However, this is costly both in financial and political terms. Evaluation of the complaints brought to the WTO dispute settlement process indicates that there are instances in which it is worth the cost to bring a single infringement to dispute settlement. Shaffer (2005) cites work estimating that a high profile trade dispute affects more than US$150 million in trade, and that recent suits have cost from $400,000 to in excess of a million dollars in legal fees. With this level of cost, it is likely that in many cases the exporter will estimate that the possible benefit from removing a single offending regulation is not worth it. It is also argued that some developing country WTO members are reluctant to bring a grievance to dispute settlement due to negative ramifications for the development assistance received from the offending party, or due to the threat of exclusion from potential free trade areas. An alternative to bringing a complaint in the WTO would be for a country to settle the issue bilaterally. The potential downfall of this approach might be that the trading partners would reach a bilateral compromise over the offending regulation that would not ensure equal access for all exporters.

It is likely that a significant component of the price gaps estimated by Bradford result from regulations that do meet WTO standards. It is possible that the WTO may re-negotiate the current SPS/TBT agreement and that a future agreement could result in more uniform standards. Currently, the WTO agreement relies on harmonization of the *principles* underlying SPS and TBT regulations. Additionally, countries can choose if they wish to use international standards. An alternative approach would be to require adoption identical rules (Leebron 1997), however, this would result in the imposition of identical quality and risk preferences on widely divergent nations, and is an unlikely outcome of negotiations. Negotiations in the Doha Round have been costly and slow, even for the relatively straight forward matter of tariff reductions, which are widely regarded as inefficient and resource-use distorting. While protectionist abuse does exist, there is a high level of support for both SPS and TBT regulations overall. Negotiations that curtail the government's ability to set regulations that reflect national preferences for health, safety and quality standards are even less likely to be successful.

Bradford's estimate of non tariff barriers to trade is likely to include both the legitimate outcomes of current regulatory processes as well as protectionism serving narrow interest groups. Separating these out, and realizing a significant portion of the gains estimated, may be beyond the ambition and the capacity of the current multilateral trade regime.

References

Bradford, S. 2005. "The Extent and Impact of Food Non-tariff Barriers in Rich Countries." *Paper presented at the annual meetings of the International Agricultural Trade Research Consortium*, San Diego, CA, December 4-6.

Bredahl, M. and E. Hollerin. 1997"Technical Regulations and Food Safety in NAFTA." In R.M.A. Loyns, R.D. Knutson, K. Meilke and D. Sumner, eds., *Harmonization/Convergence/Compatibility in Agriculture and Agri-Food Policy: Canada, United States and Mexico*. Proceedings of the Third Agricultural and Food Policy Systems Information Workshop, University of Guelph, in press.

Economic Research Service (ERS) 2003. "International Trade and Food Safety: Economic Theory and Case Studies." *Agricultural Economic Report 828*, United States Department of Agriculture, Washington DC, November.

Josling, T., D. Roberts and D. Orden. 2004. *Food Regulation and Trade: Toward a Safe and Open Global System.* Washington DC: Institute for International Economics.

Leebron, D.W. 1997. "Lying Down with Procustes: An Analysis of Harmonization Claims." In J.N. Bhagwati and R.E. Hudec eds., *Fair Trade and Harmonization: Prerequisites for Free Trade?* Cambridge, MA: MIT Press.

Otsuki, T., J. Wilson, and M. Sewadeh. 2001. "A Race to the Top? A Case Study of Food Safety Standards and African Exports." *Policy Research Working Paper*, WPS 2563, Development Research Group, World Bank, March.

Oyejide, T.A., E.O. Ogundkola, and S.A. Bankole. 2000. "Quantifying the Trade Impact of Sanitary and Phytosanitary Standards: What is Known and Issues of Importance for Sub-

Saharan Africa." Paper presented at *Quantifying the Trade Effect of Standards and Regulatory Barriers: Is It Possible?*, World Bank, April 27.

Reardon, T. and J.A. Berdequé. 2002. "The Rapid Rise of Supermarkets in Latin America: Challenges and Opportunities for Development." *Paper presented at the meetings of the International Agricultural Trade Research Consortium,* Monterey, CA, December 15-17.

Shaffer, G.. 2005. "Weaknesses and Proposed Improvements to the WTO Dispute Settlement System: An Economic and Market-Oriented View." Paper prepared for *The WTO at 10: A Look at the Appellate Body*, San Paulo, Brazil, May 16-17.

Stigler, G.J. 1971. "The Theory of Economic Regulation." *Bell Journal of Economics and Management Science* 2:3-21.

Thilmany, D. and C. Barrett. 1996. "Regulatory Barriers in an Integrating World Food Market." *Review of Agricultural Economics*, 19(1):91-107.

United Nations Conference on Trade and Development. 2005. "*Methodologies, Classifications, Quantification and Development Impacts of Non-Tariff Barriers*." Note by the UNCTAD Secretariat. TD/B/COM.1.EM.27/2, 23 June.

United States International Trade Commission (USITC). 2001. "Processed Foods and Beverages: A Description of Tariff and Non-tariff Barriers for Major Products and Their Impact on Trade." *USITC Publication Number* 3455, October.

Wilson, J.S. 2001. "Advancing the WTO Agenda on Trade and Standards: A Developing country Voice in the Debate." Paper presented at the *African Economic Research Consortium Conference on Trade*, Geneva, March 8-9.

INDEX

A

B

C

D

E

P

Q

R

U

V

W

Y